South West
Trail Running

Mark Rainsley

 Pesda Press LTD   www.pesdapress.com

First published in Great Britain 2018 by Pesda Press

Tan y Coed Canol

Ceunant

Caernarfon

Gwynedd

LL55 4RN

© Copyright 2018 Mark Rainsley

Maps by Bute Cartographics
Contains Ordnance Survey data © Crown copyright and database right 2018

ISBN: 9781906095673

Printed in Poland, www.lfbookservices.co.uk

Introduction

With thanks to Susie Allison

'And nearly every time – especially when I was really rather surprised to have survived at all – I ended up looking back on the experience with wonder and warmth, feeling happier and more alive than I did before I set out'.
Richard Askwith, Running Free

This book is about running for fun in beautiful places. Each route has been selected for its inspirational landscapes and runnable terrain. The range of routes is deliberately diverse – these runs follow rivers and coastlines, go up hills and along ridges, weave through leafy woodlands, cross barren moors and heathland. The selected routes include many of South West England's most enjoyable trails, but this is not a definitive collection! Hopefully these routes will encourage and inspire further personal exploration of South West England's trails.

Hunter's Tor (Route 23)
Photo: Claire Pinder

Contents

South rim of Cheddar Gorge
(Route 40)

About the Author

Mark Rainsley

Mark Rainsley lives and works in Dorset. As a keen trail runner (and also kayaker, surfer and mountain biker), he has explored every corner of the wild and wonderful South West, in all its moods and seasons. He has been known to survive the occasional ultra-marathon, but largely he runs sensible distances, purely for the joy of exploring the landscape.

Mark took on the challenge of researching the South West's trail running potential as a means of recovering physically and mentally from major surgery to correct a genetic heart defect. He hopes that this book demonstrates that these wonderful places are accessible to all runners, and that this book offers useful information and maybe even a bit of inspiration.

Why Trail Running?

Moving fast and light through and engaging with the landscape is what trail running is all about. All that is required is just you and a pair of running shoes! Trail runners leave roads and traffic behind in search of the quieter and wilder, sometimes hidden, paths and tracks that criss-cross the outdoors. Leafy woodland, meandering river banks, winding ridges, dramatic sea cliffs, remote moorland; South West England has all of these in abundance and all are fantastic places to run.

Trails are everywhere

The beauty of trail running is that it combines the speed and ease of running on roads with fresh air and wide-open spaces. Trails enable runners to move quickly over ground that might otherwise be too rough or boggy for a speedy passage. Trails enable runners to explore all over South West England; from the inner reaches of suburban woodlands to remote high moorland.

Trails are for everyone

Trail running is a simple activity which is accessible to everyone wishing to give it a go. Great off-road running trails are found anywhere and everywhere; in cities and towns as well as in the countryside. Anyone can take up trail running. Many trails are easily tackled by the most novice of runners and just as many trails will delight experienced runners seeking new challenges. Trail running is an activity that fits and grows with the experience and skill of the individual runner.

Definition of a running trail

A trail is simply a path or a track. Some are boggy or muddy, some are stony or sun-baked … but all are easier on the joints and (in this author's humble opinion!) far more interesting and enjoyable than running on tarmac or concrete. The routes in this book all have public access. Most follow footpaths or bridleways. Many utilise unsurfaced roads such as farm access tracks. Some are on Access Land, where you may roam freely. A number of routes follow beaches; a fantastic surface to run on, as long as it is firm wet sand rather than pebbles! Tarmac paths and roads do inevitably feature from time to time, but only when there is no alternative way to approach or complete a great trail run.

Guidebook scope and purpose

This guidebook sets out to describe trail runs all over South West England, including several islands; all are enjoyable, many are sublime! The routes presented here are selected to showcase the available spectrum of trail running experiences to be found in each of the South West's diverse regions, and to present physical challenges ranging from mild to superhuman. Inevitably, the choice of routes reflects the author's prejudices; for example, I love coastal running, I love running across open heath or moor, I love running through landscapes which tell a story of geology, history or prehistory and I especially love running along Southern England's incredible chalk ridgetops.

Why Trail Running?

Stert Combe (Route 34)

Many of the routes are easily accessible trails close to towns, cities and popular holiday destinations. These runs range from short, straightforward circuits to longer, half-day outings. The remaining routes strike out into more remote terrain taking runners into the heart of South West England's wildest landscapes. Some routes require a little road running and at the other end of the spectrum some routes have short unrunnable sections, usually where extreme gradient is involved. Likewise, some routes follow waymarked trails, others require map and compass to stay on track. The routes in this book have been selected to cover a wide range of running experiences so that runners can develop their ability in whichever direction they want: to run further, to climb higher, tackle trickier ground or navigate more complex terrain. Developing these skills opens up a whole new world of opportunities for exploring the rich and varied landscapes of South West England.

Disclaimer

Every effort has been made to ensure that the information supplied is accurate. However, mistakes happen and trails are frequently subject to change. The author welcomes updates and corrections.

As with any activity, trail runners must accept responsibility for their own actions, stay within their own limits and avoid harming other people or property. The author, publisher and distributor of this book do not recognise any liability for any injury or damage to person or property arising from the use of this guidebook.

How to Use This Book

This book is for reading in the armchair at home or for storing in the car glovebox. It has been designed so that the turn-by-turn route description and map can be photocopied and taken on the run. Each route is laid out in the same format.

Quick reference

This section lists the length of the route in kilometres and miles as well as the cumulative ascent (height gain) in metres and feet. Distances are given to the nearest 0.5km for routes under 10km and to the nearest kilometre for routes over 10km. Ascent is given to the nearest 25m. A mixture of computer, GPS and paper mapping has been used to calculate distance and ascent. Although every effort has been made to supply accurate information it is inevitable that there will be inconsistencies with readers' own plots and GPS tracks. Ascent calculations are liable to vary much more than distance, especially along coasts. Relevant maps are listed along with the start (and end) point(s) of the route with grid references and postcodes. The grid reference gives the precise location of the start of the route. The postcode is approximate and is provided to help Sat Nav users reach the right general area; rural postcodes cover a much larger area than urban postcodes. Each route is rated to indicate the level of navigation required, the roughness of the terrain underfoot and the likelihood of getting wet feet.

Tintagel mud (Route 7)

How to Use This Book

Rating system

Three aspects of the route are rated to set appropriate expectations. The rating is based on the section of the route which requires the highest level of navigation, has the roughest terrain and the highest probability of wet or muddy feet.

Navigation ●○○	These routes are relatively easy to follow, usually with full or partial way-marking or signposts.
Navigation ●●○	Some care is needed to stay on the described route as there are multiple junctions without waymarkers or signs. Some routes are graded ●●○ if they are technically easy to navigate but in a remote area where the consequences of getting lost could be serious. Map and compass are advisable.
Navigation ●●●	These routes cross remote regions where the consequences of getting lost are serious. A map, compass and the ability to use both are required in addition to the route description. The route may not always follow obvious land features. The path may not always be obvious on the ground and may depend upon the season and weather conditions.

Terrain ●○○	Smooth paths or tracks which are easy to run. There may be a few short rougher patches.
Terrain ●●○	Fairly easy to run but stones, tree roots or uneven path sections merit care at times.
Terrain ●●●	These routes are almost entirely runnable provided sufficient attention is paid to foot placement. They may be rocky, boggy or generally uneven. A few routes have sections where walking is unavoidable. This grading also encompasses routes where there are repeated very steep climbs.

Wet Feet ●○○	On a dry day, wet or muddy feet are unlikely. There may be occasional and avoidable muddy puddles or patches of shallow mud.
Wet Feet ●●○	Damp or muddy feet are likely, particularly in autumn and winter. During drier spells, puddles and muddy patches can often be avoided. In normal conditions streams can be crossed by jumping or on stepping stones.
Wet Feet ●●●	Wet or muddy feet are inevitable due to unjumpable stream or river crossings and/or boggy areas.

Map

The route maps are based on Ordnance Survey mapping with the scale varied in order to fit the whole route onto the page. They are intended to be complementary to, not substitutes for, Ordnance Survey or other published maps.

Route description

The route description is divided into two parts; a scene-setting preamble followed by functional, turn-by-turn instructions. The numbering in the description matches the numbers on the route maps.

Compass directions given in the route directions are intended to be used as a *rough indication* alongside the map, not for precise navigation!

Types of trail

All of the routes in this book have legal access. However, it is important to understand the distinctions between the different kinds of trails used. In the route descriptions, the following language is used:

Path: if the word 'path' is used alone, it describes a trail which is not a footpath, bridleway or byway (see below).

Footpath: this word is used to describe a trail marked on Ordnance Survey maps as footpath, i.e. a public right of way. These are marked by a line of short dashes – red on 1:50K Landranger maps, Green on 1:25K Explorer maps. In practice, footpaths can range from a narrow trail to a wide track.

Bridleway: this word is used to describe a trail marked on Ordnance Survey maps as a bridleway, i.e. a public right of way. These are marked by a line of long dashes – red on Landranger maps, green on Explorer maps. In practice, bridleways can range from a narrow trail to a wide track. If the route description says, 'bridleway path', this simply indicates that the bridleway is narrow, if it says 'bridleway track' it simply indicates that the bridleway is wide.

Byways: this word is used to describe a trail marked on Ordnance Survey maps as a byway, i.e. a public right of way. These are marked by a line of red crosses on Landranger maps and a line of green crosses on Explorer maps. Byways are (in theory) driveable, so tend to be relatively wide. Many have firm or tarmac surfaces. Unsurfaced byways are often heavily rutted and liable to flooding. Some byways are marked on maps by a line of 'T' dashes: these are Restricted Byways, where motor vehicles are not allowed.

Permissive: if a footpath, bridleway or byway is described as 'permissive', this means that the landowner has 'allowed' access and that it could potentially be withdrawn.

Access Land: if an area is described as 'Access Land', this means that you are allowed to run freely within it, without restriction (see page 21).

Lane/Road: the word 'lane' is used to describe a tarmac public highway where cars may be encountered, but traffic is usually light. The word 'road' is used to describe busier highways.

Trip planning

This section outlines the logistics involved in running this route. Driving directions and parking information may be supplied. Where public transport is important in shuttling a route, details will be provided. Conveniently located shops, pubs or cafés may be mentioned. Any particular local conditions requiring consideration will also be mentioned in this section.

Useful websites for trip planning are listed in the resources section at the back of the book.

Camel Estuary (Route 6)

Other routes

Every runner is different, so this section aims to help those looking for longer, shorter or just plain different routes as well as runners staying in the area for more than one day.

Events

The Events section is a non-comprehensive list of trail races held on the route or in the local area. Distances for events can be given in either kilometres or miles, depending upon whatever the organiser uses.
More detailed event listings can also be found at websites such as *www.tra-uk.org, www.runnersworld. co.uk, www.therunningbug.co.uk, www.southernrunningguide.com, www.100marathonclub.org.uk, www.fellrunner.org.uk* and *www.sleepmonsters.com*

GPX files

GPX route files are popular with many runners, who upload them onto their GPS devices to assist with navigation. The route descriptions in this book are written to enable runners to complete the route using map and compass, without the need for a GPX file. However, GPX files for all of the routes are available for download from the Pesda Press website *www.pesdapress.com*. The GPX files should be used using common sense and appropriate caution! Always first navigate based on what you see on the ground ahead.

Getting Started

Running is one of the simplest and most satisfying activities in the world: just head out of the door and put one foot in front of the other. There are just a few things it may be helpful to think about first.

Why run?

People run for all sorts of reasons. Some view running as just a means to an unexciting end: becoming fitter, losing weight, achieving performance targets. Trail runners soon come to understand that the activity is greater than the sum of its parts. Your experiences along the trails will help you in maintaining mental wellbeing. They will help you to achieve a sense of mindfulness. You will have fun. You will share adventures and bond with your buddies. You will immerse yourself in beautiful and engaging landscapes and learn how to 'read' the story they tell of geology, prehistory and history. You will become more resilient and now when the photocopier breaks at work, it won't be an apocalyptic scenario. You will become a happier person*.

Coast path freedom
(Route 17)

If all of this is accompanied by side-effects such as stronger muscles, improved cardiovascular fitness and speedier performance, then that's just great.

First steps

Those who have tried road running and found it uncomfortable (or developed injuries) will be pleased to hear that trail running – even in the driest conditions, when the ground is baked hard – is much less stressful on joints and muscles than road running.

All of the routes in this book are just as well walked as jogged or run (or walk-jog-run, the author's preferred style), so there is no fitness barrier to getting started. Just get out there and give them a go! Start off by only running the downhills. Even the world's best runners walk steep uphill sections. As with any activity it is sensible to start small and gradually increase the effort required. Check the suitability of a route by looking at the distance, ascent (height gain) and profile chart (steep or gradual climbs?) given in the route description.

Steady progress

Increase activity levels gradually to give both your muscles and brain time to adapt to the demands of running on trails. Running on uneven trails engages a wider range of muscles than running on smooth roads and pavement. On slippery or rocky trails, the brain needs to work quickly to pick the most secure foot placements. There is also an abundance of information on running-specific training and technique available from medical professionals and running coaches as well as from books and magazines.

Possibly via some truly miserable and masochistic moments!

Muddy feet

Footwear

Well-fitting shoes suitable for the terrain are essential for enjoyable and injury-free running. The fundamentals of choosing the right footwear are comfort and grip. Comfort depends on the way the shoe fits, stabilises, supports and cushions the runner's foot. The right shoe is a very individual decision. Shoe manufacturers use differently shaped lasts and have different ideas about the ideal amount of stability, support and cushioning. Specialist running shops can analyse your running gait, advise on these differences and suggest appropriate footwear.

Road shoes usually have the most stability, support and cushioning. They have a smoother sole which will give adequate grip in dry conditions for well-constructed paths and tracks. On uneven terrain this can make it more difficult to place feet accurately.

Fell shoes have comparatively little cushioning and an exaggerated knobbly sole which helps runners stay secure on steep wet grass. They can be an uncomfortable choice on anything harder than earth or grass paths, particularly during longer runs.

Further still along the 'little cushioning' spectrum are so-called 'barefoot' running shoes. Their minimalist soles are controversially claimed to reduce injury supposedly caused by padded soles. These are definitely an acquired taste.

Unsurprisingly, trail shoes are usually the best compromise for trail running. These have a rugged sole giving better grip making each step much more secure, particularly on wet days. Many models have waterproof and breathable Gore-Tex membranes, expensive but well worth considering if you will be tackling muddy or boggy conditions.

Clothing

There is plenty of technical clothing available from specialist running shops. Synthetic materials are recommended as cotton takes a long time to dry and can rub badly when wet. Multiple thin layers are more flexible for regulating temperature than one thick layer. Zip-neck tops are good for the same reason. Ankle socks are better at preventing stones and dirt from entering shoes than low cut trainer liners. Well-fitting underwear is essential for both men and women: for women this means a high impact-level sports bra.

Weather in the upland and coastal areas which feature heavily in this guidebook can be fickle. Hence, lightweight and breathable waterproofs are an important element of the runner's wardrobe. Hats and gloves should be carried in colder weather. Runners must wear enough to stay warm. It can be tempting to wear less clothing on the assumption that running will help keep the body warm. However in wet, cold conditions thinly clad runners are prone to developing hypothermia, particularly when they tire.

High-visibility reflective clothing is a must, even if (as with the routes in this guidebook), road time will be a small proportion of your run. Those worried about fashion sensibilities may be interested to know that a number of manufacturers now utilise modern materials which reflect light extremely efficiently despite being conventionally coloured (i.e. not Day-Glo).

What to carry?

For short routes there is little need to carry anything at all. For longer routes, especially those in remote areas, food, water and additional clothing are the basic extras. It is most comfortable to carry these in a lightweight rucksack or bumbag designed especially for runners and sold in specialist running or outdoor shops.

It is important to stay well-fed and hydrated. While out on routes lasting several hours, runners should aim to eat a small amount regularly. What to eat is a matter of personal preference. Muesli bars, sandwiches, jelly babies, malt loaf and gloopy energy gels are just some of the foods popular with experienced runners. Drink when thirsty. The amount of fluid needed varies between individual runners and also depends upon the conditions. Water, squash or energy drink can be carried in either a bottle or a bladder and hose.

Map, compass and the ability to use both are essential for some of the routes. A mobile phone is recommended for safety reasons although coverage is limited in many areas. A basic first aid kit containing at least a crepe bandage, wound dressing and a few sticking plasters is recommended, as are a lightweight survival bag and whistle. Head torches weigh very little and prove their worth more often than anticipated. Use common sense when packing for a run. Running with a week's supply of muesli bars, three litres of water and five spare tops will not be much fun. On the other hand, omitting waterproofs and a spare warm layer could lead to a wet, cold and exhausting epic. Go fast and light ... and well-prepared.

Getting Started

Suggested kit list

	WEAR (CONDITIONS DEPENDENT)	CARRY (CONDITIONS DEPENDENT)
SHORT RUNS	SHOES	(ROUTE DESCRIPTION)
	SOCKS	(MAP AND COMPASS)
	SHORTS OR LEGGINGS	(MOBILE PHONE)
	SUPPORTIVE UNDERWEAR	(MONEY)
	SHORT- OR LONG-SLEEVED TOP	(FOOD)
	(CAP)	(WATER)
	(WARM LAYER)	
	(WIND OR WATERPROOF TOP)	
	(HAT, NECK BUFF AND GLOVES)	
	(SUNSCREEN)	
LONGER RUNS	SHOES	LIGHTWEIGHT RUCKSACK OR BUMBAG
	SOCKS	ROUTE DESCRIPTION
	SHORTS OR LEGGINGS	MAP AND COMPASS
	SUPPORTIVE UNDERWEAR	MOBILE PHONE
	SHORT- OR LONG-SLEEVED TOP	MONEY
	(CAP)	FOOD
	(WARM LAYER)	WATER
	(WIND OR WATERPROOF TOP)	(EXTRA WARM LAYERS)
	(HAT, NECK BUFF AND GLOVES)	(WATERPROOF BOTTOMS)
	(SUNSCREEN)	FIRST AID KIT
		WHISTLES
		SURVIVAL BAG
		HEAD TORCH
		(SUNSCREEN)
OVERNIGHT CAMPING RUNS	SHOES	LIGHTWEIGHT RUCKSACK (25L IS GOOD)
	SOCKS	ROUTE DESCRIPTION
	SHORTS OR LEGGINGS	MAP AND COMPASS
	SUPPORTIVE UNDERWEAR	MOBILE PHONE
	SHORT- OR LONG-SLEEVED TOP	MONEY
	(CAP)	FOOD
	(WARM LAYER)	WATER
	(WIND OR WATERPROOF TOP)	EXTRA WARM LAYERS INCLUDING FULL-LENGTH LEGGINGS
	(HAT, NECK BUFF AND GLOVES)	WATERPROOF TOP AND BOTTOMS
	(SUNSCREEN)	FIRST AID KIT
		WHISTLES
		SURVIVAL BAG
		HEAD TORCH
		(SUNSCREEN)
		TENT OR BIVVY BAG
		STOVE, PAN, FUEL AND LIGHTER/ MATCHES
		GROUND INSULATION E.G. CLOSED CELL MAT
		SLEEPING BAG
		(TOTAL WEIGHT 4-7 KG)

Swyre Head bivvy (Route 50)

Hypothermia

Hypothermia is a serious medical condition which occurs when a person's core body temperature drops abnormally low. Look out for stumbles, mumbles and fumbles – key signs of the onset of hypothermia – and make sure these are addressed immediately by putting on more clothes and heading for home.

Ticks

Ticks are a serious danger to trail runners. Ticks can carry Lyme Disease, a life-threatening condition. Even if wearing long sleeves and leggings, ticks are liable to sneak in and find a spot to bite. Always do a full-body check as soon as possible after running in potentially tick-infested areas such as heathland, moor or forest where deer graze. Unfortunately, all of the South West is assessed as 'High Risk' according to Bristol University's 'Big Tick Project'. See their risk map for more details: *www.bigtickproject.co.uk*.

The NHS-recommended removal method is to grab the tick as close to the skin as possible using tweezers, then extract by pulling straight up gently. See a GP immediately if a target-shaped rash or flu-like symptoms develop.

Skills Development

Trail running technique

There is a real joy and satisfaction to running fast over uneven ground. This is a skill that can be learnt through conscious thought and experience. Running on trails requires concentration and can be mentally tiring. It is important to adapt speed to the terrain and to stay within personal limits. Looking ahead and 'reading the trail' to choose the best foot placement is the key to moving swiftly. There may be uneven ground, tree roots, muddy puddles, soft boggy areas, patches of gravel or larger rocks. The skill lies in selecting the clear area among gravel, varying stride length between tree roots, pushing off firm earth rather than soft bog, and landing a footstep precisely on top of a rock instead of slipping awkwardly off its side.

Navigation

The routes in this book range from city centre parks to remote wilderness areas. They cover the whole spectrum from runs where going off-route is no problem at all, to those where getting lost could be very serious. Confident navigation is essential for progressing to the more remote routes included in this guidebook. Each route is graded to indicate the level of navigation required. Confident navigation comes through practice and the ratings system is intended to help development of the required skills.

The route descriptions should be read and used in conjunction with maps. Basic map reading starts by relating the hills, valleys and features such as rivers, buildings and boundaries seen on the ground to the contour lines and symbols marked on the map. Orientate your map to the direction of travel so that the features line up with those on the ground. Whilst moving, keep a mental tick list of features on the map which must be passed in order to reach the next key point on the route. Get into the habit of memorising your tick list and consulting the map only at key points. It helps enormously to know where one is all of the time, rather than spending time figuring out the location from scratch at every stop.

The level of navigation required often changes dramatically with weather conditions. A straightforward trot over moorland to a trig point may require counting paces and following a compass bearing when the cloud rolls in.

Navigators must constantly challenge their own assumptions. Look for features that disprove an identified location. It's all too easy to make features fit with the map and inadvertently 'confirm' an incorrect location. Estimate the width and height of a feature as well as the distance to it before consulting the map. Map measurements should corroborate the estimations. If not, alarm bells should ring!

Developing an awareness of distance and timing is very useful. Try identifying features at varying distances – say 100m, 500m and 1km – and timing how long it takes to run to each of them. Try timing the same distances on rougher terrain.

No times are given for the routes in this book as running time varies so much from person to person. Keep a record of how long each route takes and work out a personalised version of Naismith's rule. This rule of thumb is used by hillwalkers to calculate the length of time a route will take, based on its distance and total ascent. The standard Naismith's rule allows one hour for every 5km plus one minute for each 10m of height gained. For runners, a good starting point is to assume one hour for every 10km plus one minute

Bonehill Rocks (Route 22)

for each 10m height gain. Rougher terrain will increase the time taken, often very significantly.

Almost all of the routes in this book use paths and tracks that are clear and easy to follow independent of the weather conditions. Some follow fainter paths and need a higher level of navigation. Path recognition is key to finding the way on less distinct routes. Developing an eye for traces of previous usage is helpful. Look out for clues such as slightly polished rocks, aligned patches of bare earth, broken, stunted or different types of vegetation. Paths often disappear into boggy or stony areas and reappear on the far side. Humans tend to follow fence lines and head to obvious features. In summertime, even usually clear paths may become overgrown and tricky to identify.

Basic navigational techniques such as orientating (also known as setting) the map, pacing, timing, and following a compass bearing can be taught through courses and by studying books (e.g. *Mountain and Moorland Navigation*, Kevin Walker, Pesda Press 2016, ISBN 978 1906095567). A theoretical knowledge of navigation is not enough. Good navigation only comes through practice. One excellent way of learning and improving navigation skills is the sport of orienteering.

Measuring distance and height

Grid squares are always 1km

OS Landranger 1:50,000 2cm = 1km, 10m contour interval

OS Explorer 1:25,000 4cm = 1km, 10m contour interval

Harvey Superwalker 1:25,000 4cm = 1km, 15m contour interval

Conversion to imperial units

10km is approximately 6 miles

10m is approximately 33ft

Naismith's rule

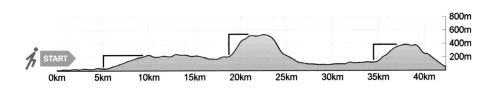

For runners a good starting point is to assume one hour for every 10km plus one minute for each 10m height gain.

EXAMPLE:
approx. 40km run = 4 hours
three climbs total 750m = +75 mins
total estimate = 5 hours 15 mins

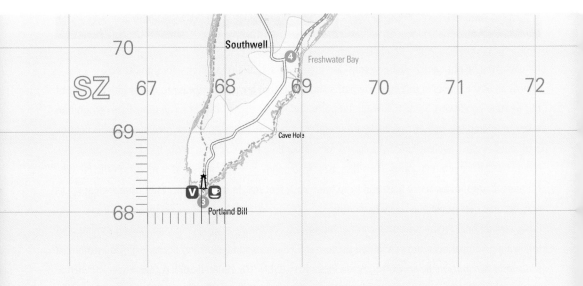

Six figure grid references

On an OS map each 1km square has a four figure reference (look for the blue grid numbers). Divide each square into ten units. Count along then up the square to find your location to within 100m².

EXAMPLE:
Portland Bill's lighthouse is in the grid square 6768;
dividing that square into tenths the lighthouse is seven tenths along and three tenths up
so the grid reference is SZ 677 683

Outdoor Access

Rights and responsibilities

The routes in this book follow trails, commons, heaths and moors where you are legally entitled to run. However, your right to enjoy these outdoor places comes with responsibilities. Adopt a minimum impact approach and leave these trails as it would be good to find them. This definitely means not dumping your gel wrappers on the trail and it may well mean carrying out other people's litter! Mesh rucksack side-pockets are particularly handy for this.

The Countryside Code

The Countryside Code is worth repeating here, as it sums up the approach that mindful and environmentally sensitive trail runners should be taking:

Respect - Protect - Enjoy

Respect other people:

> *consider the local community and other people enjoying the outdoors*

> *leave gates and property as you find them and follow paths unless wider access is available*

Protect the natural environment:

> *leave no trace of your visit and take your litter home*

> *keep dogs under effective control*

Enjoy the outdoors:

> *plan ahead and be prepared*

> *follow advice and local signs*

The full version with advice on each section is of course available online.

Access Land

Access Land is a splendid thing, created in 2000 by the CRoW (Countryside and Rights of Way) Act. On Access Land, you have a right of access on foot for various forms of open air recreation, including trail running. Note that camping is not included. Access Land can be identified using Ordnance Survey Explorer maps, where it is coloured pale yellow and marked AL. Up-to-date maps can also be found on the Natural England website. If you find yourself unsure (or in dispute) about Access Land, call the Open Access Call Centre on 0845 100 3298.

Large tracts of Access Land can be found in Dartmoor and Exmoor National Parks, on Bodmin Moor and generally anywhere where there is unenclosed heath or common.

Most enclosed fields and farmyard areas will not be Access Land. The CRoW Act exempts the following areas from becoming Access Land: land ploughed or drilled within the previous year, land within 20 metres of a dwelling, parks, gardens and golf courses.

Muddy byway

Enjoy

Have fun! Above all, this book is intended to encourage runners get out and explore the South West's amazing and diverse landscapes and trails. There are a great many hours of trail running contained within these pages. Some are easy, some are tough. Sometimes the weather will cooperate and sometimes it will hurl horizontal rain. Sunny day trail runs make the world feel a better place, but a hard run through foul weather can paradoxically be even more satisfying. Going running is always the right decision: there is no such thing as a bad run.

West Cornwall

Here at England's westernmost fringes, the sea is impossible to ignore or avoid. The land reaches out into, resists and is shaped by the booming Atlantic waves. Every route in this section includes some coast, but the diversity of scenery, culture and running experience is surprising. The Scilly archipelago offers days of running among sublime beaches and coastal heath. Land's End and The Lizard are justly famous headlands with very different geology, whilst in between them The Loe is characterised by sheltered woodlands and shingle beach. Running around St Agnes Beacon immerses you in a landscape of historic mining, preserved as a World Heritage Site. Finally, the Trevose Head route takes in the astonishing north coast, with the potential for a multi-day adventure.

Gunver Head (Route 6)

Hugh Town local

Bant's Carn burial chamber

1 The Isles of Scilly

Distance		16km (10 miles)	Ascent	375m (1230ft)
Map		OS Landranger 203 OS Explorer 101		
Navigation	● ● ●	Easy to follow coast path		
Terrain	● ● ●	A variety of surfaces and gradients, mostly grassy heathland		
Wet Feet	● ● ●	It's usually dry on Scilly!		
Start/Finish		Hugh Town quay TR21 0HY/SV 901 107		

Rugged and varied coastal trails in the 'Fortunate Isles'

The Isles of Scilly are a tiny archipelago of low-lying islands, located 40km off Land's End. They are indisputably one of the most beautiful places in Britain. Whilst many are drawn by the blinding white beaches, sub-tropical climate and regular sunshine, few are aware that the isles are a wonderful spot in which to enjoy several days of mild trail running. Outlined here is a run exploring the largest island, St Mary's. It starts directly from the quayside in Hugh Town where you disembark the ferry, and takes in prehistoric tombs, granite cliffs sculpted into outrageous shapes by the wind, and the walls of The Garrison, an extensive set of coastal defences stemming from the sixteenth century. Following this up with runs around the nearby quieter and smaller islands is highly recommended.

Route Description

START Follow the seafront E along the beach – stay on the road and ignore the lifeboat station track, it's a dead end. **1** At the second beach (Porth Mellon), take a track off to the left, leading through the hamlet of Porthloo. **2** When the road turns sharp right whilst climbing a hill, follow the path off to the left. Follow this past Carn Morval Point (option to take higher or lower path) to a junction just past a telegraph mast. **3** Turn left and follow the path downhill and along the beach, before turning left again to reach Bar Point (northern tip of island). **4** Many paths follow the E side of the island, keep choosing the nearest to the sea! **5** Continue around Porth Hellick Bay – check the traffic lights before crossing the end of the airport runway! Continue around Old Town Bay, turning left off Old Town road onto the coastal track past the Old Church to Peninnis Head Lighthouse. **6** Follow the craggy coast N from the lighthouse into Hugh Town and along Porth Cressa's seafront. **7** Turn left to follow the walls all the way around The Garrison. There is a 300m break in the walls from Steval Point (westernmost point), just follow the coast. The walls are rejoined, then follow a short road back to the quay.

St Martin's old quay

Trip Planning

This run starts from the quay in Hugh Town, Scilly's biggest (only) town. Getting to this spot requires a 2 hours 45 minute ferry crossing on the Scillonian III from Penzance. The expensive alternative is a short flight from Land's End Airport, followed by a 2km walk/taxi ride. Both are booked through Isles of Scilly Travel.

Hugh Town has all shops and amenities. Otherwise, the only refreshment on this route is a café at Old Town Bay.

Although it is possible to complete this route as an adventurous day trip from West Cornwall, it's highly recommended to stay longer and explore the other islands; they offer great trail runs around their shores and in any case, Scilly is just wonderful. Further information and accommodation options from the Isles of Scilly Tourist Office.

St Agnes, secret spot!

Other Routes

Having made it to the Isles of Scilly, it would be rude not to run the coastal trails around the other inhabited isles! All bar Samson can easily be accessed by inter-island ferries from Hugh Town.

The Isles of Scilly

Isles of Scilly

Events

The Isles of Scilly Triathlon takes place on Tresco, and there is also a demanding run-swim event organised by Otillo which encompasses all of the main islands.

The other Isles of Scilly

St Martin's: The coast of St Martin's is about 10km long and is notable for the high hedges surrounding flower gardens. At low tide there is a possible extension to adjacent White Island.

Tresco: Tresco is also a 10km run, with craggy heathland at the northern end, and breathtaking sandy beaches around the southern half. Wear sunglasses, the sand is blinding!

Bryher: A favourite of the author's. The complex and indented coast of Bryher is about 8km in length, with amazing views over the jagged Norrard Rocks to the west.

St Agnes and Gugh: St Agnes' coast is longer than it looks (7km), with craggy interludes and a (low tide) crossing of the sand spit to explore adjacent Gugh.

Samson: If you can get a boat (from Bryher or Tresco) to uninhabited Samson, do it! The trails over Samson's two hills are short in distance and restricted in scope (note signage about nesting birds) but the experience of running among abandoned cottages on a desert island is priceless.

Gwennap Head

2 Land's End

Distance	18km (11 miles)	Ascent	625m (2050ft)
Map	OS Landranger 203 OS Explorer 102		
Navigation ●●●	Easy on the South West Coast Path (SWCP), care needed on the inland section		
Terrain ●●●	Rocky footpaths, steep descents and ascents		
Wet Feet ●●●	A few squelchy farmland sections		
Start/Finish	Sennen Cove Harbour car park TR19 7DB/SW 350 263		

Heathland trails over granite cliffs, at the edge of the world!

Land's End completely lives up to its evocative name, offering an exhilarating run among breath-taking environs. Above heaving seas, gulls wheel around castellated towers of golden granite sparkling with quartz, feldspar and mica. Running atop these cliffs as the sun sinks into the Atlantic is a numinous experience. This route starts by bridging the peninsula inland, through fairly fast and direct rural trails. Once the sea is reached at Porthcurno Bay, it is all highlights; glassy seas and golden sands at Porthcurno, the headland of Gwennap Head topped by a Coastwatch lookout station, glorious Nanjizal Bay with its distinctive vertical cave running through the cliffs, the twin sea stacks of Enys Dodnan (pierced by a vast arch) and the Armed Knight, the Longships Lighthouse blinking offshore and the backdrop of Whitesand Bay and Cape Cornwall as you descend into Sennen Cove.

Sadly, Land's End itself is occupied by a theme park: keep your eyes out to sea as you pass this gaudy dump.

Land's End

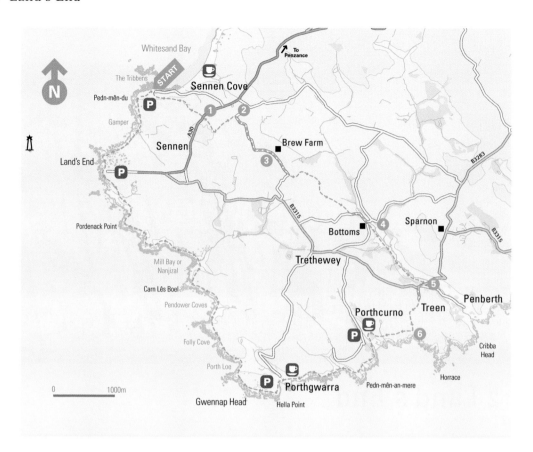

Route Description

🏃 **START**   Leave the harbour car park past the circular wooden capstan building, and turn right (uphill) along Stone Chair Lane. Continue ahead (E) for 400m following footpath signs to reach Maria's Lane. Cross the lane to the footpath opposite and follow this for 500m to the A30. **1** Cross and follow the track ahead to pass through a gate marked 'Mayon Farmhouse B&B'. Follow the footpath leading out of this yard (SE) for 200m and then turn left (NE) onto another footpath, which crosses two fields to reach a lane after 400m. **2** Turn right onto the lane and follow it for 1.4km to a sharp right bend beside a radar installation. **3** Take the bridleway on the left and follow it for 1.4km through Trengothal Farm to a lane. Turn left onto the lane and follow it 300m downhill to a junction. **4** Take the footpath directly opposite, across the junction. Follow it along the Penberth Valley for 1.4km until you reach the B3315. Turn right (steep uphill) to follow the B3315 for 120m to a lane signposted 'Logan Rock/Treen' (second turning on the left). **5** Follow this lane through the village of Treen and keep going until it becomes a track taking you past campsite buildings to the SWCP. **6** Turn right (W) and follow the SWCP for 11km back to Sennen Cove.

Trip Planning

The car park at Sennen Cove is pay and display, reached at the very end of the road past the harbour buildings. It is also possible to start from the car parks at Porthcurno TR19 6JY/SW 384 225 or Porthgwarra TR19 6JR/SW 370 217 (or even at Land's End itself, predictably exorbitant). Sennen Cove has the pleasant Little Bo Café and also a chip shop. There is a shop and post office uphill in Sennen village. Should you require refreshment en route, there are cafés at Porthcurno and Porthgwarra; you could experiment to test the effects of ice cream on your performance.

As cliff-top runs go, this is relatively safe; the heathland atop the cliffs is crisscrossed with numerous alternative paths and in windy conditions, there is usually an option which keeps you safely away from the edge.

If you just want to run the coast path, a 30-minute bus ride can shuttle you between Treen or Porthcurno and Sennen Cove, also calling at Land's End. This is the 1A service, a fitting number for the 'first' bus service in England.

Porthcurno

Pendower Coves

Other Routes

Perhaps predictably, all of the South West Coast Path around the Penwith peninsula (St Ives to Penzance) offers fantastic trail running. The path east from Treen to Mousehole is less spectacular than that around Land's End but constantly interesting and challenging, with boulder scrambles at places like Lamorna Cove and Boskenna. The section leading north to Cape Cornwall traverses some steep-sided slopes above beaches and reefs; don't miss Ballowall Barrow just after Porth Nanven, an amazingly preserved prehistoric tomb.

Above Sennen Cove

The SWCP between Cape Cornwall and St Ives (CC2STI) is just incredible; it was a difficult choice whether to include this or Land's End in this book. Both make for outstanding runs, but Land's End was finally chosen on account of its unique granite cliffs and spires. CC2STI is much more challenging, stretching nearly 30km with some seriously rugged paths and soul-sucking bogs, through a landscape of ruined mines perched atop basalt cliffs.

Penwith is also stunning, inland. The moorland above CC2STI is accessible through various short footpaths.

Land's End

This author expended considerable energy trying to locate the Holy Grail: a circular route which would link up the best of the cliff path and the high moor behind. All he found was deep gorse and bogs; if you do better, please tell me!

A short and accessible run with huge views can be enjoyed by ascending and exploring Carn Brea, England's western-most hill. Park at TR19 6JD/SW 388 283.

Land's End

Events

A number of fairly extreme races take in Land's End. Votwo's 3-day 127km Atlantic Challenge starts at Padstow and ends at Land's End. Endurance Life's Classic Quarter is 44 miles from The Lizard to Land's End, with solo and team categories. Rat Race's macho-named Man vs Coast is 20 miles long including some coasteering (jumping into the sea).

The South West Coast Path National Trail

The South West Coast Path is Britain's longest* National Trail, stretching from Minehead in Somerset to Poole in Dorset, via Land's End at its westernmost extremity. The SWCP is unquestionably the jewel in the crown of trail running in the South West, and it is no hyperbole at all to suggest that it ranks among the very best trail running experiences in the world. A continuous 1014km/630-mile path with simple access and good transport links, following ever-changing but regularly breath-taking cliffs and beaches along the Atlantic-facing shores of the South West peninsula ... there is simply nothing like it.

Planning *South West Trail Running*, there was a strong temptation to simply divide the 1014km into 70 discrete routes and fill the whole book! For sure, there are few sections of the SWCP that would not justify inclusion. However, the following approach has been taken; sections of the SWCP are utilised in many of this book's routes, but those selected are included here because they specifically showcase a particular (and usually unique) highlight of the National Trail. In most cases, a 'loop' route is suggested. The routes which are simply 'A to B' sections of the SWCP are included because the author deems them unmissable, because public transport offers a way to shuttle back to the start and because in his opinion the inland part of a 'loop' route wouldn't be of justifiable quality compared to the coastal part.

At time of writing (2018), the record for completing the entire 1014km and 35,000 metres ascent of the SWCP is 10 days, 15 hours and 18 minutes, achieved by Damien Hall in 2016. Julie Gardener set the women's record of 14 days, 14 hours and 44 minutes in 2013. Typically, I'd throw in a joke or mildly amusing comment at this point ... but I simply have no words.

* *The England Coast Path, expected to be completed in 2020, will of course be much longer. See page 176*

Loe Bar

3 The Loe

Distance		10km (6 miles)	**Ascent**	200m (660ft)
Map		OS Landranger 203 OS Explorer 103		
Navigation	●●●	Just keep the lake on your right …		
Terrain	●●●	Tarmac, followed by stony estate tracks, footpaths, grassy fields and soft gritty sand		
Wet Feet	●●●	Gets pretty muddy on the east shore, good chance of sandy shoes too		
Start/Finish		Penrose Hill National Trust car park TR13 0RE/SW 638 258		

A variety of trail surfaces circumnavigating Cornwall's largest natural lake

The Loe is Cornwall's largest freshwater lake, formed from a ria (drowned river valley) which became cut off from the sea by a shingle bar. Estimates of its age range from 700 to several thousand years old. Today, it is part of the Penrose Estate, administered by the National Trust. The lake is surrounded by marsh, farmland and woodland, threaded with trails which make for great running on a variety of surfaces. Running through the sand and shingle atop Loe Bar is heavy-going, just concentrate on the sea views and the crashing waves and try to keep going! For company you will have the wildfowl and maybe the occasional deer. Although Penrose is popular with tourists, you will have no problem finding peace and quiet once you get past the surfaced sections.

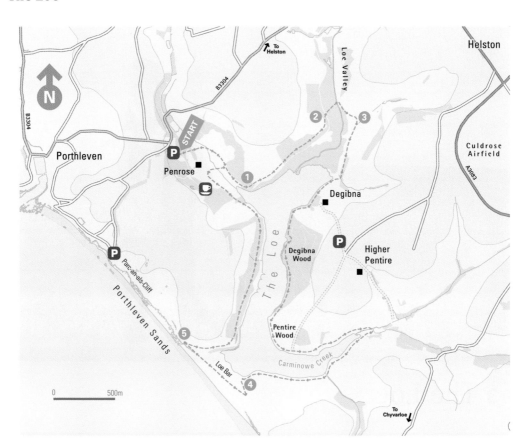

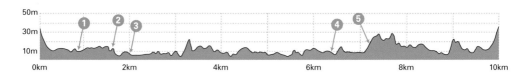

Route Description

START Follow the path leading from the downhill end of the car park and descend steps to a tarmac road. Turn right and follow this downhill to the lakeside. ❶ Pass through gates and past a building. Follow the track NE past the end of the lake. ❷ Turn right onto the first footpath signposted off the track. Cross the bridges and ascend steps to a track beside an engine house. ❸ Turn right onto the track and follow it S along the lakeshore; this alternately changes from a path to a track. Turn right at all junctions! ❹ When you reach the beach, ascend the sand bar and cross between the sea and lake, aiming for the crumbling concrete path at the far end. ❺ Ascend the path to a junction beside a house where you turn right (inland) away from the sea. Follow this estate track paralleling the W shore of the lake until you rejoin your original route; follow it uphill to the car park.

Loe Bar

Trip Planning

The car park at Penrose Hill (signposted off a bend on the B3304) asks for donations. Similar NT car parks are found at Degibna TR12 7PR/SW 653 250 and Chyvarloe TR12 7PY/SW 651 236, and it is also possible to park outside the estate at Helston TR13 0RA/SW 654 270 or Porthleven TR13 9ES/SW 635 249 to access this route. The Stables Café serves local cakes and ice cream and is passed near the start of this run, a good place to refuel and recuperate afterwards. Only open weekends in the winter months.

The Penrose Estate supposedly closes at dusk, although this author encountered no problems with running past sunset. More information about the estate (including a detailed map) can be downloaded from the National Trust website.

In times of strong winds and stormy seas, Loe Bar may be a dangerous place to be. Use your judgement.

Loe Bar sunset

The Loe

The Loe

Other Routes

Starting from Helston or Porthleven will extend your run by about 2km. There are numerous other paths within the estate, see the NT's downloadable map.

The South West Coast Path leads 5km south-east from Loe Bar to Poldhu Cove, from where it is only another 13km (Route 4) to the very bottom of Britain ...

Events

A 5km 'parkrun' is held every Saturday on the tarmac sections of the estate. Freedom Racing organise a 10K trail race from Poldhu Cove along the SWCP to the edge of the Penrose Estate, and back.

Above Ogo-dour Cove

4 The Lizard

Distance	13km (8 miles)	**Ascent**	550m (1800ft)
Map	OS Landranger 203 OS Explorer 103		
Navigation ●●●	Follows clear paths along the South West Coast Path		
Terrain ●●●	Grassy heathland and rocky steps		
Wet Feet ●●●	A few small swampy areas to negotiate		
Start	Poldhu Cove car park TR12 7JB/SW 666 199		
Finish	Lizard Point TR12 7NU/SW 701 115		

Cliff-top trails leading to the base of Britain

This iconic section of the South West Coast Path is a particularly fine playground for trail runners. A succession of imposing headlands leads you further and further south until you can go no further! The paths are just technical enough to negotiate without distracting you from the views. The cliffs are particularly amazing; you won't need to be a geologist to enjoy the Technicolor slates, schist, gneiss, granite, gabbro, and serpentine. Sandy Poldhu Cove is followed by the Marconi Monument, commemorating his pioneering wireless radio experiments on The Lizard. You pass through the wave-battered harbour of Mullion Cove, backed by dramatic Mullion Island. Further south, Kynance Cove is a famous beauty spot, with a strand of sand linking tall Gull Rock and Asparagus Island to the shore at low tide. Finally you round the corner at Lizard Point and the very base of Britain opens up. Atop the cliffs are the twin octagonal towers of the Lizard Lighthouse, whilst sawtooth reefs extend out to sea.

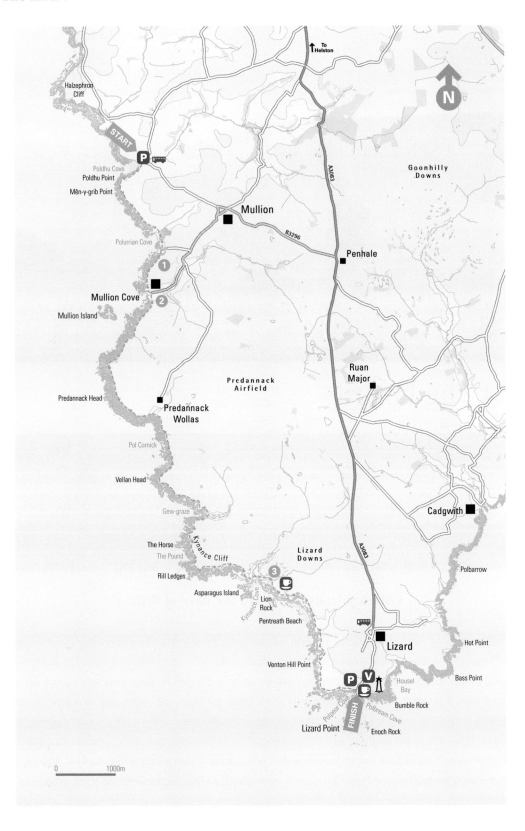

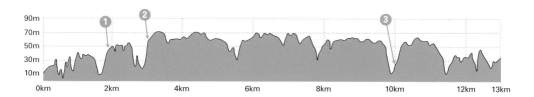

Route Description

🏃 START From the bus stop and car park at Poldhu Cove, follow the SWCP uphill along the road to a care home. Circumvent this via the footpath along the cliffs, which passes the Marconi Monument before descending to Polurrian Cove. ❶ Ascend from Polurrian Cove – there is a brief tarmac interlude – and continue S to the parking area above Mullion Cove (you'll see the harbour walls below). There are various path options down to Mullion Cove, descend with care. ❷ Climb out of Mullion Cove. The 7km to Kynance Cove are mostly level, broken up by two mild descents and ascents and one rockier descent to the valley of Gew-graze, before climbing back up to Kynance Cliff. The winding descent into Kynance Cove follows a choice of paths, some requiring you to jump the stream at the bottom. ❸ Climb out of Kynance Cove. The last 3km S are more undulating and closer to sea level. When you round the corner at Lizard Point, you will see a cluster of buildings and the lighthouse; finish at the café, or (for completeness' sake) descend the track to Polpeor Cove and dip your toes in our most southerly waters.

Trip Planning

This run can be shuttled using the Number 37 bus service, which runs between the start and finish every hour or two. The car park at Poldhu Cove is pay and display, run by Cornwall Council. Buses stop opposite the car park. At the other end, buses depart from Lizard Green which is a kilometre inland from Lizard Point.

The Polpeor Café is located right on Lizard Point where you finish. It looks ramshackle and 'greasy spoon' but it actually serves rather nice fare. The Kynance Café is en route, should you be able to cope with a cream tea mid-run.

The Lizard Lighthouse Visitor Centre is worth a peruse after your run, especially if you sign up for a tour of the towers.

Lizard Point

Other Routes

The South West Coast Path along the east side of the Lizard peninsula is similarly dramatic, certainly as far as Kuggar. By happy coincidence, the bus service also calls here, meaning that this run can be extended by 8km past Lizard Point.

Predannack Head

Mullion Cove

Goonhilly Downs National Nature Reserve offers an inland (and flatter) alternative. From the Natural England car park at Goonhilly on the A3293 (TR12 6EA/SW 729 211), explore open heathland dotted with wild flowers, prehistoric standing stones and WWII building remains. Maps available at the car park.

Events

Endurance Life's Classic Quarter ultramarathon is an über-hard 44 miles from The Lizard to Land's End, with solo and team categories. Freedom Racing organise a 10K trail race from NW Poldhu Cove along the SWCP to the edge of the Penrose Estate (Route 3) and back.

St Agnes Beacon

5 St Agnes Beacon

Distance	11km (7 miles)	Ascent	425m (1400ft)
Map	OS Landranger 203 OS Explorer 104		
Navigation ●●●	Inland paths are clear and obvious, the SWCP is followed in the second part		
Terrain ●●●	Stony tracks and paths, rocky exposed sections on the coast path		
Wet Feet ●●●	The paths dry well and there are few mud patches		
Start/Finish	Porthtowan Beach car park TR4 8AA/SW 692 480		

Ghostly mining ruins and a summit with expansive coastal views

The landscape around St Agnes Beacon is scarred and littered by the traces of centuries of tin mining. Don't be put off, however! The mining ruins unquestionably add to, rather than detract from, the already stunning coastal scenery.

Leaving the surfers at Porthtowan and Chapel Porth behind, you ascend St Agnes Beacon, giving you a magnificent panorama over the landscape that inspired the 'Poldark' novels and TV series. You then drop down to follow the cliffs around St Agnes Head. These are rather vertiginous, avoid if you don't like heights! The highlight is perhaps the Wheal Coates mine where a complex of ruined chimneys and engine houses overlook the waves crashing far below.

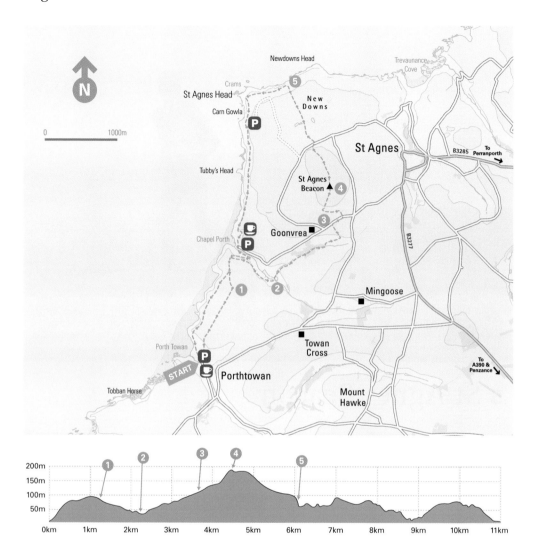

Route Description

START Follow the bridleway signposted out of the back of the car park, steeply uphill heading N. From the top of the hill, follow the bridleway (which parallels the SWCP about 200m inland) for 700m until it reaches a crossroads at the edge of overgrown heathland. Continue ahead for another 130m to another junction, then turn left (towards the sea). ❶ After 350m the bridleway begins to steeply descend towards Chapel Porth. Look for a rough but straight path on your right, leading inland along the side of Chapel Combe valley. This path leads gradually downhill (if you miss this rough path, you can follow the footpath from Chapel Porth car park along the valley floor). ❷ When you reach the valley floor take the footpath on the left (heading NE) across the stream. Follow the footpath uphill. After 850m it bends left; turn right at the next junction (60m away) and left at the following junction (200m away). After another 200m the path reaches a road. ❸ Turn right onto the road and follow it for 150m, then take the footpath leading uphill on the left. Follow this, taking the uphill option at all junctions until you reach the summit trig point of St Agnes Beacon. ❹ From the summit, follow the ridge N. Various paths lead downhill at the end of the ridge; keep going ahead (N) as much as possible. When you reach the road you should be almost opposite a footpath track continuing N. Follow this ahead until you reach the cliff top. **5** Turn left and follow the SWCP W to St Agnes Head, then turn left (or fall into the sea) to follow the SWCP S for the remainder of the run. Initially the path is quite exposed – not for those with vertigo! There are various path options around the mining ruins at Wheal Coates, all re-converge before descending steeply to Chapel Porth. Climb back up out of the cove following the SWCP, and follow this back to Porthtowan.

Trip Planning

Apart from the pay and display car park, there is some parking on the sandy road towards the beach, only early birds need apply. Another possibility is to start from the National Trust car park TR4 8AL/SW 697 494 at Chapel Porth, where there is also a small café. There are also various free parking areas TR5 0ST/SW 699 512 up on St Agnes Head itself.

Runners above Chapel Porth

Your cup will runneth over for refreshment choice in Porthtowan; there are numerous cafés and pubs to choose from, as well as a shop and chippie.

A number of times along this route, you will spot conical cages. These are covering unsealed mine shafts, so don't investigate too closely! For similar reasons, avoid the temptation to cut corners or stray off paths. There are several places along the clifftop where a bad misstep could lead to you taking the Four-and-a-half-second Tour (I've done the maths, that figure is correct), so perhaps avoid very wet or windy conditions.

St Agnes Head

Chapel Porth

Other Routes

From Porthtowan south to Portreath along the South West Coast Path is 6km and it is another 10km to Godrevy/Gwithian (look out for the huge seal colony basking in Mutton Cove); all this magnificent cliff-top running can be shuttled using the A4 Atlantic Coaster bus service.

Events

Freedom Racing's Porthtowan 10K follows a similar route to this one.

Porthtowan

Wheal Coates

Cornish Mining World Heritage Site

The landscape around St Agnes is part of the above-named World Heritage Site, which celebrates and pre-serves the mining heritage of Cornwall and also the Tamar Valley (see Route 25). This is a post-industrial landscape of waste heaps, scarred hillsides, crumbling chimneys and gutted engine houses; not an entic-ing prospect, on paper! However in practice these remains are a hauntingly beautiful sight, blending as integral components of the landscape.

'Hard rock coastal mining' was profitable on account of Cornwall's unusually rich tin and copper lodes. Early in the nineteenth century the introduction of steam pumps led to astounding expansion. For example, Levant Mine near Cape Cornwall reached 600m below sea level, with tunnels extending 1.5km out under the sea and worked to within metres of the seabed. Accidents were common and a miner's life expectancy was under 40.

Porthmissen

6 Trevose Head

Distance	21km (13 miles)	**Ascent**	600m (1970ft)
Map	OS Landranger 200 OS Explorer 106		
Navigation ●●●	Entirely following the (well-signposted) SWCP		
Terrain ●●●	A few rocky steep patches, mostly mild gradient. Some beach sections		
Wet Feet ●●●	Fairly slippery after rain. Shallow streams on beaches to jump or wade		
Start	Porthcothan Bay PL28 8LW/SW 858 719		
Finish	Padstow Bus Depot PL28 8DW/SW 920 751		

Atlantic perfection, enjoyed via mildly challenging trails

Seriously, where do I even start? There is just so much to enjoy and experience along this route that summing it up in a paragraph seems heretical. Ask yourself whether you enjoy any of the following: running along clifftops above reefs and sea stacks; striding across wet sand, whilst waves pound the beach alongside; weaving through sea pink-covered maritime heath; lighthouses and towers topping airy headlands. Presumably some of these things appeal, in which case you really should come run here.

To be fair, the characteristics outlined above are not exactly unheard of in Cornwall. What makes this route especially engaging is the constantly varying scenery. The indented coast north of Porthcothan is followed by wide beaches and rocky reefs. Trevose Head and Stepper Point jut into the Celtic Sea, with high cliffs exposed to the Atlantic breakers and offering vistas far along the north coast. In between the two, Harlyn

Trevose Head

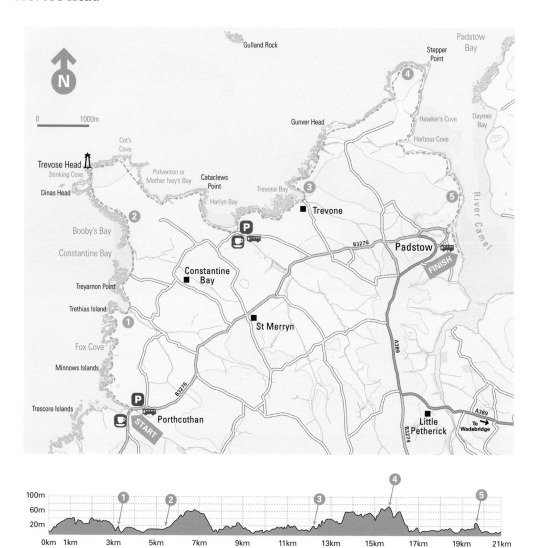

Bay is sheltered from the south-west swell, as are the River Camel estuary's vast sands leading to the fishing port of Padstow.

This can be enjoyed by all trail runners; the going is generally easy with few steep sections and not too much technical challenge, and it is simple to break into shorter sections.

Route Description

This route is waymarked throughout, as it is part of the South West Coast Path: follow the acorn symbol. This description just outlines the main features of the route. START From Porthcothan to Treyarnon Beach, you follow low cliffs around numerous coves and inlets, above many stacks and tiny islands. ① Treyarnon Bay is crossed on the sand, as is Constantine Bay shortly after. ② The ascent onto Trevose Head is mild, followed by easy trails around the Head to Harlyn Bay. A short section of sand in Harlyn Bay is followed by more easy trails to Trevone Bay. ③ The ascent from Trevone Bay is the steepest of this route,

followed by another steep ascent to Gunver Head.
④ From the tower on Stepper Point, you descend to
sea level and follow the Camel Estuary south to Padstow. ⑤ From the War Memorial, the paths are tarmac.
Follow the road past Padstow Harbour and then continue following Riverside Road along the seafront
until you reach the bus depot, opposite Rick Stein's
Cookery School.

Trip Planning

This route's start and finish points are just 7km apart,
conveniently served by the A5 bus service. Buses depart
every 90 minutes (less frequently on Sundays) and
take about 30 minutes. The A5 route also serves Harlyn
Bridge at the halfway point, and points along the coast
south to Newquay, should a longer run be desired.

There are cafés and other seaside eateries at Porthcothan, Treyarnon, Constantine, Harlyn and Trevone; the
burger stall at Treyarnon Bay gets my vote. Padstow
is pretty upmarket nosh-wise, due to the Rick Stein
effect. Even his chippie (close to the bus stop) serves
langoustines and champagne.

A regular passenger ferry connects Padstow with Rock,
across the estuary. This opens up the possibility of combining this route with Route 7 to create a world-class
fastpacking adventure ...

Other Routes

The car park at Harlyn Bridge PL28 8PD/SW 879 753
is at the halfway point, perfectly dissecting the route
into two. If choosing which 10.5km half best suits
your prejudices, note that the second half has steeper
ascents and slightly rockier trails.

A lovely 8km circuit of Trevose Head can be enjoyed
by starting at Harlyn Bridge and crossing the headland
via 2km of lane and footpath, to join the SWCP at
Constantine Bay. Similarly, a 14km loop around Stepper
Point is possible by following lanes and tracks from
Padstow to Trevone Bay ③.

Pepper Cove

Stepper Point

Mother Ivey's Bay

Trevose Head

Trevose Head

Bedruthan Steps

Starting from Bedruthan Steps National Trust car park PL27 7UW/SW 849 690 or Mawgan Porth car park TR8 4BJ/SW 849 671 will extend your run to 27km or 29km respectively. The extra mileage is worth considering as it encompasses the spectacular stacks on the beach at Bedruthan Steps.

The Camel Trail leads inland for 29km from Padstow to Wenfordbridge on Bodmin Moor, unsurprisingly following the River Camel. This former railway is mostly hard-surfaced and popular with cyclists.

Events

The Big Run Cornwall follows the Camel Trail and finishes at Padstow with 5.5, 11 and 17.3-mile options. For the somewhat motivated, Votwo's 3-day 127km Atlantic Challenge starts at Padstow and ends at Land's End.

East Cornwall

This region includes coastal running adventures every bit as spectacular as those found in West Cornwall, most obviously in the epic Atlantic frontage between Polzeath and Boscastle, less showily around the coves, headlands and inlets facing the more benign English Channel. Between these two contrasting shores, Bodmin Moor rises starkly, characterised by bleak eminences and rough-going bog. Although less well known and frequented than Exmoor and Dartmoor, Bodmin can be equally wild in both landscape and climate and has much to offer runners prepared to endure some seriously heavy-going terrain.

Polridmouth (Route 8)

Kellan Head

Port Isaac Bay

7 Tintagel

Distance	36km (22.5 miles)	Ascent	1850m (6070ft)
Map	OS Landranger 200, 190 OS Explorer 106, 111		
Navigation ●●●	Entirely along the SWCP; follow the acorns!		
Terrain ●●●	Numerous steep climbs and descents, your knees will despise you		
Wet Feet ●●●	Slippery and muddy sections in winter		
Start	New Polzeath long stay car park PL27 6UG/SW 936 795		
Finish	Boscastle Bridge bus stop PL35 0AQ/SX 098 912		

The ultimate South West Coast Path adventure

Bit of a brave title, right? We're not claiming that this long section of the SWCP is the best long trail run along the SWCP*, simply that tackled over two days, it offers the perfect mini-expedition. Any part of this route is well worth the journey to trail run. But you really must cram your sleeping bag and mat into your rucksack and plan on tackling the entire 36km and 1850m of ascent as a single adventure, broken up by an overnight bivvy. Trust us on this one.

Whilst there are evenly-spaced spots where civilisation intrudes and refreshment is available, the going is consistently tough and for the most part out of sight of roads and houses. The trails regularly offer challenging narrow single track (with admittedly a few too many flights of steps). In particular, the middle section between Port Gaverne and Trebarwith Strand feels remarkably wild; the path grinds up and down

*Although as it happens, it might well be ...

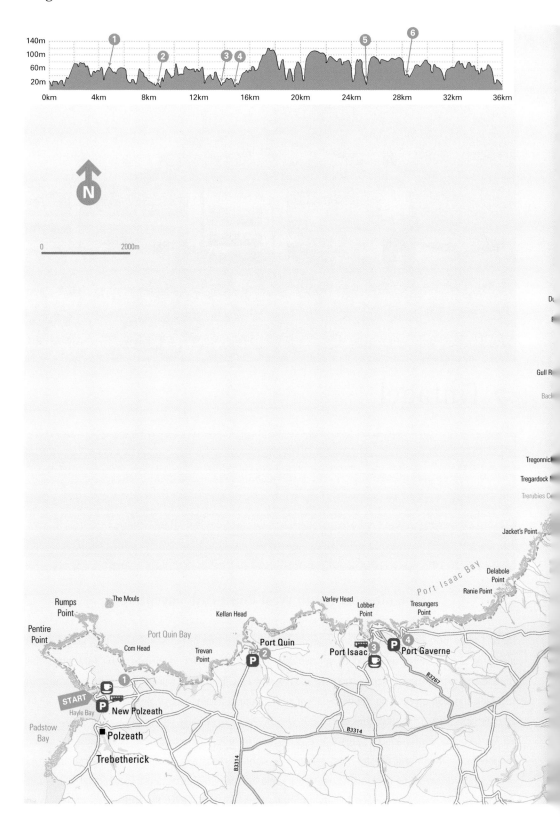

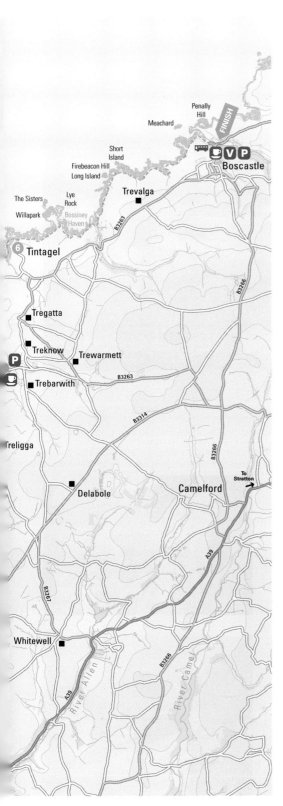

endless steep valleys descending to the Atlantic shore and we met literally no one on our last run.

The coastal scenery starts off as breathtaking, yet somehow manages to *keep getting better* along the route. By the time you make it to soaring Tintagel Head (topped by a ruined castle and supposedly the site of King Arthur's Camelot), your mind will be properly blown ... and you still have the deep waterfall-adorned cleft of Rocky Valley and rugged sea stacks around Boscastle's winding gorge-like harbour to savour.

Route Description

This route is waymarked throughout, as it is part of the South West Coast Path; follow the acorn symbol. This description just outlines the main features of the route. **START** Head towards the beach from the car park and turn right when you reach the coast path! Ascend gradually to Pentire Point and continue around the headland, passing the Iron Age earthworks across Rumps Point. ❶ From Pengirt Cove, you leave the headland and head east above and sometimes along the cliffs, dropping to sea level at Epphaven Cove. ❷ From the handful of buildings at Port Quin, the path winds around Kellan Head and then Varley Head, before a steep descent and ascent at Pine Haven, just before Port Isaac. ❸ Reaching Port Isaac, there is about 1km on road through the village around to Port Gaverne. ❹ At Port Gaverne, the SWCP heads steeply uphill, but continue following the coast path around the harbour (towards Main Head) for a pleasant short detour. Between Port Gaverne and Trebarwith Strand is 10km of steep ascents and descents, the most challenging section of the route. ❺ From Trebarwith, the path climbs above disused quarries. At Tintagel Head, there is a choice of paths; the steep path down to the bridge connecting the 'island' to the mainland is spectacular but may be busy with tourists. ❻ The final 8km to Boscastle Harbour is mostly along clifftops, with one steep descent and ascent at Rocky Valley.

Rumps Point

Trip Planning

The key to making this work logistically is the 95/96 bus service, which serves Polzeath, Port Isaac, Tintagel (some way inland) and Boscastle. The ride between Polzeath and Boscastle involves a change at Wadebridge or Camelford and takes nearly two hours. Leave your car at New Polzeath long-stay car park or hide it on a side street; alternatively, park at Boscastle and ride the bus shuttle first.

Rocky Valley

Polzeath, Port Isaac and Boscastle have plenty of options for food and shops. Port Quin has only a water tap, which you may appreciate on a hot day. There is a pub and café at Trebarwith Strand; the Port William Inn serves good food and might be an ideal place to fuel up in the evening, before bedding down a little further along the trail! English Heritage also run a café beside Tintagel Head. Note that there are zero facilities for the toughest 10km, between Port Gaverne and Trebarwith Strand.

Additional car parks along the route: Port Quin PL29 3SU/SW 971 805, Port Isaac/Port Gaverne PL29 3SB/SW 999 810, Trebarwith Strand PL34 0HB/SX 053 864.

Tintagel Castle

Sunset near Bossiney

Other Routes

If you have time and energy, a highly recommended extension is to start from Porthcothan and first run Route 6, perhaps making for a full weekend's outing. This coast is less wild and milder in terms of terrain but makes for a perfect warm-up. Route 6 is 21km and the dune-strewn coast between the Rock Ferry and Polzeath adds another 5km. If you want to continue past Boscastle(!) you face another strenuous and spectacular 10.8km to Crackington Haven, with over 700m of ascent. This includes High Cliff, at 223m the highest point on Cornwall's coast.

If you insist on breaking this route down, then Polzeath to Port Quin ❷ is 9.2km, Port Quin to Port Isaac ❸ is 5.1km, Port Isaac to Trebarwith Strand ❺ is 11.1km and Trebarwith Strand to Boscastle is also 11.1km.

The loop around Pentire Point headland (turning inland towards Polzeath on the footpath at ❶) is a popular and classic 6km run.

Port Quin Bay

Pentire Point
Photo: Chris Eden

Events

The Polzeath 10K, organised by Freedom Racing, involves a circuit of the Pentire Point headland.

Fastpacking

What is fastpacking? It's simply a buzzword dreamt up (by the outdoor gear industry?) to describe the zone of overlap between backpacking and trail running. Whatever you think of the name, it describes a means of accessing some amazing mini-adventures. Fastpackers move fast and light through the landscape, carrying the minimum gear to sleep and eat. You sleep wherever you wind up when the sun sinks and the stars come out. When dawn rises you quickly pack up, head off again and cover as much ground as your legs will allow; running, jogging, walking.

The key to this being practical is travelling lightweight. A trawl through the internet will reveal that ultra-light fastpackers will forgo sleeping bags and shelters and sleep under their waterproof capes! This author takes a less hypothermic approach; 2-season down sleeping bag, inflatable mattress and Gore-Tex bivvy bag. These weigh under two kilos, can be laid out quickly – literally wherever you stop on the trail – and offer decent protection and comfort outside the winter months. Carrying cooking gear and evening meals etc. is possible, but a non-purist approach is to utilise pubs and other eateries along your route …. eat well, sleep rough!

Haytor (Route 22)

East side of Gribbin Head

8 Gribbin Head

Distance	11km (6.5 miles)	**Ascent**	500m (1640ft)
Map	OS Landranger 204 OS Explorer 107		
Navigation ●●●	Mostly on the SWCP		
Terrain ●●●	Narrow footpaths, various steps and short climbs		
Wet Feet ●●●	Nothing worse than the occasional puddle jump		
Start/Finish	Readymoney Cove Long Stay car park PL23 1JD/SX 116 513		

Splendid mild coastal trails in Daphne Du Maurier country

The coast of low cliffs and craggy beaches that you explore here is that which inspired Daphne du Maurier's novels. This route starts from Fowey, where she lived from 1926 to 1943 writing *Frenchman's Creek*, *Rebecca* and *Jamaica Inn,* and crosses the peninsula to loop around Gribbin Head and the Menabilly estate, her home from 1943 and *Rebecca*'s 'Manderley'.

This run becomes progressively more scenic as you clock up the kilometres. The first (cross-country) section to Polkerris follows clearly defined paths on the Saint's Way. You then speed south towards Gribbin Head on narrow winding footpaths, never far from or above the sea, with the 'Cornish Alps'* as a backdrop across the bay. The distinctive striped square tower on Gribbin Head which rises 104m above the sea is a Trinity House daymark from 1834. A series of tiny coves lead back towards Fowey, interspersed with short

Artificial hills of waste from china clay mining.

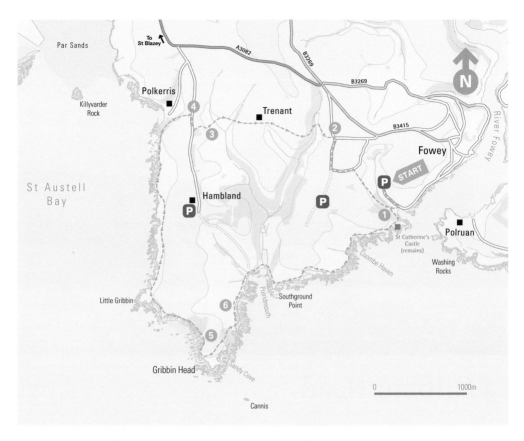

steep climbs. Be wary of electric fences, the author managed to electrocute himself in the head hereabouts (long story). The final landmark is St Catherine's Castle guarding the entrance to Fowey Harbour, which you can explore via a quick detour.

Route Description

START Take the path leading out from the back of the car park and descend to Readymoney Cove. Cross the cove behind the beach and follow the rocky footpath leading uphill out of the cove on the far (SW) side. Ascend 75m to a T-junction with a bridleway. **1** Turn right and follow this bridleway uphill to a lane. Turn left onto the lane. After 225m, turn right at a T-junction and descend on this lane to another junction. **2** Take the footpath on the left, directly after the junction (signposted as Saint's Way). Follow this 1.5km to Tregaminion Farm. **3** Pass through the farm to a lane. Turn right onto the lane and then after 150m turn off left again onto a footpath. **4** Follow the footpath towards the coast (don't descend into Polkerris) and then 3km S to Gribbin Head, following the SWCP acorns. **5** At Gribbin Head (striped

Gribbin Head daymark

tower) you have the option of a short deviation off the SWCP if you follow the footpath further S towards the headland. ⑥ When the paths rejoin, follow the SWCP 3.5km NE back to Readymoney Cove and then ascend back to the car park.

Trip Planning

Readymoney Cove long stay car park is found on Tower Park, just SW of Fowey, and is pay and display. Parking within Fowey itself is a brutally competitive experience; good luck if you try. Other possible places to set out from are the car parks at Tregear's Wood PL23 1HP/SX 109 511 or Hambland PL24 2TN/SX 096 510, either of which would enable you to join the route at Polridmouth Cove, a short distance after ⑥.

Ice cream is available at Readymoney Cove and all other forms of sustenance can be obtained within Fowey, 1km from the car park.

Readymoney Cove

Fowey

Gribbin Head

St Austell Bay

Other Routes

The Saint's Way is a scenic 48km coast to coast path joining Padstow to Fowey, although the final section around Fowey is mostly on roads.

Across the Fowey River to the east, the South West Coast Path enjoys a particularly stunning 19km section between Polruan and Looe, including the picture-postcard inlet of Polperro after 8km, which can be easily shuttled by bus.

Further up the Fowey River along the tidal creek around Lerryn, some extremely attractive waterside trails can be explored, mostly on National Trust land.

Atop Rough Tor

9 Brown Willy

Distance		15km (9.5 miles)	Ascent	425m (1400ft)
Map		OS Landranger 200 OS Explorer 109		
Navigation	•••	Plenty of unmarked moorland, compass essential		
Terrain	•••	Tracks, paths, moor, bog, some scrambling on granite		
Wet Feet	•••	If you don't find a bog, you're not trying hard enough		
Start/Finish		Lane near St Breward PL30 4PN/SX 116 789		

A strenuous yomp into Cornwall's wilderness

This route takes you into the heart of Bodmin Moor, ascending both the craggiest (Rough Tor, 400m) and highest (Brown Willy, 420m) of Cornwall's hills. Surveying Bodmin Moor's bleak expanses from these summits, you'll appreciate that it can be every bit as wild and unforgiving as its much larger cousin, Dartmoor. The lack of human presence is a modern thing; literally everywhere you stumble across clues to a populous distant past; boundary walls, cairns, standing stones, hut circles and so forth.

Don't expect to log any personal bests on this run ... the going is often slow and at times you will mutter and curse as you attempt to locate the sheep path of least resistance through bracken, boulders, peat bog and grassy tussocks.

Oh, and that name? Stifle those childish sniggers ... 'Brown Willy' is derived from the Cornish *Bron Wennyly*, meaning 'hill of swallows'.

Brown Willy

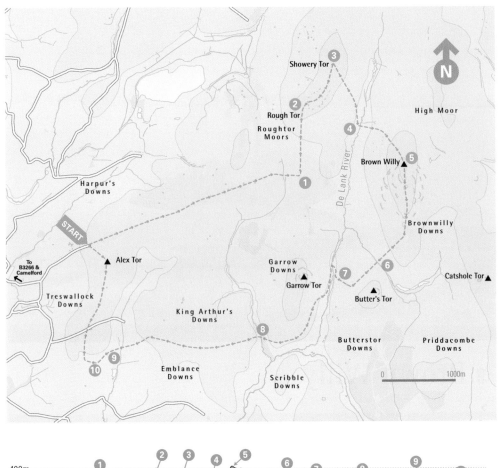

Route Description

🏃 **START** Follow the road, which becomes a track, for 3km ENE. **1** 100m after the track descends and crosses a stream, turn off left onto the moor and head N past a stone circle towards the summit of Rough Tor. Scramble through the bracken and boulders to the summit. **2** Follow the summit ridge for 700m over Little Rough Tor to Showery Tor. **3** Descend roughly SSE to the De Lank River and cross the bridge at **SX 153 805**. **4** Follow the permissive path 1km to the summit of Brown Willy (trig point). **5** Follow the permissive path S along the ridge and then SW to a track at the valley floor. **6** Cross the track and the stream behind by a footbridge, still following the permissive path. Follow the permissive path SW (uphill) following the fence closely. After 450m the fence bends right (WNW), follow it downhill to a track. **7** Turn right (N) onto the track and follow it 100m to a footbridge across the De Lank River. Cross the river and take the path which follows the river downstream, gradually climbing. After 900m you reach buildings

Rough Tor from Brown Willy

(Garrow Farm); pass them on the downhill (E) side, don't go through the farmyard. Continue on the footpath (now a track) and pass through a small wood after 700m. ❽ Leaving the wood, follow the footpath W; this runs alongside a stone wall for 400m, then heads across open moor for 800m to another stone wall. Follow the wall (on your L) to a stile, cross this and follow the footpath to a farm (Lower Candra). ❾ Pass the farm on the right (N) side, then follow the farm's drive 200m to the farm's front gate. ❿ Turn right (W) off the track and follow the stone wall 200m until it bends N. Turn N and cross the moor for 2km N (crossing a lane after 400m and the summit of Alex Tor after 1.3km) back to the car.

Trip Planning

The web of lanes above St Breward are unnamed and unsignposted; you will have to consult a map or use a Sat Nav to find the start point. When you pass a gate on the right marked 'White Meadows' just after a junction, you have found the correct lane; continue for around 750m to where there is open moor on either side. This quiet lane is not geared up for tourist invasion; there are just a handful of rough roadside spaces to leave a car. A sign suggests that there is no right of access along the track leading from the end of the road; this is not the case, it is within designated Access Land.

A map, compass and gear appropriate for the upland environment are necessary. One quirk of this route (indeed, of Bodmin Moor: see page 64) is that there are few official footpaths, and even these do not always correspond on the ground to the 'permissive path' you are invited to follow.

Downhill in St Breward (the highest village in Cornwall), there is a shop and Post Office, as well as Cornwall's highest pub, The Old Inn.

Brown Willy

De Lank River

Other Routes

Want something easier? The 'tourist' route to the summit of Rough Tor is only about 1.5km long and starts from Rough Tor car park at PL32 9QJ/SX 138 818. Tacking on an out-and-back to Brown Willy's summit makes for a satisfying but short run totalling 6–7km.

Those for whom this route is insufficiently masochistic will eye the utterly empty hills north and east of Brown Willy with interest. Go explore by all means, but note that these are the headwaters of the De Lank and Fowey Rivers, effectively an extended marsh.

Also relatively close (for days when the weather on top is uninviting?) are Cardinham Woods (see page 72) and also the National Trust's Lanhydrock Estate, which organises a 5km parkrun on Saturdays and an annual 10K race.

Events

Truro Running Club's Brown Willy Run is held every New Year's Day and follows a rough-going out and back route from Jamaica Inn beside the A30.

Access to Bodmin Moor

Bodmin Moor suffers from a noticeable surfeit of signs telling you where you can and can't go (mostly the latter). The good news is that in many (most?) cases, you can regard this signage as an historical curiosity. The vast majority of Bodmin's moorland has been designated as Access Land (see page 21), meaning that there are few restrictions to responsible runners. An up-to-date copy of OS Explorer Map 109 will clearly indicate which areas are Access Land.

The Hurlers

10 The Hurlers

Distance	8km (5 miles)	**Ascent**	175m (575ft)
Map	OS Landranger 201 OS Explorer 109		
Navigation ●●●	No marked routes, map and compass recommended		
Terrain ●●●	Grassy moorland, with rocky or uneven patches to negotiate		
Wet Feet ●●●	As long as you avoid Witheybrook Marsh!		
Start/Finish	The Hurlers car park, Minions PL14 5LW/SX 259 711		

An engaging introduction to Bodmin Moor's charms

The comically-named village of Minions is the start point for this short 'highlights' tour of Bodmin Moor. All the ingredients which characterise Bodmin are here; prehistoric remains, mining ruins, sheer-sided quarries, wild ponies and tors sculpted by wind into fantastical shapes. The Hurlers are the three impressive stone circles at the start and end point of this run; supposedly a group of young men played Cornish Hurling on the Sabbath and were turned to stone as punishment. Folk musician Seth Lakeman has recorded a song about them. Behind on Stowe's Hill, the prominent tor which seems to defy gravity is the 'Cheesewring', but equally impressive is the five-metre high Neolithic wall enclosing the summit. The landscape you run through is frequently churned up and pitted by old mining works; you will cover more distance than advertised! Large bites have been taken out of the hillsides by quarry cliffs; the result is not unattractive, and you might find yourself tempted to strip off for a wild swim in the second quarry.

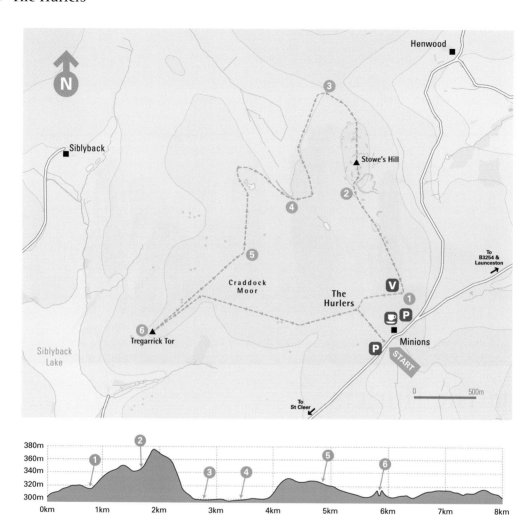

Route Description

🏃 START Head 300m NW from the car park to The Hurlers (a series of three stone circles). From the third circle, head 300m roughly E to the prominent engine house and chimney. ❶ Ascend the ridge leading NNW following faint paths, detouring around old mine pits, ravines and suchlike. ❷ When you reach the large quarry, bypass it on the left (W) side and ascend past the prominent Cheesewring rock to the summit of Stowe's Hill. Continue N to cross the stone enclosure wall and then descend towards Wardbrook Farm, visible 350m to the NW. ❸ Do not enter the farm (signs will dissuade you in any case), instead follow the boundary wall leading S alongside Witheybrook Marsh. After 550m, a muddy track passes through a gap in the wall; continue past this gap following the boundary wall for 400m S to its end, then follow the wall 300m W until its end. ❹ Head NW, climbing uphill with the quarry spill on your left. At the top, turn left and follow the rim of the quarry (deep and unfenced!), then turn S across Craddock Moor. ❺ After 500m is a (fallen) stone circle; when you reach this, head SW for 1km to the summit cairn of Tregarrick Tor. ❻ Backtrack 500m along your route and then head to the ruined engine house and chimney you see 850m to the ESE. The Hurlers are 500m ENE across rough ground, head to these and then back to the car park.

Trip Planning

Although this route doesn't take you far from civilisation, you are finding your route across open moor; take a map, compass and gear appropriate for the hills. Much of the route can be run 'line of sight' to the next feature but if visibility is poor, this will be rather more tricky. Be alert for the shafts, pits and ravines which pepper this landscape of past mining industry, and take special care around the quarry cliffs!

The car park is free, located on Minions Row a few hundred metres south-west of the village centre. In the village, The Cheesewring Hotel is friendly and serves decent food. The first engine house passed on this route is open to the public as the Minions Heritage Centre, well worth a visit after running. It has a car park; hence you don't need to retrace the running route.

Other Routes

Those wanting a shorter (5–6km) run can turn right at Wardbrook Farm ❸ and follow the disused railway which skirts the east side of Stowe's Hill back to Minions. This track incidentally continues around Caradon Hill (south of Minions), offering an alternative/additional loop.

It is possible to extend this route northwards from Stowe's Hill, potentially taking in Sharp Tor, Bearah Tor and the extremely rugged Twelve Men's Moor. Passing through Wardbrook Farm (one obvious approach to these tors) is not permitted, however.

Events

East Cornwall Harrier's 5 Tors fell race follows a 13km off-road route which takes in parts of this run as well as the tors to the north.

Stowe's Hill

The Cheesewring

Disused quarries

Mining remains

Stowe's Hill

Tors

Tors are the rocks found piled atop or around most hills in Dartmoor and Bodmin Moor, stacked in horizontal layers with an impacted-turds appearance, sometimes sculpted into fantastical shapes. These stacks can be tiny or truly massive, and a tor singly named on an OS map will often turn out to in fact consist of numerous stacks extending over a wide area. Running among tors is splendid fun. Running over them is even better, the granite is grippy underfoot and often inclined at shallow angles (be careful, usual disclaimers apply). Also, there is a law stating that whenever they see a tor, trail runners have to ascend it and take a selfie. Fact.

Most tors acquired their current form less than 100,000 years ago; a blink in geological time. However, they originated 280 million years earlier when a batholith of magma (molten rock) welled up underneath the bedrock of Devon and Cornwall. This cooled underground into coarse-grained granite speckled with feldspar crystals. As it cooled it shrank, split by vertical joints which allowed water to ingress, rotting the granite. The surface rocks above the granite finally eroded away, exposing it to the elements. Wind, rain and frost did their worst, exploiting the weaknesses of the joints. Where tors have been particularly heavily eroded, or have eroded away completely, fields of uneven boulders persist known as clitter; this stuff is not fun to run on.

Hound Tor (Route 22)

Hawk's Tor

11 Hawk's Tor

Distance	8km (5 miles)	Ascent	275m (900ft)
Map	OS Landranger 201 OS Explorer 109		
Navigation ●●●	Some open moorland where care is required		
Terrain ●●●	Uneven and rough paths, scrambling over boulders near the summit		
Wet Feet ●●●	Add a star in the winter months		
Start/Finish	North Hill Village Hall PL15 7PB/SX 270 767		

A gruelling ascent exploring a quiet corner of Bodmin Moor

This route leads you up onto Hawk's Tor, an isolated 329m summit on the NE fringe of Bodmin Moor. The upper River Lynher valley is sparsely populated and doesn't see many visitors, so you'll likely work your way up through the woods above the river and out onto the open moorland with little company. The summit ridge comprises a series of complex tors offering a degree of scrambling, should you be so inclined; decide which outcrops you want to run over, and which you wish to bypass. The descent back to the village of North Hill is simple and fast, indeed this whole route is ideal for those looking for a short but intense taster of the wild. The terrain is rougher and heavier going than that around the Hurlers (Route 10).

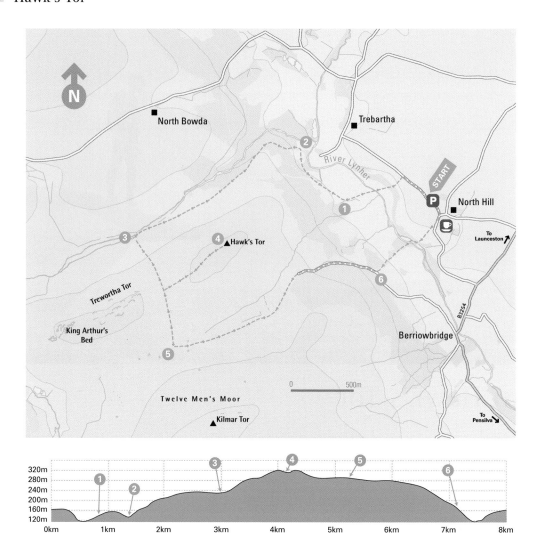

Route Description

🚶 **START** From the car park, follow the main road (Lynher Way) NW for 290m to where a footpath leads off on the left. Follow this footpath downhill, across a bridge over the River Lynher and uphill across two fields to the edge of a wood. **1** Turn right and follow the footpath leading NW across two fields and through Castick Farm, where it becomes a track. When the track bends downhill, take the bridleway leading steeply uphill on the left. **2** Follow the bridleway uphill through Castick Wood onto open land. Keep going ahead (SW) through successive field boundaries, although the bridleway becomes indistinct. **3** About 1.2km after leaving the woods, the bridleway reaches a wall blocking further passage. Turn left and follow the wall uphill (SSE) to a gate on the ridgetop. Turn left (NE) and follow the ridge to the summit tors of Hawk's Tor. **4** Retrace your steps back to the gate and pass through it. Descend S to the obvious track, 450m away. **5** Turn left (ENE) and follow this bridleway track. After 1km it becomes surfaced, and after another 1km a footpath leads off on the left; take this. **6** Follow the footpath downhill to cross the river, and then uphill into North Hill village. Turn left when you reach the road to return to the start.

Hawkstor Downs

Trip Planning

North Hill Village Hall's car park is free. Fact: the author spent several post-run hours sheltering from the rain in the Village Hall porch, shivering in shorts and t-shirt, after locking himself out of his car.

The Racehorse Inn in North Hill is a 'gastro-inn' but also caters to the masses by offering takeaway chips and pizza. Otherwise, your best bet for shops and other facilities is the town of Launceston.

Hawk's Tor

Other Routes

An easy 2km extension is to follow the ridge ESE from Hawk's Tor onto Trewortha Tor.

Across the valley, the serrated skyline of Twelve Men's Moor looks very tempting indeed ... however crossing direct to it from ❺ involves a very steep root-clinging ascent to the summit, and the ridge itself requires a bit of scrambling to traverse. This makes for a great adventure, but stretches the definition of trail running.

Trewortha Tor

Hawk's Tor

Twelve Men's Moor from Hawk's Tor

Cardinham Woods

The Forestry Commission's Cardinham Woods are on the fringes of Bodmin Moor, just outside Bodmin itself. The FC pay and display car park is at PL30 4AL/SX 100 667. Four different marked trails follow wide tracks through mixed woodland around the valley of Cardinham Water, ranging from 3km to 5.5km. There is also the Woods Café for afters; their scones are expensive but admittedly rather fine. More details and downloadable trail maps from the Forestry Commission website.

Descending to Kingsand

12 Mount Edgcumbe Country Park

Distance		10km (6 miles)	Ascent	250m (820ft)
Map		OS Landranger 201 OS Explorer 108		
Navigation	●●●	Partly following the South West Coast Path		
Terrain	●●●	One long steep climb to enjoy/endure		
Wet Feet	●●●	Some paths can get muddy		
Start/Finish		Cremyll Mount Edgcumbe Ferry Landing PL10 1HX/0 454 534		

Cornwall's forgotten corner, just minutes from central Plymouth

What a great way to escape the city bustle! Mount Edgcumbe Country Park covers nearly 4 square kilo-metres of the Rame Peninsula, located on the south and west shores of Plymouth Sound. The park and sixteenth-century Edgcumbe House (restored after WWII bombing) have belonged to Plymouth Council since 1971. Whilst the park is (understandably) popular with day-tripping city folk, you don't have to venture far from the Cremyll Ferry and main buildings to enjoy peace and quiet.

This run traverses a variety of landscapes, starting with the quiet north shores of the peninsula, before climbing through meadows and woodland out of the park to hilltop Maker Church, with views up the River Tamar, across Plymouth Sound and out to sea. You descend back into the park at Kingsand, before following the shores of Plymouth Sound around to your start point. En route you pass various coastal fortifications and defences, dating from Henry VIII through to Victoria's reign. In the last 2km, you pass

Mount Edgcumbe Country Park

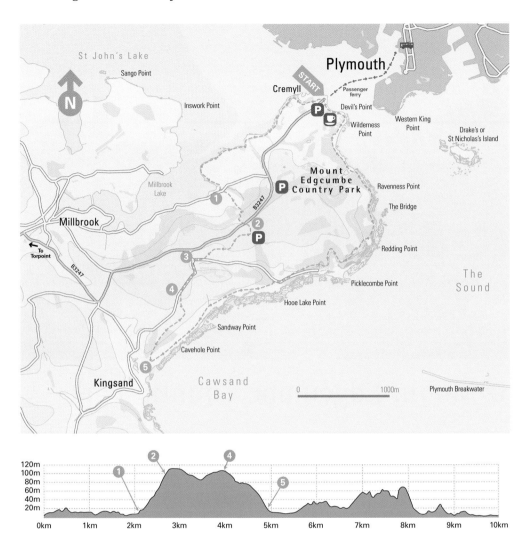

through a parkland landscape of rhododendron bushes, ornamental gardens, ponds and artificial temples. Shortly before the end are the beautiful Orangery gardens, now a café where it is highly tempting to stop for refreshment before returning to Plymouth on the ferry.

Route Description

START Follow the B3246 road inland and take the footpath just past and behind the Edgcumbe Arms, signposted for Empacombe. Follow this along the waterfront for 2.1km to a lane. **1** Cross the lane and follow the footpath uphill across the field and into woods. Keep heading uphill, following footpath markers and ignoring side paths until you reach the B3246. **2** Cross the B3246 and head towards the church. When you reach the churchyard gate, turn right and follow a path along the hedge. After 140m and directly after a gate, the footpath turns left and downhill. Follow the footpath (crossing one lane) until it terminates at a lane. **3** Turn right along the lane, and after 100m turn left at a junction. Follow this lane for 280m until you see a footpath leading off to the left. **4** Descend along this footpath until you reach the village of Kingsand after 1km. Turn left onto the South West Coast Path through a gate signed 'Welcome to Mount Edgcumbe'. ⑤ Follow the SWCP for 5km back to your start point. Note that after the path veers inland around Fort Picklecombe, a landslip diverts the SWCP steeply uphill (2018), eventually descending back to the coast via steps.

Climbing to Maker Church

Trip Planning

It's possible to arrive by car from the west; there are pay and display car parks at Cremyll PL10 1HU/SX 452 533 (150m along the B3247 from the ferry) and in the centre of the park PL10 1HZ/SX 452 526 (follow park signs from the B3247). It is also possible to park free at Maker Church ② PL10 1JA/SX 445 519, although this would mean finishing the run with the big climb!

Barn Pool

By far the easiest approach from Plymouth is to take the cheap passenger-only Cremyll Ferry, which runs every half hour across the fast-flowing 300m wide River Tamar. The crossing from Admirals Hard in Stonehouse takes just eight minutes. Citybus Number 34 connects this to the city centre.

Mount Edgcumbe Country Park has plenty of interest if you wish to stay longer, not least visiting Edgcumbe House; see their website for details. The Orangery Café mentioned above is near the ferry, and despite reasonable prices, is more luxurious than you probably deserve. There is also a café and the Edgcumbe Arms near the ferry.

Mount Edgcumbe House

Other Routes

A 10km extension out from ⑤ to Rame Head and back via the South West Coast Path would be simply splendid. Within the park, there is a large network of paths and tracks to explore; download a leaflet from their website for ideas.

Empacombe

Events

Mount Edgcumbe Park hosts a weekly 5km parkrun, partly on unsurfaced trails.

Maker Church

Mount Edgcumbe Country Park

Plymouth Sound

Plymouth trail running

Plymouth is of course extremely close to Dartmoor, but should you be unable to escape, there are some decent trails to explore within the city.

The Plymouth Cross-City Link is an 11km chain of surfaced and unsurfaced trails along the northern part of the city, passing through some pleasant enclaves such as Forder Valley and Bircham Valley Local Nature Reserves. The PCCL connects the Tamar Valley Discovery Trail in the west (this is mostly on tarmac) and the West Devon Way in the east. The WDW near Plymouth is also called the Plym Valley Trail and also Drake's Trail, for no apparent reason than to confuse everybody. This snakes up the glorious wooded valley of the River Plym, with riverside trails and glimpses of industrial ruins among the trees. A parkrun is held at Plym Bridge, and upstream of here the east bank is Cann Woods, 230 hectares of Forestry Commission trail running freedom.

East of the River Plym, Saltram Park is maintained by the National Trust, who organise a Trust10 run. The trails around the park give splendid views of the estuary. The South West Coast Path around to Wembury is a great salty-air-infused run, and it's possible to return to town using the Erme-Plym Trail. This passes through Radford Woods LNR (Local Nature Reserve), another useful spot for a short run.

North Devon

All of the routes featured here are near the Bristol Channel coast, because that is indisputably where North Devon's best scenery and trails are to be found ... and then some! Close to the Cornish border, the convoluted Hartland Heritage Coast is unlike anything else in the UK, whilst the golden granite of Lundy Island is visible, promising a great offshore adventure. To the east, the massive bulk of Exmoor looms. Exmoor National Park uniquely offers moorland hill running comparable to that found in Dartmoor to the south, only mixed in with epic cliffs falling vertiginously to the sea. Between these two areas, Braunton Burrows is England's largest dune system, a remarkable landscape in which to immerse yourself.

Below Little Hangman (Route 16)

West coast of Lundy

Church and Marisco Tavern, Lundy

13 Lundy Island

Distance	11km (7 miles)	Ascent	300m (980ft)
Map	OS Landranger 180, Explorer 139		
Navigation ●●●	Unsignposted but obvious paths along the cliff top		
Terrain ●●●	Grassy/stony paths, some steep steps		
Wet Feet ●●●	Firm going, a couple of boggy streams to hop across		
Start/Finish	Marisco Tavern EX39 2LY/SS 137 440		

An airy island circuit atop spectacular granite cliffs

Lundy Island is located 20–30km offshore of North Devon, depending upon where you're measuring from. Is it worth the four-hour round trip by ferry, just to run around this 5km long island? Absolutely! Lundy is a unique place, a 140m high granite monolith rearing out of the Bristol Channel. The ground is littered with ancient monuments, mining ruins and listed buildings, and there is an amazing lighthouse which is freely open to explore. As you run, you'll encounter sika deer, soay sheep, feral goats and an infinite number of rabbits, whilst puffins wheel above the crashing waves below. The cliffs on the west coast are phenomenal, with smooth granite descending into the Atlantic. The indented nature of the coast means that you get great views of these cliffs. When you've finished, the Marisco Tavern is a fine place to refuel and relax, whilst waiting for the ferry back.

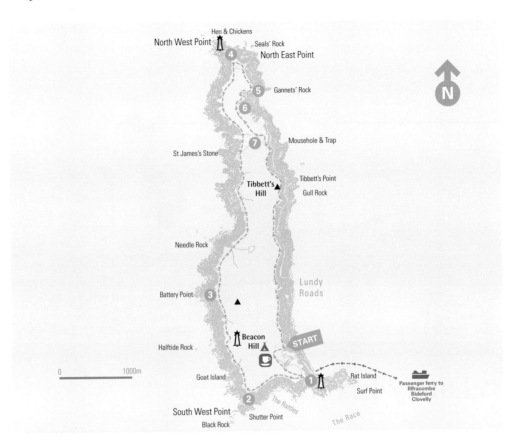

Route Description

START From the Marisco Tavern, follow the track past the church to the castle. ① After passing the castle, turn right and follow Lundy's S coast. Take care; after about 700m the path veers N to avoid the Devil's Limekiln, a huge collapsed cave. ② Follow Lundy's west coast N through a gate past the Old Light (disused lighthouse). ③ Shortly before reaching the Quarter Wall, you have option of a detour down steep steps to visit The Old Battery; 400m after passing the Quarter Wall, the path descends to a boggy stream. After crossing this, the route N is straightforward along the clifftop. ④ When you reach the North Light, explore as far down the steps as you dare and then retrace your route and continue around the coast heading SE. ⑤ When the path turns inland at Gannets' Bay, resist the temptation to take a short cut across – the ground is steep, damp and tussocky. ⑥ Turn onto the island's central track, follow it S for 250m, where the coast path leads off left. ⑦ You can either stay on the track which takes you direct to the finish in 3km, or turn left onto the coast path and follow this atop the cliffs S to the Marisco Tavern.

South tip of Lundy

Trip Planning

Ferries leave Bideford or Ilfracombe for Lundy on at least three days a week from April to October. The crossing is around two hours and you are dropped off at the pier beside The Landing Beach, leaving you with a 130m climb following a track up to the shop, campsite and Marisco Tavern. Year-round, it is possible (for the affluent) to access Lundy by helicopter.

The Marisco Tavern serves food and drink, but woe betide you if you fall foul of their 'no mobiles' rule! Should you wish to stay (and enjoying sunset from Lundy, ideally whilst running the west coast, makes this an appealing option) camping is available for a limited number of tents. Most of the island's quirky properties are available for rent from the Landmark Trust, albeit at eye-watering prices.

Marisco Tavern, Lundy

Other Routes

The island is open access so feel free to explore any paths. An alternative route on the east side is to follow the lower track through the old quarry sites; join this old tramway by turning left just after ⑥, south of Gannets' Bay.

The Old Battery, Lundy

Lundy Island

East coast of Lundy

Events

pureTrail organised the first Lundy Island Race, around the coast, in 2018. The entries for the 2019 event, including ferry charter, filled up in an hour.

Exploring Lundy

Despite having just a dozen or so permanent residents, Lundy has a small shop and Post Office, a church, a castle, three lighthouses and possibly the finest pub in the UK, the Marisco Tavern. It even has its own beer, 'Lundy Experience'.

Lundy is South West England's largest seabird breeding colony and a stopping-off point for innumerable migratory species. Guillemots, razorbills, gannets and Manx shearwaters abound. The name 'Lundy' derives from Old Norse, Puffin. Puffins have unfortunately taken a battering in the past from non-indigenous rats, but are now recovering well and you have a good chance of spotting some. Up on top, look out for Soay sheep, Lundy ponies and Sika deer. Finish a run by enjoying sunset atop the Old Light, Britain's highest lighthouse; amazingly, you can enter freely and climb to the top at any time.

Lundy Old Light

Blegberry Cliff

14 Hartland Point

Distance	10km (6.5 miles)	**Ascent**	525m (1725ft)
Map	OS Landranger 190 OS Explorer 126		
Navigation ●●●	Well-signposted, clear junctions, uses SWCP		
Terrain ●●●	Some steep climbs and descents on rocky paths		
Wet Feet ●●●	Well-churned farm tracks, coast path susceptible to muddiness		
Start/Finish	Hartland Quay EX39 6DB/SS 222 247		

Challenging ups and downs amongst incredible cliffs and jagged reefs

The Hartland Heritage Coast is one of the South West's scenic highlights. Here, forbidding cliffs face the ocean, fronted by expanses of sawtooth reefs. Rushing streams have incised deep clefts into these cliffs, ending abruptly in waterfalls freefalling onto the reefs. However much coast and cliff running you have experienced, be prepared to be amazed by this savage landscape. Indeed, on the author's most recent run here (a bleary-eyed dawn excursion on New Year's Day), which was far from being his first, he was still literally stopped in his tracks by the vista of Atlantic rollers smashing into Blegberry Beach.

This run departs from Hartland Quay, which is somewhat inaccurately named. There *was* a quay, commissioned by Raleigh and Drake no less, but it was destroyed by a storm in 1896. A short hop over the hill to Blackpool Mill gives you a taster of the coast scenery before you venture inland with notable ups and downs through farmland to reach the coast near Hartland Point Lighthouse. The tide flows strongly below

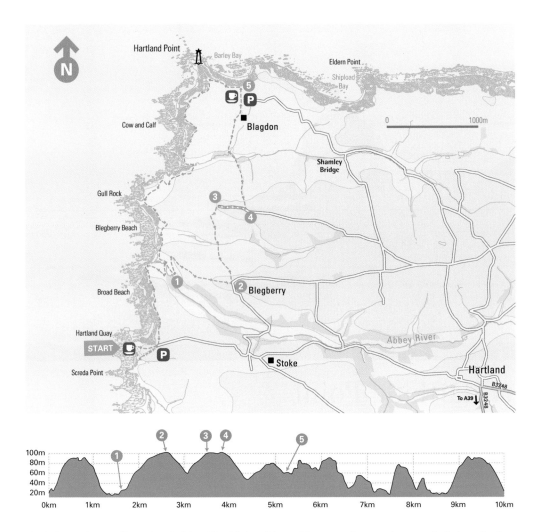

the Point and magnificent Lundy Island is visible offshore. If you run here at dawn or dusk from April to September, you'll witness a spectacle; large numbers of Manx shearwaters (so-named for their tendency to almost graze the water with their wingtips) fly past en route to their burrows in Pembrokeshire. The record is 15,000 counted in one morning! Below the lighthouse, hefty chunks of the *Johanna* (shipwrecked in 1982) are visible. The trails back south to Hartland Quay closely follow the clifftops, with care needed on steep sections. The views are ineffable.

Route Description

START Head uphill from the car park following the SWCP N (N is left, looking inland). Follow the SWCP along Warren Cliff past the ruined tower and downhill to a valley. After crossing a bridge, follow the SWCP 100m to a junction just before Blackpool Mill. ❶ Turn right off the SWCP and follow this footpath uphill. At the top of the hill turn right (inland) and follow the footpath 750m to a lane. ❷ Take the track directly to the left (signposted 'unsuitable for motor vehicles') leading N off the lane. Follow this downhill and then uphill to Blegberry Farm. ❸ Take the lane leading off to the right (E) and follow it for 350m to where a track (signposted as a bridleway) leads off on the left. ❹ Take this track and follow it N downhill and uphill and through Blagdon Farm to reach the SWCP. ❺ Turn left (W) and follow the SWCP for 5km around Hartland Point and then back S to Hartland Quay.

Trip Planning

The car park charges; if you are there early, you can claim a spot in the scenic lower car park which is convenient for the pub but of course means a bigger climb to start your day. Another possible start point is the car park for Hartland Point Lighthouse EX39 6AX/SS 235 275 at ❺, or alternatively you could park in the village of Stoke, adding an extra 1km at either end of your run. Hartland Quay has just one street, called … The Street. The Wrecker's Retreat bar serves decent pub food; eating chips outdoors beneath the zig-zagged cliffs of Warren Beach makes for a not-dissatisfying post-run carb-load. A small gift shop sells ice-cream and other beach-related items; for anything more, visit The Pop In Store 4km east in the village of Hartland. There is also the Shipwreck Museum at Hartland Quay, if you fancy a dose of local heritage.

Should you require refreshment mid-run, there is a tiny café shack beside the Hartland Point car park, grandiosely named The Point @Hartland.

Other Routes

The coast south of Hartland Quay offers more of the same fabulousness. An additional/alternative 5km loop can be completed by following the coast to the double-waterfall at Speke's Mill Mouth and then looping inland via Kernstone Cross and Stoke. The Heritage

Hartland Point

Smoothlands

View from Dyer Lookout

Coast continues to amaze for 25km south to Bude (you cross into Cornwall at Marsland Mouth). If you survive that distance, you'll probably want to be aware of the 219 bus service serving both Bude and Hartland. The South West Coast Path undergoes a notable change of character east of Hartland Point. The cliffs are higher but generally more level, making the trails easier going. An interesting loop would be to cross the peninsula from Hartland Quay via lanes to the beach at Mouth Mill (unmistakeable on account of towering Blackchurch Rock) and then follow the SWCP west to reach Hartland Point at ❺.

Hartland Point

Hartland Quay

Events

The Hartland Hartbreaker (see what they did there?) is organised by North Devon Road Runners and has 9 or 18-mile options, following a similar route to this one. If you wish to go further, pureTrail run the Tsunami Coastal Races between Westward Ho! and Bude, offering 16, 26 and 36-mile distance events. Votwo's Devon Coast Challenge starts at Hartland Point; see Route 16.

The Hartland Heritage Coast

The Hartland Heritage Coast stretches between Bude and Bideford, characterised by cliffs protected by a wave-cut platform; in plain-speak, a bedrock reef up to 250m wide extends into the sea. The reef's character is explained by the dramatic zigzagging patterns in the cliffs. Geologists who know about these things explain that, around 290 million years ago, the two continents of Eurasia and Gondwana collided in this general vicinity, the impact causing the zigzags. Waves eroded softer mudstone away from the zigzags and the harder sandstone remains, pointing to the sky. The resulting effect was best described by local author Charles Kingsley in his 1855 novel *Westward Ho!*: *"Each cove has its black field of jagged shark's-tooth rock which paves the cove from side to side ... one rasp of which would grind abroad the timbers of the stoutest ship. To landward, all richness, softness and peace; to seaward, a waste and howling wilderness of rock and roller."*

Braunton Burrows

15 Braunton Burrows

Distance	12km (7.5 miles)	Ascent	100+m (325ft)
Map	OS Landranger 180 OS Explorer 139		
Navigation ●●●	Little signage but this route follows obvious landmarks. Take a map in case you		
	decide to stray off-route.		
Terrain ●●●	Grass, sand, sand, sand, sand, more sand		
Wet Feet ●●●	As long as you avoid the waves on the beach		
Start/Finish	Broadsands car park EX33 2NX/SS 468 328		

Sandworld

This is an exceptional run in an exceptional setting. Braunton Burrows are a vast sandscape of towering dunes, interlaced by a network of inviting trails. The diversity of terrain within the Burrows might surprise you, including brackish marsh, grassy pasture and pure soft sand. Despite being close to the town of Braunton and the popular surf beach of Saunton, it is possible to run for hours without encountering a soul. Be prepared to empty your shoes once or twice, and be wary that 12km on sand will likely feel more like twelve miles. Marathon Du Sable veterans will be in their element!

The route here follows a relatively simple course through the dunes, mostly sticking to the larger trails and obvious landmarks. The second part follows the seashore along the beach and up into the Taw and Torridge estuary. This is really something: whilst hundreds of surfers crowd the far extremity of the beach,

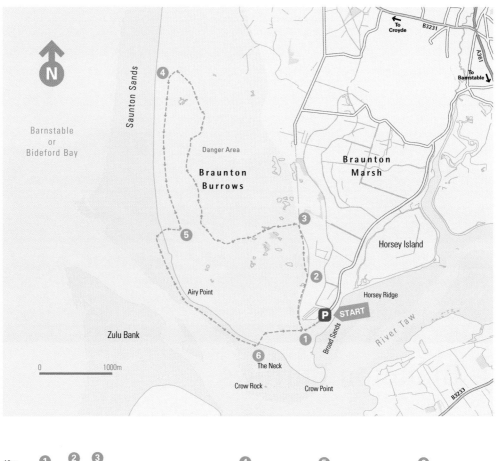

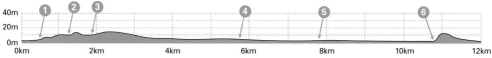

you weave alone through heaped driftwood following the strandline's firmer sand, with waves lapping insistently at your heels. Care is needed; the wildness comes at the price of no marked trail and no lifeguards.

Route Description

START Follow the paths out of the SW end of the car park for 450m to a T-junction with a gravel track (American Road, also the SWCP). ❶ Turn right (N) and follow the track 700m past two gates on the left, to a stile on the left signed 'Zone 3'. ❷ Cross the stile and follow the bridleway N (the clearest path visible). After 700m a junction of tracks is reached. ❸ Take the track leading left (W) and follow this for 4km, ignoring all turn-offs. After 1.5km the track is heading N; look out for the most prominent/highest dune beside the track on the left and detour 100m to ascend it before returning to the track. After 4km a gate is reached which obviously leads over a dune to the sea. ❹ Don't go through the gate, but turn left (S) and follow the rough undulating path along behind the coastal dunes. After 2km the track is following a wire fence on the right and reaches a gate in the fence. ❺ Climb over the gate and run up and over the obvious tall dune to the right to reach the beach. Turn left (S) and follow the beach (be careful to stick to landward, following the water's edge can lead you into dead ends). After 2km you pass broken wooden groynes and then brick and concrete remains. Look for a single bridleway sign pointing inland. ❻ Turn left (inland) and follow the bridleway for 1km back to the car park (there are several parallel paths including a boardwalk).

Trip Planning

To reach the car park, follow signs from Braunton for Crow Point (toll road). The correct road leaves Braunton at a roundabout beside the Saltrock Factory Outlet. The toll road is signposted off to the left after a kilometre, and winds interminably out across marshes (via a toll booth, of course) to Broadsands car park at the end of the road. The toll is not expensive.

You'll note from the OS map that the southern half of Braunton Burrows is marked as a 'Danger Area'. The MOD carry out training exercises here and access restrictions apply during these. For details of exercise times, call 01271 375101 and ask for Fremington Training Camp, Barnstaple. Obey warning signs and don't pick up any suspicious metal objects you see around the dunes ... duh!

The wonderful latter part of this run – along the beach and into the estuary – will almost certainly be simple and worry-free. There is however the potential for things to go very wrong, so apply common sense. If the tide is exceptionally high, i.e. lapping the dunes, then do not attempt this part and retrace your steps. Similarly, if the waves are particularly violent and rushing quickly up the beach, stay well clear. Finally, as you turn into the estuary the area of tidal sand widens and at low tide you can encounter multiple sand bars with pools of water between them. It is possible to follow a bar only to reach a dead end ... and you could conceivably then be trapped by the rising tide. Stay alert and keep to the most inshore route.

The Taw and Torridge Estuary

Braunton has various pleasant cafés and useful shops, as well as more surf shops than you'll ever need.

Other Routes

The route possibilities exploring Braunton Burrows are possibly infinite, explore at your leisure! To shorten this route, perhaps head direct from ❸ to ❺. The most obvious way to lengthen it is to continue N as far as Saunton, perhaps returning along the full length of the beach.

Braunton Burrows

Slightly further north, the headlands of Morte Point and Baggy Point both offer wonderful coastal running with obvious inland routes to complete the loop. We found a mysterious 'fairy door' in a rock out on the tip of Baggy Point when we were there last, all answers on a postcard ...

Approaching Airy Point

An alternative 6–7km of beach and dune running can be enjoyed by following the length of Woolacombe Sand and Putsborough Sand before returning (to either Woolacombe or Putsborough) along the path through the dunes behind the beach. The bridleway (part of the Tarka Trail) which parallels this further uphill is partly surfaced and hence a bit dull.

The American Road

Events

The North Devon AONB* Marathon & Half Marathon grinds along the South West Coast Path around the headlands of Morte Point and Baggy Point, as well as some hilly inland sections. A friend recently ran this and noted that, halfway round on a hot day, he had to, "Give myself a stern talking-to". The event is run for North Devon Hospice. The Woolacombe 10K Beach Run is exactly what it sounds like, laid on by the Rotary Club of Ilfracombe.

*Area of Outstanding Natural Beauty

Braunton Burrows

The landscape and ecosystem of Braunton Burrows is considered so important that in 1976 it was designated by UNESCO as a Biosphere Reserve (the UN expanded this designation in 2002 to encompass a larger area, centred on Braunton Burrows). England's largest dune system sprawls across 1,000 hectares of the Christie Estate and encompasses a range of habitats hosting a huge variety of flora and fauna. In summer, over 470 species of flowering plant, including eleven species of orchid, add colour to the dunes. Some 33 species of butterfly flutter by, whilst adders lurk among the drier inland dunes.

The historical legacy is surprising; during WWII 10,000 US troops trained for D-Day, when it was designated the 'Assault Training Centre'. Amidst the dunes, you come across a concrete edifice which was used for simulating bazooka attacks on Nazi bunkers, whilst near the estuary towards Crow Point are three blocky structures which were practice landing craft.

Bazooka training wall

Exmoor Coast from Great Hangman

16 Great Hangman

Distance	17km (10.5 miles)	Ascent	850m (2800ft)
Map	OS Landranger 180 OS Explorer OL9		
Navigation ●●●	Sections of open moor, compass necessary in case of low visibility		
Terrain ●●●	Some ascents probably unrunnable, steep rocky descents needing care.		
Wet Feet ●●●	Some trails double as streams(!) after rain, moorland usually waterlogged		
Start/Finish	Kiln car park, Combe Martin EX34 0DN/SS 577 472		

A hard grind over steep coastal hills and moorland

Great Hangman is the hill looming 318m above the seaside village of Combe Martin. It is the best known (but not the highest!) of the chain of coastal Exmoor hills which this route traverses. What makes these hills particularly interesting is their proximity to the sea; the high moorland summits are just a few hundred metres from the sea, with some of Britain's highest sea cliffs in-between.

This is one of the tougher routes in this book, relative to the distance; somewhere in the middle you get to feeling that all you have ever done is claw your way up desperately steep inclines. Actually it's not all suffering; there are some lovely sprints through woodland and upland farmland, and stretches of open moorland where you can open out your battered legs and stride, and the finale is a wonderful long descent following the rim of the cliffs.

Great Hangman

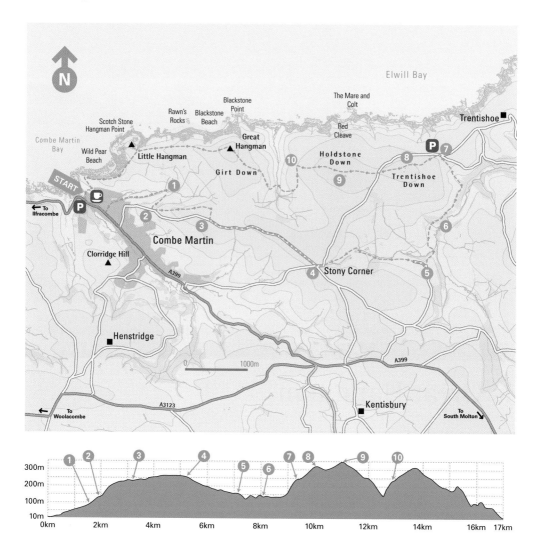

Route Description

START From the car park (or seafront), head up the A399 High Street for 400m to where a footpath turns off left up steps (opposite Kingston House). Follow this footpath up to a lane (Shackhayes), continue 150m ahead on the lane to join West Challacombe Lane. After 100m you reach a junction with a signpost; take the footpath to the right signed 'Great Hangman via Knap Down'. **1** Ascend on the footpath to a T-junction with a track. Turn right (again signposted 'Great Hangman ...') and ascend to a lane. **2** Turn left and follow the lane 80m uphill to where a footpath turns off left. Take this footpath and follow it (still uphill!) to a T-junction where you turn right to reach the lane again. **3** Turn left (E) onto the lane (Vellacot Lane) and follow it for 2km to a junction. Turn off left and follow this lane 100m to a sharp left bend with a bridleway on the right, signposted for Verwill Farm. **4** Take the bridleway on the right and follow it (blue markers) downhill, through the farm and along the valley to join a lane. After 200m a track leaves the lane on the left; take this. **5** Follow the track winding N. After 900m the footpath 'Ladies Mile' is signposted off on the left, take this. **6** Follow Ladies Mile 800m to a crossroads of paths. Turn left (uphill), signposted for

Approaching Little Hangman

Trentishoe. Climb steeply until you reach the road. ❼ Choose one of the faint paths ascending Trentishoe Down (to the ESE) and follow it to the summit. ❽ Descend WSW to the road, cross this and continue W to ascend Holdstone Hill by the obvious path. ❾ Follow the path downhill to the W until you reach the SWCP. ❿ Turn left (S) onto the SWCP and follow it down into the valley of Sherrycombe, up to the summit of Great Hangman and downhill to the finish (after 3km Little Hangman is passed, ascend it via a short side-tour).

Holdstone Down summit

Trip Planning

Combe Martin is busy in summer and Kiln car park (being close to the beach) may fill quickly. Arriving early also gives you the option of the limited parking spaces available along the A399, some of which are free on Sundays. The only other viable spot from which to set out is the free parking area on Trentishoe Down EX31 4QD/SS 635 480, which would mean finishing your run with the hardest of all the climbs!

Combe Martin has the distinction of having the longest main street of any village in Britain, along which all manner of shops and eateries can be found.

Ladies Mile

Climbing Trentishoe Down

View from Little Hangman

The village is sheltered and mild, yet half an hour later and a few hundred metres higher, you might find yourself enduring mountain weather. Set out equipped for the wilds, regardless of how oddly the beach-goers may look at you. A compass is definitely recommended, in case the clouds close in.

Other Routes

Those who feel that this route lacks sufficient steep climbs can peel off at ❻ to follow the road down the valley for 2km to Hunter's Inn, knock off Route 17 and then return to complete this route. I salute you. This route can be shortened in various ways, for example following signs to ascend Great Hangman direct, after ❷. But all options of course will still involve steep climbs …

Events

North Devon Road Runners organise a series of 5K and 10K trail races (by both night and day!) at the nearby National Trust property of Arlington Court. Votwo's Devon Coast Challenge is three successive day marathons, following the South West Coast Path from Hartland Point to Porlock. Enjoy.

On the South West Coast Path

17 Heddon's Mouth

Distance	10km (6 miles)	Ascent	475m (1560ft)
Map	OS Landranger 180 OS Explorer OL9		
Navigation ●●●	Hard to stray from the path		
Terrain ●●●	Stony paths, care needed at precipitous points		
Wet Feet ●●●	Well draining paths, however a couple of rivers to cross		
Start/Finish	Heddon Valley National Trust car park EX31 4PY/SS 655 480		

Precipitous trails traversing Exmoor's plunge to the sea

The River Heddon follows a deep and steep-sided cleft through Exmoor's hills, opening onto the sea at the beach of Heddon's Mouth. Cliffs soar on either side, as the hills of Exmoor meet the Bristol Channel rather abruptly. Trails traverse this upended landscape and there are few more exhilarating locations to open out your legs and sprint, than halfway down a 200m cliffside. Don't miss your footing, though!

This route starts with a dash down and up the Heddon Valley, fording the river en route. A long but gradual climb takes you high above the beach before traversing one of the most vertiginous parts of the South West Coast Path. A short section of tarmac at Woody Bay interlopes before you retrace your route, 100m higher up. Needless to say, the views along the Exmoor coast are epic.

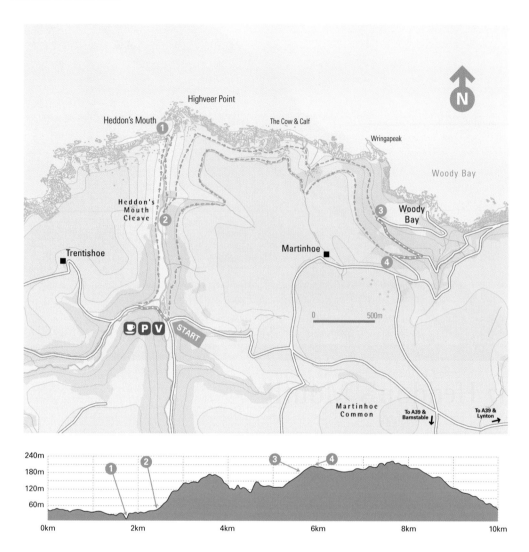

Route Description

🏃 **START** From the Hunter's Inn, follow the lane leading NW. After 250m it crosses a bridge, take the footpath on the right directly after. Follow this down the valley until you reach the sea. ❶ Cross the River Heddon by the stepping stones (if the river is too high for this, backtrack 300m to a footbridge) and head back up the valley until a footpath (the SWCP) leads steeply uphill on the left. ❷ Follow the SWCP uphill and along the coast (note: some precipitous bits) until it meets a tarmac lane. ❸ Turn right onto the lane and follow it uphill until it joins another lane. Turn right and follow this uphill to a left bend. ❹ Two footpaths leave the road on the outside of the bend; take the righthand one, nearest the sea. Follow this for 4km back to the Hunter's Inn.

Trip Planning

The National Trust car park is free to members, of course. The NT also lay on an information centre, toilets and shop (useless of course, unless you urgently need pot pourri). Alongside the car park is the Hunter's

Heddon Valley

Inn, which is a perfect place to refuel and reflect on the gobsmacking geography around you.

The walk from the Hunter's Inn to Heddon's Mouth is popular in summer, you may have to set out early or late to enjoy an unobstructed run along the valley.

The word 'precipitous' used in the subtitle is a fair description of the paths in the middle part of this route, but as long as you don't suffer vertigo, you should have no problems. You probably want to avoid strong winds however ...

Heddon's Mouth

Other Routes

If you haven't had enough of big hills and big climbs, it is possible to link up with Route 16. Either continue along the lane W right at the start, or turn off left onto the South West Coast Path 500m down the Heddon Valley.

The SWCP between Woody Bay and Lynmouth is disappointing; most of it follows roads, and the exposed path traversing the cliffs from The Valley of the Rocks has been Health and Safety-fied with a tarmac surface.

Descending towards Woody Bay

View past Woody Bay

Below The Beacon

Events

Endurance Life base the Exmoor leg of their popular Coastal Trail Series (CTS) from the same start point as this route. The distance options range from 10K to ultra-marathon, and unsurprisingly this is regarded as the toughest of their race series. Votwo's Devon Coast Challenge passes through here; see Route 16.

The Heddon Valley

You may struggle to imagine the modest stream that is the River Heddon carving out the spectacular deep V-shaped valley that you see today ... but it did, albeit in an expanded state. During the last Ice Age, glacial flood waters gouged their way down from Exmoor's high ground. The scree slopes which incongruously litter both sides of the valley were formed by the freeze-thaw process: meltwater seeped through the bedrock, before freezing and expanding, generating enough pressure to shatter rock away from the valley walls.

Heddon's Mouth is still a relatively remote spot today, being a rare beach with no vehicular access. Captains of German U-Boats have claimed that they landed here unnoticed during the Second World War, to replenish their water stocks and allow their men to stretch legs.

Heddon's Mouth

Dartmoor

Whilst this book's other sections are divided by county, Dartmoor National Park gets a whole extended section to itself, because ... because Dartmoor. Nowhere else in England is there such a vast expanse where you can roam, run and wild camp freely. The landscape is characterised by bleak and boggy peat hills topped by 'tors' – granite stacks of engaging variety and complexity. This high moorland includes inaccessible and inhospitable terrain that truly warrants the title 'wilderness', yet sheltered adventure is also available in the ancient forests covering Dartmoor's river valleys and eastern third. Dartmoor offers trail runners a wide range of running surfaces ranging from pathless peat and soul-sucking bog through to boulder-paved path and grippy granite tor. Sometimes, all in one run.

Haytor (Route 22)

South Hessary Tor

The climb onto the moor

18 Princetown and Burrator Reservoir

Distance	21km (13 miles)	**Ascent**	300m (1000ft)
Map	OS Landranger 191, 201, 202 OS Explorer OL28		
Navigation ●●●	Mostly easy, some care needed around Burrator		
Terrain ●●●	Hard surfaced tramway, rooty paths, rocky tracks		
Wet Feet ●●●	Firm surfaces and minimal mud		
Start/Finish	High Moorland Visitor Centre car park PL20 6QY/SX 589 734		

A classic all-weather loop encompassing high moorland and deep forest

Versions of this loop are popular with walkers and mountain bikers, due to its simple navigation, great views and firm going; this is the closest thing Dartmoor has to an all-weather trail on the open moor! The route starts on the high moor near Princetown's infamous prison and descends gradually via a long disued tramway. Naturally, this winds among the remains of quarries it once served. There are expansive views across the Walkham valley and out to Plymouth Sound.

The forests above Burrator Reservoir envelop the central part of the route, where you tread more technical trails. Eventually you emerge above the treeline to follow a rugged bridleway up the valley of the River Meavy back onto the high moor, where a die-straight bridleway leads over South Hessary Tor back into Princetown.

Princetown and Burrator Reservoir

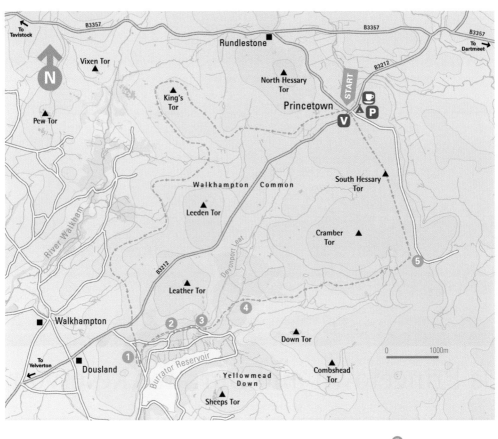

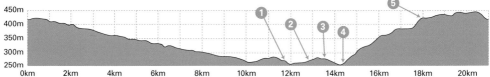

Route Description

START Follow the road leading W out the back of the car park. After 100m take the path on the left just after the fire station. Follow this onto a disused tramway. Continue on the tramway for 11.5km! After 9.5km you reach gates and farmland, after 11km you cross the B3212 via a bridge and then cross a lane. **1** After you cross a second bridge, continue ahead for 100m, looking for a footpath sign on the left. Turn left (downhill) when you see this. Descend a short distance and cross a lane to continue on the footpath. Follow the footpath 500m along a leat (a man-made stream) to a lane, cross this to rejoin the footpath and continue another 500m to where it reaches the lane again. **2** Follow the footpath another 500m to where it rejoins the lane, or run along the lane. **3** Where a track leads left off the lane, follow the footpath along the leat stream close by. After 270m turn right (downhill) onto the track which crosses the leat via a bridge. After 700m cross the stone bridge and turn left (uphill). After 60m take the bridleway leading off to the right. **4** After 500m bear right and then immediately left, following signs for Older Bridge. Follow this bridleway 3km uphill to a crossroads. **5** Turn left (N) and follow the bridleway for 3km back into Princetown.

Trip Planning

High Moorland Visitor Centre car park is pay and display and is located on Station Cottages, just off the B3357 beside the visitor centre. Free parking is possible on the B3357, Princetown's main street.

Princetown has a shop selling basic provisions. Refreshment options in Princetown include the famous Plume of Feathers Pub (indulge yourself with a mixed grill) and close by the Fox Tor Café which is popular with cyclists and runners. The pub has a campsite behind, and this and the café have bunkhouses.

The National Park's High Moorland Visitor Centre is worth a visit, with displays on the park's landscape, history and wildlife. Plus, you get to dress up in prison clothes.

Local resident

Other Routes

The route can be shortened by 2.5km by taking the obvious bridleway on the left which appears after 2.8km; this lops off the 'sticky-outy part' of the tramway. Many runners just do the downhill part (cheating, surely?) and continue 1km from ❶ on the tramway to reach the ice cream van at Burrator Reservoir's dam. This makes for a 13km run, obviously you need a pick-up waiting at the end. A 2-4km longer variation is to descend to the dam, cross and then ascend lanes through Sheepstor to explore the bridleways around the upper Plym valley on the way back to Princetown.

Burrator Reservoir

A popular 11km loop from Princetown with less gradient is to follow the Dartmoor Way to the Swincombe valley, follow the bridleway SW to Whiteworks, then join the last part of this route from ❺.

From ❺ this route is on part of two long-distance trails; the Abbots Way and the Perambulation of 1240 (see Route 24).

Near Princetown

Events

Something Wild have established an annual Trail Running Festival which is based at Hexworthy near Princetown. This weekend includes races from 5K to ultra-distance.

Meavy valley

The climb onto the moor

Dartmoor wild camping

Dartmoor is the only area of England where the right to wild camp is legally enshrined. This is allowed on areas of open moorland making up about half of Dartmoor, encompassing huge swathes of the park's

north-west and south, as well as patchy parts of the park's east. A useful leaflet map is available from National Park visitor centres (such as that at Princetown), also there is an online map on the National Park website.

A maximum stay of two nights is allowed, at least 100m from any road or enclosure. It should go without saying that you must leave zero trace; don't light fires and after you leave, nothing should indicate that you were ever there.

Sharpitor bivvy (Route 23)

Looking towards High Willhays from Yes Tor

19 Yes Tor

Distance	15km (9.5 miles)	Ascent	500m (1650ft)
Map	OS Landranger 191 OS Explorer OL28		
Navigation ●●●	Some compass work necessary		
Terrain ●●●	Very rough ground, often pathless, one extremely steep climb		
Wet Feet ●●●	Many boggy patches, enjoy!		
Start/Finish	Meldon Reservoir car park EX20 4LU/SX 561 917		

Fell running through a stunning valley to Dartmoor's highest point

The valley of the West Okement River is among the most beautiful spots on Dartmoor, hidden from the crowds by Meldon Reservoir. In the upper valley, the river tumbles among boulders with open banks allowing you to run directly alongside. The gnarled oaks of Black-a-tor Copse National Nature Reserve are a fantastic backdrop; this fairytale wildwood is strewn with lichens only otherwise found in Scotland. Rearing above the clitter-strewn valley sides (clitter is loose boulder debris) are High Willhays and Yes Tor, the highest points in Southern England. The scramble up to this plateau-ridge is harsh but it's over quickly and the views pay dividends. High Willhays is inconspicuous, yet 2m higher than Yes Tor which is impossible to miss with its tors, huts, trig point and flag pole. The descent is mostly on stony tracks used by the military.

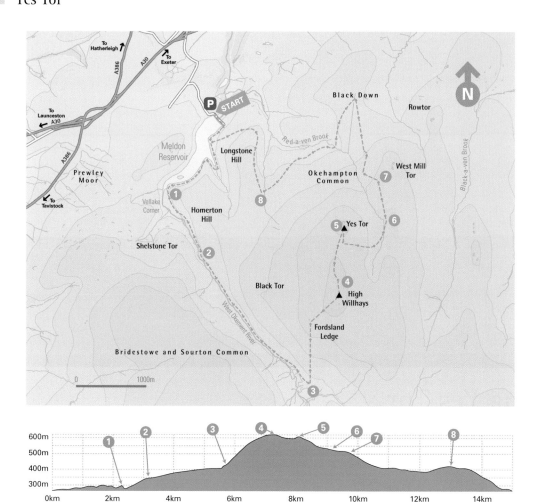

Route Description

START Turn left out of the car park entrance towards the reservoir. Cross the dam and follow the reservoir up the valley on the path just uphill from the fence. **1** At the reservoir's end, you reach a large meadow; cross this to a track going uphill alongside and above the river's gorge. **2** When the gradient eases, keep following the river upstream following the faint path close alongside. Continue upstream along the woods (Black-a-tor Copse NNR). About 800m after the last trees, the valley opens out. **3** Zig-zag uphill steeply heading N, keeping to areas free of clitter (glacial boulders). After about 900m (and 180m of ascent), you reach some military huts and a mast at Fordsland Ledge (**SX 576 888**). Follow the track heading NE onto the summit ridge; High Willhays is the tor with a large cairn. **4** Head 700m N to Yes Tor's large summit tor and trig point. **5** Backtrack 200m S and take the stony track leading downhill and E. Follow this for 1km. **6** Shortly after crossing a tiny stream (and where the track begins to turn NE), turn left off the track and cross 600m of rough ground to a track (**SX 584 908**) heading ENE and then N. **7** Follow this track downhill for 1km to a junction, turn sharp left and then left again after 120m. After 1.3km ignore a smaller track leading off right, take the lefthand fork going uphill. **8** At a T-junction, turn right and follow the track downhill back to the reservoir and dam.

Trip Planning

It's the highest part of Dartmoor, and you will be venturing off-piste: a map, compass and gear appropriate for the upland environment are necessary. This run needs care after heavy rain or snowmelt, when the West Okement may be flooding upstream of the dam.

Check whether the area will be used for military activity before setting off: search online for 'Dartmoor Firing Programme'.

Meldon Reservoir car park, signposted off the A30 west of Okehampton, invites voluntary contributions for parking. The nearest food and services can be found downhill in Okehampton.

Other Routes

If you do not fancy the climb up to High Willhays, returning down the West Okement valley again is no hardship, making for a beautiful 10km run. Note that there isn't a right of way along the west side of Meldon Reservoir back to the car park, whatever older maps might imply.

Black-a-tor Copse NNR

This run can be extended by following the West Devon Way from Okehampton Castle to Meldon Reservoir, about 4km each way.

If you want to run Yes Tor by the easiest route, drive uphill from Okehampton past the army camp to the parking area at EX20 4LT/SX 591 913. From here, military tracks make possible a 5km out and back route climbing just 170m.

Yes Tor

This route just dips a toe into the huge wilderness of North West Dartmoor. Following the West Okement for around 6km up to its source will bring you to Cranmere Pool Letterbox*, located in a vast bog and reputedly the wildest spot on Dartmoor. The East Dart River drains south from Cranmere Pool and one challenging route would be to reach Postbridge, perhaps bypassing Cranmere Pool using the peat pass on Black Ridge.

Meldon Reservoir

Events

Okehampton Running Club organise a series of trail events on North Dartmoor, including the 8km Great West Fell Run up Yes Tor. Dartmoor High Ground organise the Yes Tor Hill Race, a 16km fell race from Okehampton. They also organise the Dartmoor Marathon and Dartmoor 50, two tough routes which include Yes Tor.

High Willhays

* 'Letterboxes' are a Dartmoor peculiarity. Hidden caches all over the moor are sought out in a pastime not unlike geocaching.

West Okement valley

The Dartmoor Training Area

The military have used Dartmoor as a training ground for over two hundred years. During occasions such as WWII, the entire moor was requisitioned, but today the Dartmoor Training Area is much reduced to 130 square kilometres. This is mostly concentrated around three training ranges on the northern half of the moor (Okehampton, Merrivale and Willsworthy). Live firing takes place on about one day in three, with

firing times available by calling 0800 4584868 or online by searching for 'Dartmoor Firing Programme'.

Live fire areas are marked out by red and white posts and warning signs. When firing is underway, red flags fly (red lights at night) and there are also lookouts stationed to stop stray trail runners entering the area. At all other times there is open access to these areas. You might still encounter soldiers 'dry' training, i.e. without live ammunition.

Dartmoor Training Area

Track up Hangingstone Hill

20 The Dartmoor Crossing

Distance		52km (32 miles)	**Ascent**	1200m (3940ft)
Map		OS Landranger 191, 202 OS Explorer OL28		
Navigation	●●●	A challenge, despite largely following mapped paths		
Terrain	●●●	Hardened tracks, indistinct footpaths and bridleways, open moorland		
Wet Feet	●●●	Numerous river and stream crossings, interminable bogs		
Start		Okehampton Railway Station EX20 1EJ/SX 592 944		
Finish		Ivybridge Railway Station PL21 0PL/SX 646 565		

A gruelling expedition along the length of Southern England's wilderness

Crossing the entire moor is a wonderfully deranged challenge, taking in a wide variety of Dartmoor landscapes in a single (or multi-day) outing. Here to be enjoyed is all of the Dartmoor experience, from the very best to the very worst. You'll ascend 600m hills, follow bearings across featureless moorland, weave through mining ruins, chance upon ancient stones, scramble over tors, jump or wade streams, fight through thigh-slashing gorse, sink into peat bogs and puzzle over the map.

Although the route suggested here attempts to follow a route of least resistance via well-defined and mapped trails, in reality many are seriously hard-going and one or two possibly exist only in the Ordnance Survey's imagination. You will at least be grateful for the final section, which utilises a firm tramway.

Inevitably, inexorably, you will become muddy, wet, tired and miserable.

You'll love it.

The Dartmoor Crossing

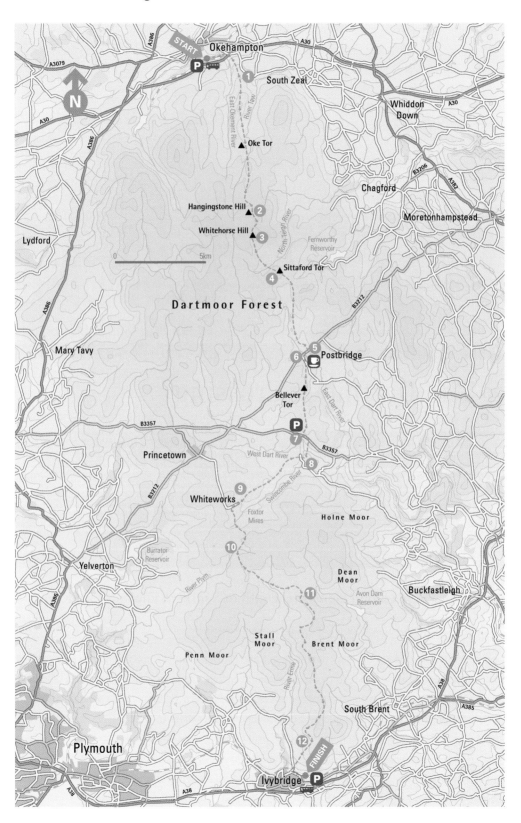

Route Description

START Leave Okehampton Station's car park via the gate marked 'Footpath to Fatherford Viaduct & Woods' and follow this bridleway E and downhill to pass under the viaduct. Turn left onto the footpath and follow the East Okement River upstream to cross at a footbridge. Follow the footpath uphill to a T-junction with a track. **1** Turn right (S) onto the track and follow it S to a T-junction: cross this track and head cross-country for 100m uphill to join a parallel track. Follow this 6km S past the summit of Oke Tor, across the River Taw via a ford, and then to the summit of Hangingstone Hill. **2** Take the track leading SE from the summit, this avoids the summit bogs by leading you to a 'peat pass' track which you follow W to the summit of Whitehorse Hill. **3** Follow the rough path S from the summit, this eventually follows a wall down to the North Teign River. Cross this and follow the wall SE to ascend Sittaford Tor. **4** Descend to the SE on rough paths to reach a N-S bridleway after 700m. Turn right (S) and follow this 4km (often overgrown and heavy going) along the East Dart River to cross the B3212 at Postbridge. **5** Cross the stone clapper bridge (why not?) before following the B3212 250m SW to a junction. Turn left onto a lane signposted for Bellever, then take the track immediately on the right (beside a Forestry Commission sign) heading S into Bellever Forest. **6** After 1.5km you reach a crossroads, continue ahead, passing Bellever Tor to the E (or ascend it) and following a footpath S to the B3357 at Dunnabridge Pound Farm. **7** Turn left (SE) to follow the B3357 300m to a bridleway on the right. Follow this bridleway S to cross the West Dart River via stepping stones, continue S and cross the Swincombe River via stepping stones to reach a lane. **8** Turn right onto the lane and follow it uphill to Sherberton Farm. Continue ahead following a faint bridleway which leads W and then SW to reach a lane at Whiteworks after 4km. **9** Follow the lane uphill for 450m to where it crosses a leat stream, turn left onto this and follow it for 1.3km to where a NW-SE bridleway crosses. Turn left (SE) and follow the bridleway (often indistinct) over Crane Hill to where a footpath descends on the left to Plym Ford. **10** Cross the River Plym and follow the rough footpath (part of Abbot's Way) over Great Gnat's Head and downhill to Erme Head. The footpath becomes a bridleway (no visible change though), follow this along the N bank of the River Erme through Erme Pits (mine wastes) and then uphill to cross Red Lake Ford. **11** When the bridleway path reaches a crossroads with a firm surface (disused tramway), turn right and follow this for 10km. **12** Take the bridleway on the right heading SW downhill and follow this down to a lane. Turn left (downhill) onto the lane, after 250m you cross the railway; take the lane on the left. After 400m, you see a path leading off on the left to the railway station.

Trip Planning

Naturally, the first priority in planning is safety; to dress and be equipped appropriately for the hostile environments you'll face. Don't forget the compass, as noted above the mapped trails don't always materialise on the ground. A day with good visibility is recommended. Some river crossings have stepping stones, some involve jumping. The West Dart River is sizeable and will be impassable if the stepping stones are submerged.

At Postbridge PL20 6SY/SX 648 789 you cross the road close to a pub and Post Office shop. If planning to break up the trip, the road at Dunnabridge is almost the half-way point, with a car park PL20 6SA/SX 641 746 close by. Camping wild is an appealing option; see page 104. It is possible to 'shuttle' back to the start using public transport. The rail route involves a change at Exeter, although trains only run to Okehampton on Sundays! This is the Sunday Rover service, run by Dartmoor Railway. At time of writing, plans have been announced to reopen the line to regular services. On days other than Sunday, the 6/6a bus services connect Exeter and Oke-hampton (West Street) in an hour. The railway stations at both ends have car parks, of course.

West Dart River crossing

East Okement valley

Other Routes

Numerous variations on the crossing are of course possible. This route does not claim to be the most direct or easiest; but if you figure out which route is, let me know! The author has also completed a shorter crossing between Belstone and Harford via Dartmeet. Another (strenuous-looking) possibility is to cross further west, via Yes Tor and Princetown.

The keen-eyed will notice that this route traces a big curve between Whiteworks and the River Erme valley, when in fact there is a bridleway leading almost direct between these two points. The reason for this dogleg detour is the infamous Foxtor Mire, inspiration for Great Grimspound Mire in the Sherlock Holmes novel,

Clapper bridge on the East Dart River

Bellever Tor

The Hound of the Baskervilles. The author has experience of this heinous swamp, and prefers the longer route. But by all means try the direct route. I double-dare you.

Events

pureTrail's Big Day Out is a 34-mile crossing from Belstone via Princetown, with the option of a 50-mile 'Crossing Extreme' route or a 'Great Escape' half marathon from Princetown to Ivybridge.

River Teign

21 Castle Drogo

Distance	13km (8 miles)	Ascent	425m (1400ft)
Map	OS Landranger 191 OS Explorer OL28		
Navigation ●●●	Mostly signposted		
Terrain ●●●	Firm trails, wide forest tracks, some stony paths		
Wet Feet ●●●	Minimal mud		
Start/Finish	Castle Drogo National Trust car park EX6 6PB/SX 725 902		

Exploring a deep wooded river valley, high and low

This is the most sheltered of the Dartmoor routes in this book, with the simplest terrain to negotiate. It can also easily be shrunk to a 6km loop. There is still worthwhile challenge from the trails, which are occasionally steep or exposed. The scenery is just wonderful, with views from on high along the winding and steep-sided valley of the River Teign competing with the more intimate views of the bubbling river, down at water level. Keep your eyes open, the author spotted an otter swimming below one of the Teign's bridges. After running, consider exploring eccentric Castle Drogo, the (currently scaffolding-clad) centre-piece of the Teign landscape.

Castle Drogo

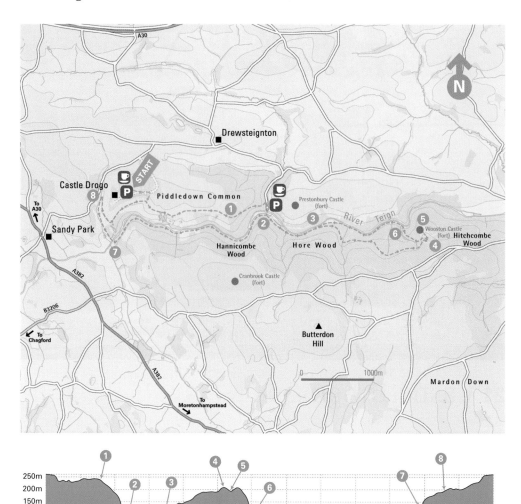

Route Description

🏃 **START** Leave the car park by a path which crosses the entrance road, signposted 'Teign Valley Trails'. This descends to a T-junction, turn left onto a bridleway following signs for 'Fingle Bridge'. ❶ After 600m, bear right at a fork, follow this bridleway steeply downhill to a road. Turn right on the road and cross Fingle Bridge after 150m. ❷ Turn left and follow the footpath track 800m along the river (downstream) to a junction. ❸ Take the track on the right leading uphill, signposted for 'Wooston Castle'. Follow this permissive path ahead at all junctions, following signposts with white arrows. ❹ After 1.8km you reach a crossroads, continue ahead and cross Wooston Castle (hillfort earthworks) to the viewpoint. ❺ Return to the crossroads and turn right onto the footpath leading steeply downhill. Descend on this path to the River Teign. ❻ Turn left (upstream) and follow the river 2.1km back to Fingle Bridge. You now have the choice of continuing upstream following either bank. The N bank path is narrower, with handrails at one point. After 2.5km you reach a footbridge, cross it if you are still on the S bank. ❼ Take the footpath signposted uphill from the footbridge, follow it for 300m until it merges with a tarmac drive and continue ahead. After another 400m a bridleway leads off sharp right (signposted 'Castle Drogo Estate'), and take this. **8** Follow the bridleway for 1km around the hillside until you reach a set of steps on the left leading steeply uphill, follow these back to the trail leading from the car park.

Trip Planning

The National Trust car park is easy enough to find, Castle Drogo being signposted from miles around. It is free to NT members, otherwise pay and display. An alternative start point is Fingle Bridge **2** EX6 6PW/SX 743 899, where there is free parking on either side of the bridge. This spot is extremely popular at weekends however.

The National Trust run a café at Castle Drogo if you need to replenish your cream tea levels, alternatively the Fingle Bridge Inn can feed you. The nearest town is Moretonhampstead, worthy of mention because it contains the Gateway Tea Rooms, simply the nicest and friendliest tea rooms on the planet.

Exploring Castle Drogo and its gardens is recommended: free to NT members, of course.

Other Routes

This route can be reduced to a still excellent 6km loop by simply turning right after crossing the river at **2** and skipping ahead to **7**. For those wishing to go further, there are at least 45km of footpaths and bridleways up- and downstream of Fingle Bridge. One excellent adventure could be to start from the village of Chagford, run to Chagford Bridge and then follow the riverside paths descending the river all the way to Steps Bridge. This route is about 16km, with the option of taking the buses back up to Chagford (change at Moretonhampstead), or of turning around and running back!

Teign valley from Hunter's Tor

The Angler's Rest, Fingle Bridge

Beside the River Teign

Events

The Deep River Trail Races by pureTrail have 6-mile and half marathon options along the Teign valley. The LDWA (Long Distance Walkers Association) run the Chagford Challenge nearby, with distances of 30, 21 or 17 miles.

Castle Drogo Estate

Castle Drogo

The 'Castle' at the centre of this route is actually an early twentieth-century mansion. It was designed by architect Sir Edwin Lutyens (responsible for everything from the Cenotaph to central Delhi), seemingly with the remit to build the most massive private residence possible (it was originally intended to be twice the size!) in the most prominent position. Inside, the first thing you notice is how rooms, corridors and doors are absurdly over-scaled, as if designed for people nine feet tall.

Unfortunately, Lutyens doesn't seem to have factored the Dartmoor weather into his granite monolith, and it leaked like a sieve from day #1. The National Trust is spending epic sums renovating it, and at time of writing (2018) it has for years been hidden from view by a vast tent enveloping a scaffolding framework. You can still visit inside; the NT has rather imaginatively filled empty rooms with (regularly updated) art installations inspired by the building and the valley, which tend to be entertaining and quirky. When the renovation is finally completed, Castle Drogo will once more dominate the skyline of North East Dartmoor.

Chinkwell Tor

22 Hound Tor and Haytor

Distance	13km (8 miles)	Ascent	550m (1800ft)
Map	OS Landranger 191 OS Explorer OL28		
Navigation ●●●	Paths are unmarked, but obvious … in clear weather		
Terrain ●●●	Multiple climbs and descents among rocky terrain		
Wet Feet ●●●	Some sections very muddy or boggy in winter		
Start/Finish	Hound Tor car park TQ13 9XQ/SX 739 791		

A grand tour of grand tors

This is the perfect introduction for trail runners to Dartmoor's terrain; the route follows a loop around high ground, passing through about ten tors. Tors are the shattered and eroded piles of granite exposed on hill tops, often being spectacular in scale and complexity. Hound Tor and Haytor are the most visited in the National Park, but you'll also be just as impressed by other relatively unknown tors along this route. The route is often as simple as following line of sight from one tor to the next (on a clear day!), and the road is regularly close by; hence this is a good run on which to test yourself before venturing into Dartmoor's wild and remote interior.

Apart from the tors, you pass various other highlights along the way: the medieval village below Hound Tor, the deep cleft of Becka Brook, the traces of industry around Haytor (deep quarries and a granite-railed tramway), the boardwalks through Emsworthy Mire (a nature reserve) and everywhere, whatever the weather, the mild and unflappable Dartmoor ponies.

Hound Tor and Haytor

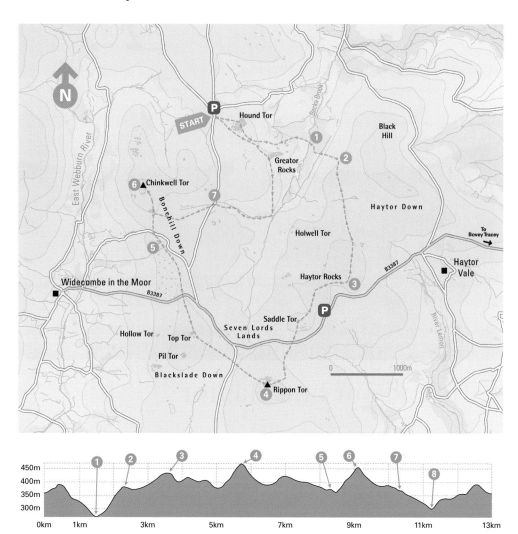

Route Description

🚶 **START** Head uphill to Hound Tor, pass between the tors. Descend past the medieval village remains to a bridleway leading to the valley bottom. ❶ Cross the footbridge and follow the bridleway for 200m until a junction. Ignore the signposts and follow the path straight ahead and uphill. When the path splits, take the right turn. ❷ When you finish climbing steeply, aim for the twin tors of Haytor, 1km S. ❸ Pass between the tors of Haytor and head 500m W to the next hill top, and then 500m SSW to the summit of Saddle Tor. Descend S to the road, cross and follow paths to the summit of Rippon Tor. ❹ Descend NW to cross the road and continue ahead to the summit of Top Tor. Descend NNW to the road, cross at a parking area and continue ahead to Bonehill Rocks. Climb to pass between these. ❺ Descend to a cattle grid in the road. Cross the road and follow the track opposite; take the path immediately branching off to the right (N) towards the rocks of Bell Tor. Pass these to the right (E) and climb to the summit of Chinkwell Tor. ❻ Backtrack downhill to Bell Tor, then take the path leading ESE which brings you to a lane after 850m.

❼ Cross the lane to a gate (entrance to Emsworthy Mire nature reserve), 25m to the left (N). Pass through the gate and follow the yellow markers downhill. ❽ When you reach the stream at the valley bottom, leave the nature reserve via a gate and follow the footpath leading uphill (N). After 700m you pass Greator Rocks (serrated cliff) to the left (W), continue uphill to Hound Tor and descend to the car park.

Greator Rocks

Trip Planning

Although you are never far from a road, you're venturing onto rough and rocky terrain and you should go equipped as for wild upland conditions. The author was reminded of this when he ran this at night and (embarrassingly) managed to run in a complete circle at one point: no compass!

Hound Tor car park is free; note that it is a popular spot and fills up quickly in summer months, as do the similar car parks near Haytor (TQ13 9XT/SX 759 767). From Bovey Tracey, follow signs for Haytor, keep going past this and then follow signs for Hound Tor.

Emsworthy Mire

The best place to eat and relax afterwards is probably the scenic village of Widecombe on the Moor, especially at the very welcoming Café on the Green. Widecombe does however suffer from the curse of coach parties.

The National Park run a visitor centre at the lower of the Haytor car parks, useful to learn more about this landscape.

Hound Tor

Other Routes

The good road access means that you can easily break this circuit down into smaller sections.

A local alternative (or a significant extension to this run if you continue 1km NE along the road from the finish and descend into the Widecombe valley by bridleway) is to run the section of the Two Moors Way from Grimspound (an amazing Iron Age village) south to Widecombe. This follows the skyline visible to the west from Chinkwell Tor.

Bonehill Rocks
Photo: Chris Eden

Hound Tor and Haytor

Haytor

Events

Teignbridge Trotters' Haytor Heller is a 'not for the faint hearted' 10km circuit. pureTrail's Hameldown Hammer half marathon starts in Widecombe in the Moor and ascends the hills across the valley from Chinkwell Tor.

Horsham Steps
Photo: Claire Pinder

23 Lustleigh Cleave

Distance	13km (8 miles)	Ascent	550m (1800ft)
Map	OS Landranger 191 OS Explorer OL28		
Navigation ●●●	Mostly signposted, clearly defined tracks		
Terrain ●●●	Paths strewn with granite boulders, one long steep climb		
Wet Feet ●●●	Some sections get muddy after rain		
Start/Finish	Pullabrook Wood car park TQ13 9LG/SX 784 793		

Woodland trails littered with granite boulders in a stunning valley

At the car park, you are confronted with an impressive view up a deep and tree-covered cleft, backed by a steep-sided hill rising 250m above the valley floor. Basically, everything you can see from here, you are going to run!

Lustleigh Cleave is the name given the central part of this valley, carved through by the River Bovey. Most of these ancient oak woodlands are protected within the bounds of the East Dartmoor National Nature Reserve. You are free to run the trails within the NNR as you please, and what trails! They are a wonderful test for your agility and focus, continually weaving around and over worn granite boulders, with the occasional fallen tree to duck or jump; boredom is impossible here. A highlight is Horsham Steps, where you cross the Bovey by leaping from boulder to huge boulder. If you don't experience trail running Nirvana at some point on this route, you never will ...

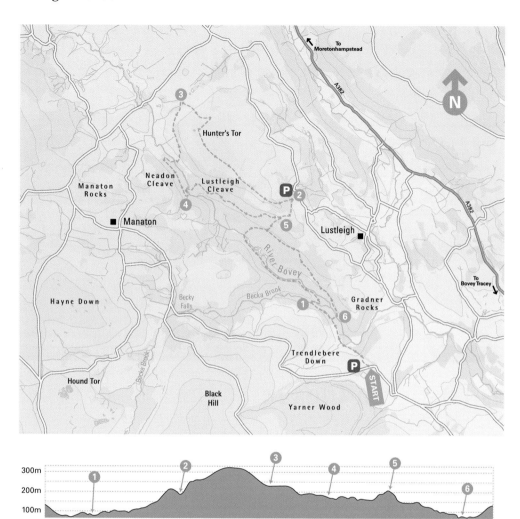

Route Description

START Take the path leading out of the back of the parking area and follow it downhill to meet a byway track (Old Manaton Road) after 150m. Turn left and follow the byway NW. After 800m you pass a gate on the right signed Hisley Wood, and after another 1km take the footpath on the right. **1** Cross Becka Brook by a footbridge, then follow the River Bovey upstream until the footpath terminates at a pair of footbridges across the river. Take the bridleway across the river and then follow it steeply uphill, ignoring any turn-offs and following signs for Hammerslake. After the bridleway begins to descend and you reach a gate, look for and take the bridleway leading off left (uphill) signposted for an 'ancient camp'. **2** Follow this bridleway uphill to Sharpitor, and then NW along the ridgetop to Hunter's Tor (highest point of hill). The bridleway descends steeply to Peck Farm; pass these buildings to the left, through a gate. 100m after Peck Farm, you reach a T-junction with a bridleway. **3** Turn left onto the bridleway, signposted for Foxworthy. When you reach Foxworthy (quaint cottages), descend to the river and cross it, then take the bridleway immediately on the left. After 140m this rejoins the road into Foxworthy; turn left onto this and then after 30m take the footpath on the left signed for East Dartmoor National Nature Reserve. After 600m, the footpath reaches a junction. ❹ Turn left (steep downhill) and then cross the River Bovey via huge boulders (Horsham Steps). Follow the footpath 200m uphill to a T-junction. Turn right (SE) onto this bridleway and follow it for 1.4km to a junction with the Hammerslake bridleway (which you ascended earlier). ❺ Turn right (downhill) and descend steeply for 350m to a junction. Take the left fork, a bridleway signposted for Pethybridge. Follow it for 1.6km (taking the downhill route when it forks) to Hisley Bridge. ❻ Cross Hisley Bridge and turn left onto the byway. Retrace your original route back to the car park.

Trip Planning

This run is much less exposed to the elements than is the Dartmoor norm, and the clear trails and signage should mean that there is little danger of getting lost ... usual disclaimers apply!

Horsham Steps should be avoided when the River Bovey is running high; if it looks dangerous, then assume that it is! At such times, from Foxworthy, use the short section of bridleway on the left before you cross the bridge there.

The car park is free. From Bovey Tracey (where the nearest food and services can be found) follow signs for Manaton. After 3km the car park is the right, just after a left bend.

Other Routes

It's easy to shorten this route, most simply by cutting off the second loop: for a 6km run, take the first bridleway on the right after crossing the River Bovey. To tackle the more strenuous second loop (7km), park roadside near Hammerslake TQ13 9SQ/**SX 774 817** and follow a bridleway 100m to join the route at ❷.

Variations or minor extensions are possible by exploring the footpaths and bridleways on the south-west side

Hisley Wood

Lustleigh Cleave from the car park

Houndtor Wood

View from Raven's Tor

Lustleigh Cleave

Trendlebere Down

of the valley, for example the bridleway which continues ahead at ① to climb the Becka Brook Valley and eventually reach Foxworthy. Across the road from the start car park is Yarner Wood National Nature Reserve (entrance is 550m downhill along the road) which has numerous extra trails to get lost on.

Deviants wanting a big day out can augment these woodland trails with some open moorland trails as Route 22 (Hound Tor and Haytor) is less than 3km from the start of this route.

Events

The 16km Bovey Beauty Fell Race, by the Woodland Trust, follows 16km of these trails. A weekly 5km parkrun takes place on mixed surfaces at Parke near Bovey Tracey, TQ13 9JQ/SX 805 785. This National Trust estate is also the headquarters of the Dartmoor National Park.

Above the Erme valley

24 The Perambulation of 1240

Distance	76+km (47+ miles)	**Ascent**	c2225m (c7300ft)
Map	OS Landranger 191, 202 OS Explorer OL28		
Navigation ●●●	A major challenge to find and follow the easiest route		
Terrain ●●●	Extremely heavy-going, plenty of off-path time		
Wet Feet ●●●	Innumerable bogs and river crossings		
Start/Finish	High Moorland Visitor Centre car park PL20 6QY/SX 589 734		

One ring to rule them all

The what? Of when? The Perambulation originated in the year 1240 as a circuit following boundary markers delineating the ancient Forest of Dartmoor, traced out by King Henry III's officials on horseback. In other words, this route follows the traditional border of Dartmoor. Except that there isn't a route, or at least no particular designated path to follow, just a series of waymarks to visit. In fact, often there is no path at all. And this isn't the rim of Dartmoor, the Perambulation leads you around the wildest heart of the upland moor. The Perambulation has had a cult following among geeky backpackers for years; the author originally learned about it through his (geeky backpacker) wife's treks.

Don't be scared off! This behemoth doesn't have to be tackled non-stop in one go; it could be achieved in separate chunks over a period of time or better still, as a fabulous multiday expedition.

In the interests of full disclosure ... at time of going to print, this is the only route in this book which the

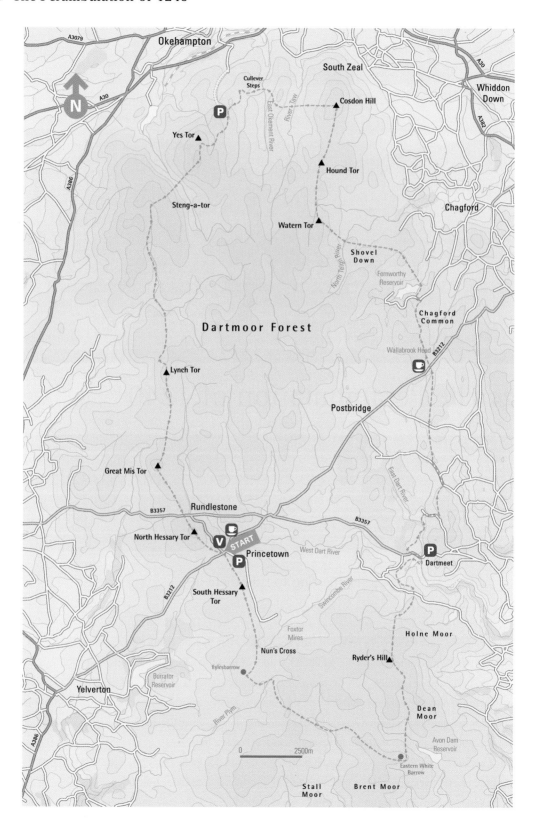

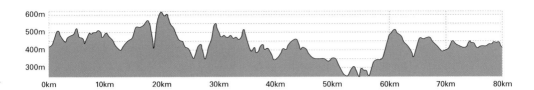

author has not yet (fully) completed. I certainly hope to, once I jiggle the right combination of fellow runners, dry moor, support team, good weather and mental/physical preparedness into place ... all of which kiboshed several planned attempts during the past year. Plus, the dog ate my homework.

A blow by blow route description of the Perambulation would defeat the whole object: those taking on this challenge need to choose their own route from each boundary marker to the next. Note that the map and profile shown here are just one interpretation of how to tackle the Perambulation!

Many of the boundary markers exist as physical objects; e.g. stones or cairns. Others are natural landmarks such as tors and river intersections. Sometimes there is an obvious route between them following the lie of the land or even existing pathways, often there isn't; expect numerous arduous climbs and some bog-fast moments.

Here are the boundary markers of the Perambulation of 1240, clockwise starting from Princetown:

#	Marker	Grid ref
1	North Hessary Tor	SX 579 742
2	Rendlestone	SX 574 750
3	Great Mis Tor	SX 563 769
4	White Barrow	SX 568 793
5	Limsboro Cairn on Lynch Tor	SX 566 805
6	Rattlebrook Foot (confluence of Rattle Brook and Amicombe Brook)	SX 561 837
7	Rattlebrook Head	SX 560 876
8	Steng-a-Tor	SX 568 880
9	Yes Tor	SX 581 902
10	Cullever Steps	SX 606 921
11	Cosdon Beacon on Cosdon Hill	SX 636 915
12	Hound Tor	SX 629 890
13	Thirlstone on Watern Tor	SX 629 869
14	Hewlake Foot (confluence of Hugh Lake and North Teign River)	SX 640 860
15	Long Stone on Shovel Down	SX 660 857
16	Heath Stone	SX 671 837
17	Metherall Marsh on Chagford Common	SX 671 830
18	King's Oven	SX 674 812
19	Wallabrook Head	SX 676 810
20	Wallabrook Foot (confluence of Walla Brook and East Dart River)	SX 672 747
21	Dartmeet (confluence of West Dart and East Dart Rivers)	SX 671 731
22	Week Ford and O Brook Foot (confluence of O Brook and West Dart River)	SX 662 724
23	Drylake Foot (confluence of Dry Lake and O Brook)	SX 660 710
24	Boundary Stone on Sandyway	SX 659 696
25	Petre's Bound Stone on Ryder's Hill	SX 659 691
26	Western Wellabrook Head (source of Western Wella Brook)	SX 665 686
27	Western Wellabrook Foot (confluence of Western Wella Brook and River Avon)	SX 665 662
28	Eastern White Barrow	SX 665 652
29	Red Lake Ford	SX 642 664
30	Erme Head Ford	SX 622 669
31	Eylesbarrow	SX 600 686
32	Siward's or Nun's Cross	SX 605 699
33	South Hessary Tor	SX 597 723

Trip Planning

Obviously, anyone attempting the Perambulation will need to be totally kitted and prepared for the wild environment they are tackling. Particular consideration needs to be given to food and drink ... carry it all, or arrange resupply en route? There are a number of spots where vehicles could meet runners; e.g. the lonely track close to Yes Tor (EX20 4LT/SX 591 913, see Route 19), the Warren House Inn on the B3212 (PL20 6TA/SX 674 809) and Dartmeet car park (PL20 6SG/SX 672 732).

River crossings are almost unavoidable; dry times are recommended, and attempting this after recent rain would be madness.

Camping spots are almost infinite; see page 104. Another factor to consider is the firing ranges; see page 108.

Everything you could ever want to know about the Historical context and significance of the Perambulation is assembled in *Dartmoor's Greatest Long Distance Walk: The Perambulation* by Roland Ebdon. This intriguing book does however contain little on the topic of actually completing it.

Observers at Erme Pits

Approaching Princetown

Yes Tor

Events

Ultramarathon events inspired by the Perambulation route have been organised in recent years, but none were operative as of 2018.

Long distance routes on Dartmoor

Below are further ideas for long runs on Dartmoor. Some are official and waymarked, others less so.

Abbot's Way – An ancient 37km route between Buckfastleigh Abbey and Tavistock Abbey (now a ruin). There is no 'official' information available, but it is marked on OS maps.

Dartmoor Ramble – An 80km circuit linking youth hostels. Little trodden as the guidebook is out of print.

Dartmoor 600 – Not a route, but a challenge! Run Venture invite runners to ascend Dartmoor's five 600m peaks in any order and record their time. A typical distance is about 35km. 'Rules' and guidelines from their website.

Dartmoor Way – Currently under development, to complement the 145km Dartmoor Way cycling trail.

Templar Way – This is a 29km descent from Haytor to the sea at Teignmouth on relatively easy terrain. An information leaflet is available from Devon Council's website.

Two Moors Way – This crosses Dartmoor for about 65km between Ivybridge and the Teign Valley (see page 156).

South and East Devon

This section covers a wide swathe of terrain comprised of the coast and adjacent inland areas stretching from west and south of Dartmoor all the way east to the Dorset border. It's impossible to simply categorise the landscape of this huge area, the runs here are selected to help you explore the highlights of the region's diverse scenery. In the far west of the region, the deep cleft of the River Tamar valley is a remarkable post-industrial landscape which has been utilised as a trail-running centre. The South Hams coast offers ineffable running experiences, with Devon's southernmost tip cherry-picked here. Devon's eastern coast is within the Jurassic Coast World Heritage Site; the routes recommended reveal two very different aspects of this. Finally, Devon's hinterland is showcased by a route in the little-visited Blackdown Hills.

View from Culmstock Beacon (Route 28)

Bedford United Trail

Wheal Maria Trail

25 The Tamar Trails

Distance	8.5km (5.5 miles)	Ascent	300m (1000ft)
Map	OS Landranger 201 OS Explorer 108		
Navigation ●●●	Colour-coded and waymarked trails		
Terrain ●●●	Steep narrow descents at first, then forestry tracks		
Wet Feet ●●●	Well draining tracks		
Start/Finish	Tamar Trails Centre PL19 8JE/SX 438 727		

Marked trails exploring a surprisingly attractive mining wasteland

The Tamar Trails are 25km of colour-coded and waymarked trails along steep slopes above the River Tamar. Suggested here is an introductory run which gives a good flavour of the trails, but this is a place that rewards repeated visits and explorations. Based around a trail-running shop, café and information centre, these trails are included in the guidebook as representing perhaps the nearest equivalent for South West trail runners to a mountain bike trail centre!

Despite being in Devon, this is part of the Cornish Mining World Heritage Site (see page 44). The landscape is churned and ravaged from five centuries of mining, most intensively in the nineteenth century. Traces of this industrial heritage can be glimpsed through the cover of coniferous forest; this route takes in mine entrances, leat streams and the epic scars and ruins of the world's largest arsenic mine. The trails are mostly broad forest tracks. However, this suggested route starts with a bang by negotiating the slightly precarious Bedford United Trail with its boardwalks, bridges and steep steps; why not?

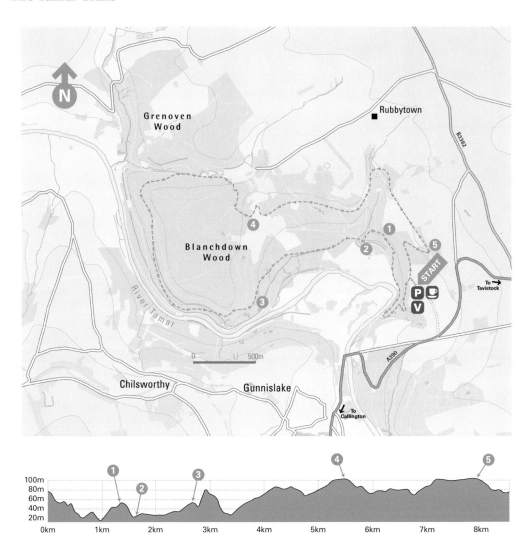

Route Description

🏃 **START** At the car park exit, turn left (over a mock bridge) onto the Bedford United Trail (brown signs). Follow this for 1.5km until it widens and reaches a crossroads with the Wheal Josiah Trail (grey signs). **①** Turn left and follow the WJT 300m downhill to a junction. **②** Take the left-hand track, signposted for Wheal Frementor. Follow this uphill for 1km to where it joins the Wheal Maria Trail (green signs). **③** Turn left onto the WMT and follow it for 2.8km to a junction with the Mineral Railway Trail (red signs). **④** Follow the MRT downhill around the ruined buildings of an arsenic mine and then continue following it for 2km until you see a right turn signposted for the Tamar Trails Centre. **⑤** Follow this 700m downhill to the car park.

Trip Planning

The Tamar Trails Centre is signposted off the A390, 1km east of New Bridge at Gunnislake. Parking is pay and display. Pick up a detailed map of the trail network for a few pence or download it beforehand from their website. The centre is based around the Beech Café, which serves sandwiches, cakes and pasties.

Tamar Trails Centre

Other activities available include bike hire and a high ropes course.

Run Venture are the small trail-running shop based at the Tamar Trail Centre. They run coaching sessions and guided runs as well as Tamar Trail Runners, a social club open to all. The trails are maintained by the charitable Tamar Community Trust.

Other Routes

Those of a nervous disposition (or just wanting to speed along wide trails) might want to skip the Bedford United Trail section of this route, by going straight ahead from the car park to ❶; continue ahead at these crossroads. There are seven Tamar Trails, adding up to 25km. This route includes the four trails north of the Tamar Trail Centre. The remaining three trails extend south as far as Maddacleave, where there is a car park PL19 8JN/SX 458 696. Chimney Rock Trail is the most challenging of these, being steep and narrow.

Wheal Josiah Trail

The arsenic works

Events

A parkrun is held every Saturday. Run Venture some-times organise races on the trails, check their website for updates.

Wheal Maria Trail

Gammon Head

26 Prawle Point

Distance	18km (11 miles)	**Ascent**	625m (2050ft)
Map	OS Landranger 202 OS Explorer 20		
Navigation ●●●	Mostly on the SWCP, otherwise well-signposted		
Terrain ●●●	Footpaths, farm tracks, tarmac, trails over boulders or bedrock slabs		
Wet Feet ●●●	Maybe just a few puddles to dodge		
Start/Finish	Pig's Nose Inn, East Prawle TQ7 2BY/SX 781 364		

Ineffable coastal trails on raised beaches above foaming reefs

One of the author's all-time favourite runs! That said: he won't forget tripping on rocks and face-planting near the end of an 80km adventure race here, right in front of the event photographer. Prawle Point is the southernmost tip of Devon, located in the region of interminable narrow lanes known as South Hams. The coastal geology is particularly remarkable here; the South West Coast Path winds close to sea level above wave-cut platforms (i.e. reefs) caused by changing sea levels, whilst the jagged crags of ancient sea cliffs soar above the trail. This (author's humble opinion) is the very best kind of trail running that the SWCP offers: constantly changing rocky narrow trails where you have to find the mental balance between maintaining pace, placing your feet safely and soaking up the surrounds; clue: zoning out is the key!

Prawle Point

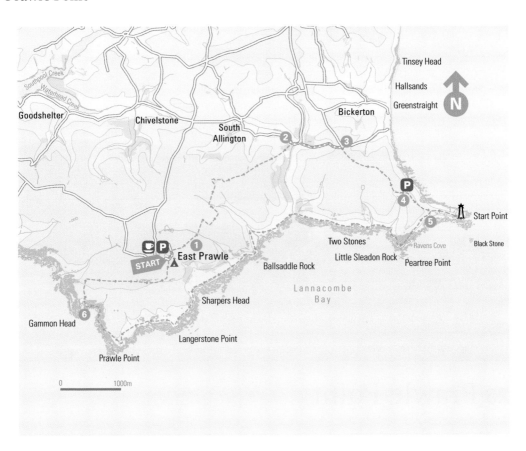

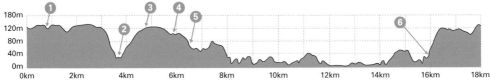

Route Description

🏃 **START** Follow the lane (Shippen) leading downhill (NE) to the right of the Pig's Nose Inn. Bear right at the first junction and then right again at the next. Follow this lane for 225m to where it becomes a track, then a bridleway. ❶ Follow this well-signposted bridleway for 2.9km, ignoring all footpaths leading off, until it descends and reaches a lane. ❷ Turn right (E) onto the lane and descend 170m to a junction. Turn right and then left at the junction immediately after. Ascend 1.1km on this lane to a crossroads (Hollow-combe Head). ❸ Turn right at the crossroads (SE) and continue ahead for 1.5km to Start Point car park, passing entrance signs for Start Farm. ❹ Follow the tarmac drive 400m downhill towards the lighthouse to a footpath sign pointing right ('Minehead 462 miles'). ❺ Turn right and follow this footpath, but first you have the option of continuing 500m to the lighthouse and back. Follow the SWCP for 8.5km W. ❻ 1km after the Coastwatch hut on Prawle Point and just before Gammon Head (first headland after Prawle Point), take the footpath leading right (uphill) off the SWCP. Ascend to a junction with a bridleway and turn right (E) onto this. After 1.2km it joins a lane, follow this 400m uphill to the Pig's Nose Inn.

Langerstone Point

Trip Planning

The Pig's Nose Inn is at the centre of East Prawle, with free parking available around the village green in front of the pub. This quirky pub is full of all manner of eccentric bric-a-brac and often hosts bands in the adjacent hall. Food is available here, and also from the combined Piglet Café and Shop across the road. The surrounding fields also offer camping options; ask at the pub.

Other Routes

There are various points at which this route could be cut shorter, e.g. turning right at the junction directly after ❷ and following this south to Lannacombe Beach. Extending to the run to East Portlemouth on the Kingsbridge estuary will offer more of the same great coastal trails. However, you would have to return mostly on lanes. Should you wish to just run the coast, you'd need to shuttle vehicles; pay parking available at Start Point car park TQ7 2ET/SX 820 375 and Mill Bay National Trust car park TQ8 8PU/SX 741 380 which is horrible in summer, being over-popular and located down ridiculously narrow lanes.

Sharpers Head

Pig's Nose Inn, East Prawle

Start Point

Prawle Point

Prawle Point

The section of the SWCP west of the Kingsbridge Estuary, between Salcombe and Hope Cove, is a wonderful run of very different character, with high cliffs and descents to tiny coves. Highly recommended if you are staying in the area!

Events

The most popular event hereabouts is Endurance Life's South Devon CTS which is usually based from Beesands and incorporates much of this route. The choice of distance ranges from 10K to Ultra. The author once entered the Ultra, but went down with Man Flu before the event ... a lucky escape. The Salcombe Coastal Marathon takes in an epic swathe of the SWCP from Torcross to Bantham, with a ferry crossing to Salcombe; with 1,400m of ascent, it's registered as a fell race! The South West Coast Path Running Challenge is located to the east of this route, starting from Dartmouth with 19km and 41km options.

Otter Estuary Nature Reserve

27 Ladram Bay and the River Otter

Distance	14km (9 miles)	**Ascent**	550m (1800ft)
Map	OS Landranger 192 OS Explorer 115		
Navigation ●●●	Mostly on the South West Coast Path, care needed on inland byways		
Terrain ●●●	Rough byways, optional steep climb to High Peak		
Wet Feet ●●●	Some muddy byways		
Start/Finish	Lime Kiln car park EX9 7AY/SY 072 820		

Beautiful riverside trails leading to spectacular sandstone cliffs

This run starts within the Otter Estuary Nature Reserve, with firm trails leading through reed beds and marshland. You follow the river upstream beyond its tidal limits, where it becomes a glorious rippling stream. Keep your eyes peeled as you might spot kingfishers, otters and – wait for it – beavers! These mysteriously appeared on the river in 2010 and have since been protected and monitored by the Devon Wildlife Trust. You next ascend through a series of sunken lanes and tracks until you rather dramatically emerge at the coast atop a 150m sheer cliff of Devonian sandstone. The remainder of the run follows the rim of these amazing burnt orange cliffs back to the Otter Estuary, with the highlight being the numerous sea stacks peppering Ladram Bay.

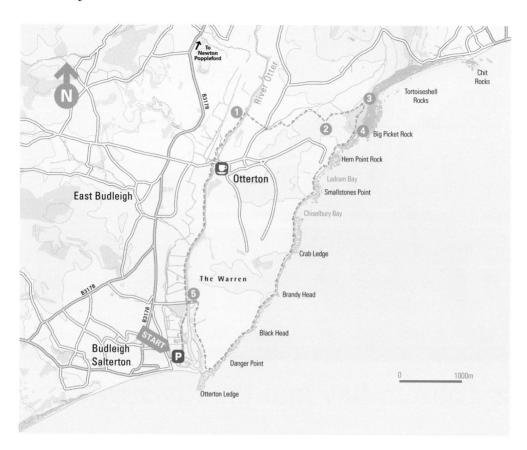

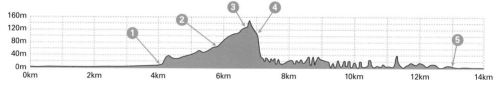

Route Description

START Follow the footpath from the car park leading upstream along the estuary. Cross lanes after 900m and 3.3km. After 4.2km, cross the river by an arched footbridge. ❶ Head uphill following the sunken byway to a lane. Cross the lane and take the byway track just to the right. Follow this around a right bend to a junction where you take the left-hand track. This leads downhill to a junction, take the right-hand (uphill) track. After 340m, this reaches a T-junction with a byway (Bar's Lane). ❷ Turn left onto Bar's Lane. After 800m, turn right onto the signposted SWCP (if you miss the turning and reach the top of the cliffs, just backtrack c50m). ❸ Follow the SWCP around High Peak. After 300m, a steep path on the left offers an optional side-tour to the summit trig point of High Peak. ❹ Continue following the SWCP for 5km S to Danger Point. The SWCP bends N along the estuary, follow this for 1km to a road and bridge. ❺ Cross the river and turn left to follow the footpath back to the car park.

High Peak

Trip Planning

Lime Kiln car park, located at the far east end of Budleigh Salterton's seafront, is pay and display. Cheap-skates might wish to know that there is limited free parking available back along adjacent Granary Road. For ice cream, stroll to Budleigh Salterton's seafront after running. Provisions can be obtained in Budleigh Salterton or at the Community Shop in Otterton, not far from Otterton Mill where lunch can be enjoyed beside the River Otter.

Other Routes

This loop can be extended by 7–8km by taking in Bulverton Hill. At ❶, continue north along the river and eventually cross near Ashtree Farm, then follow a lane north for 1km before ascending the track past Northmosttown. Follow the ridge south to the coast and rejoin the SWCP.

Woodbury Common is about 5km west of Otterton. Numerous parking areas give easy access to this attractive heathland which is Access Land and conveniently crisscrossed by many trails.

Events

The Jurassic Coast 10K covers the southern half of this route. Nearby, The Big Dipper is a 24km out and back race on the Sidmouth-Beer section of the SWCP. The LDWA run the Devonshire Dumpling hereabouts, with distances of marathon or 17 miles. 'JP's Exe to Axe' is a 44-mile coastal ordeal organised by Sidmouth Running Club.

OTTERTON

Here be otters

Ladram Bay

Exeter trail running

The Exeter Green Circle is a 12-mile loop of trails through mainly green spaces within the city, much of which is surfaced. Parts of the Circle make pleasant spots to enjoy a short run, such as Ludwell Valley Park, a working farm reaching between Heavitree and the River Exe. The Circle also includes Mincinglake Valley Park in Stoke Hill, although the trails are mostly surfaced here and the much more interesting Stoke Woods (Forestry Commission) are only a kilometre away, served by several parking areas.

The trails following both banks of the Exeter Ship Canal offer an excellent easy run, starting from Haven Bank Quay in the city centre and leading 8km south along the River Exe Estuary. The popular Double Locks pub is passed en route (a possible start point) as well as Riverside Valley Park and various nature reserves. If you continue past the canal's end to Starcross (including some road time) you can return into Exeter by train.

The National Trust estate of Killerton is 5km north-east of Exeter, with plenty of space (2,600 hectares) to run, a parkrun on Saturdays and an annual 5km Fun Run, 19km run, and a half marathon. Climb The Clump for some 'lurvely' views, or even extend your run to nearby Ashclyst Forest (Forestry Commission). Haldon Forest is 6km south of Exeter, sprawling over 1,400 hectares of hilly woodland with various marked trails and much more for the adventurous to explore. The Forestry Commission manage Haldon and there is a café and various other facilities.

On Black Down Common

28 Culmstock Beacon

Distance	10km (6 miles)	**Ascent**	225m (740ft)
Map	OS Landranger 193 OS Explorer 128		
Navigation ●●●	Well sign-posted, but plenty of junctions to keep track of		
Terrain ●●●	Forest, farm, heathland and bog underfoot		
Wet Feet ●●●	A few sections are appallingly muddy, even in summer		
Start/Finish	Scotts Shute, Culmstock EX15 3HP/ST 108 154		

The nicest East Devon hill that no one has heard of

Whilst there was a temptation to squeeze in just-one-more-amazing-coast-run here, the author instead has decided to instead direct you inland to Culmstock Beacon. The Beacon is a stone beehive hut with an opening in the roof, from which fires were lit to warn of the Spanish Armada. It sits on Black Down Common atop a lonely and little visited hill. Most of the travellers whizzing past on the M5, a few miles away down in the valley, will be oblivious to this rather lovely corner of the Blackdown Hills AONB.

This route initially grinds around the hillside through some rather 'quaggy' farmland, but once you climb into the woods of Culm Davey Plantation, your run becomes increasingly rewarding. The plateau up on top is a heath rimmed and criss-crossed by numerous trails to try out, with commanding views across the vale to the Quantock Hills and Exmoor. Go see and explore; but please keep this place a secret ...

Culmstock Beacon

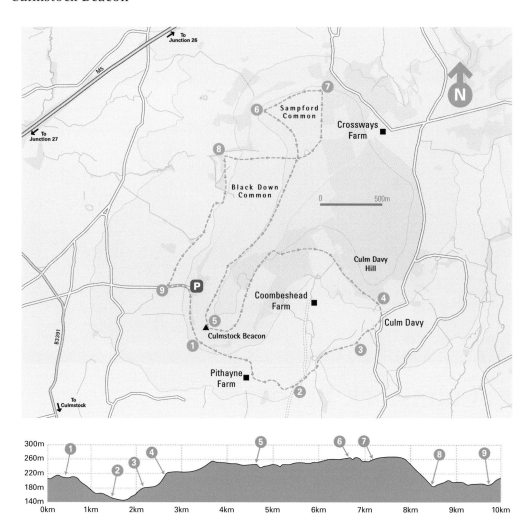

Route Description

🚶 START From the parking spot, descend 50m along the lane and take the lane leading off left (S) beside a tin shed. Follow this past a house to where it becomes a footpath, continue ahead (muddy) until you see a footpath sign leading left (uphill). Follow this uphill until a junction beside an orange post and then take the right path leading downhill (a sign at the bottom explains that this was a diversion around an SSSI bog). ❶ Follow the footpath along three fields and then down a steep track to Pithayne Farm. At a junction, take the footpath leading left (E) and follow this track for 400m to a lane. ❷ Turn left (uphill) and follow the lane for 150m before turning right onto a byway track. Follow this for 500m to another lane. ❸ Turn left (uphill) onto the lane, follow it for 400m to a junction. Take the track leading straight ahead (N, uphill). After 100m this splits; take the left fork which shortly after passes an FC sign for Culm Davy. ❹ Follow the track uphill for 1km to a gate where it reaches the hilltop. Turn left (SSE) and follow the path along the rim of the hilltop for 1km to Culmstock Beacon (circular stone hut). ❺ Continue following tracks around the rim of the hilltop for 2km to Sampford Point (prominent jutting spur). ❻ The path continues to a track descending from Sampford Point, do not take this; instead take one of the paths leading off to the right just before and follow this 500m along the rim of the hill to the forest boundary, where you turn right (S). ❼ Follow the forest boundary 350m S and then SW across the heath until it crosses your earlier route beside a pond. Continue ahead heading E on the track which descends steeply downhill to a gate. ❽ Cross the gate and turn left (S); follow this footpath for 1.25km across two fields (turning right and descending in the middle of the second one) along a track and along more fields to the lane you started on. ❾ Turn left and follow the lane uphill to your car.

Culmstock Beacon from Sampford Point

Trip Planning

The start point is located at the end of an obscure lane; you will likely need a map or Sat Nav to find it. When you reach a crossroads on the lane between Culmstock and Nicholashayne, take the turn-off uphill signposted for 'Beacon' and follow this lane right to the end where it terminates in a stony track where you can park.

There are no amenities on or close to this route; Culmstock is your nearest bet with pubs and a café/shop, the Strand Store.

The nearby Wellington Monument (maintained by the National Trust) is a glorious viewpoint, worth a visit after your run.

Culm Davy Plantation

Other Routes

It is possible to extend the run by 4km through starting from Culmstock village and following footpaths to join at Pithayne Farm, just before ❷. Another possibility extending the run by around 6km is starting at the National Trust Wellington Monument car park TA21 9RE/ST 143 167 and reaching Black Down Common just after ❺. This would however mean following 2km of busy road.

There are plenty of options for further exploring up on Black Down Common and in the adjacent Forestry Commission land. Don't be tempted to short-cut to the finish via the bridleway descending from Sampford Point, however; the footpath shown on the map is in reality an impassable bog!

Culmstock Beacon

Bog diversion

Wellington Monument

Culmstock Beacon

View from Culmstock Beacon

The Blackdown Hills Area of Outstanding Natural Beauty

The Blackdown Hills are a range of steep-sided and often wooded ridges broken up by idyllic valleys and bubbling streams. The AONB sprawls along the Devon/Somerset border; to locate it more crudely – these are the hills to your left as you head down the M5 past Taunton.

Devon local

Few know about or visit this unspoilt area. This is forgivable as there is little tourist infrastructure and no central 'hub' to help visitors make sense of the region. It is a shame however, as this is a huge natural playground waiting to be enjoyed. On the bright side, you'll likely have it to yourself! The two routes in this book (28 and 36) just scrape the surface of the area's trail-running potential. The Blackdown Hills AONB and the Neroche Scheme websites both suggest numerous walking routes which should also suit trail runners.

The Undercliffs

29 The Undercliffs

Distance		c11km (c7 miles)	Ascent	c350m (c1150ft)
Map		OS Landranger 193 OS Explorer 116		
Navigation	●●●	Impossible to get lost (probably)		
Terrain	●●●	Roots, rocks, steps, all runnable		
Wet Feet	●●●	Mud galore, usually jumpable		
Start		Seaton seafront EX12 2LN/SY 244 898		
Finish		Marine Parade, Lyme Regis DT7 3JE/SY 342 920		

Fantastic rooty trails winding and undulating through Devon's jungle

The Undercliffs are a series of huge landslips dating from the eighteenth and nineteenth centuries, and indeed still occurring: the path was blocked by a landslip from 2014 to 2016. This inaccessible No Man's Land between cliffs and sea has reverted to wilderness with trees, creepers and dense undergrowth forming a humid jungle. Running through is just sublime. The narrow path continuously contorts, climbs and falls. The path is far too complex for an OS map to do justice to, so treat the distance and ascent stated above with a pinch of salt. Roots, rocks and mud patches test the grip of your trail shoe's soles. Steep sections have wooden steps, there are a couple of boardwalks and a short surfaced section late on, but this doesn't distract from the untamed and remote feel of this unique landscape.

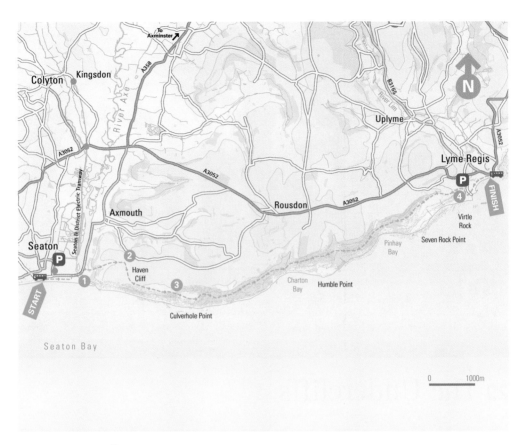

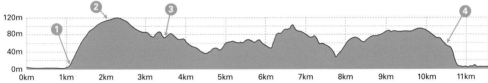

The start is unpromising, with a dull climb along a surfaced road and through a golf course. Once you've descended the cliffs into the jungle, however, it's all good. Eventually emerging from the Undercliffs (into Dorset) and running past the sunbathers on Lyme Regis's beaches is a surreal experience, requiring intake of ice cream to properly absorb.

Route Description

START Head E along Seaton's seafront and cross the B3172 bridge over the River Axe. ❶ Turn right onto Squire's Lane, follow it uphill to its end. Continue ahead through the golf course. ❷ 300m after joining a track (Barn Close Lane), turn right following the SWCP signage. Cross several fields to the cliff edge, the path continues along this for about 700m. ❸ Follow the path down into the Undercliff – henceforth the path is obvious and when there are alternatives (rarely) the SWCP is signposted clearly. ❹ Follow the SWCP downhill to Lyme Regis Harbour and along the seafront to the bus stop OR continue ahead 200m to Holmbush car park.

The Undercliffs

Trip Planning

The start and finish points named above (Seaton seafront EX12 2LN/SY 244 898 Marine Parade, Lyme Regis DT7 3JE/SY 342 920) are bus stops. The easiest way to organise this run is to park at one end and use the 9a bus service to shuttle to the other. Hence, it makes sense to check bus times and plan around these! In Lyme Regis, Holmbush car park DT7 3JW/SY 336 919, is conveniently close to where the path emerges from the Undercliffs. If you are running in the other direction, Seaton Jurassic car park EX12 2LX/SY 247 902 is on The Underfleet, 250m from the seafront.

There are very few points at which you can escape from the Undercliffs, and none are rights of way. Once you enter, you're committed to either finishing or turning back. Take extra water as the temperature and humidity can be surprising, even in winter!

Other Routes

You can (of course!) turn around when you reach the car park in Lyme Regis and do it all again. No shuttle required ...

Events

Axe Valley Runners' Grizzly is a well-established and notoriously hilly trail race starting in Seaton. The full race is 32km and the accompanying 'Cub Run' is 15km. Albion Running's Ham and Lyme Race is a 50km/100km trail ultramarathon along the Liberty Trail. The 100km option goes from Lyme Regis north to Ham Hill Country Park in Somerset.

Seaton

The Undercliffs

Approaching the Undercliffs

Goat Island and the Chasm

The grassy patch of open ground that you ascend onto early on is Goat Island, undisturbed land somehow left high and dry by the 'Great Landslip' of 1839 which created the Undercliffs. The path has only ascended Goat Island since the 2016 reopening. Throughout this adventure, you will glimpse the overgrown Chasm below to your left, between the ridge that the path follows and the high cliffs behind. When this land sunk in 1839, a ridge of land simultaneously surfaced out to sea, part of the same geological syncline. Discussions were held in Parliament as to whether this might serve as a harbour for the Navy! However, it soon eroded away.

West Somerset

West Somerset is dominated by the high moorland and deep valleys of Exmoor National Park. There was a temptation to give Exmoor its own chapter (as with Dartmoor), but arguably Exmoor in Somerset is noticeably different in character from Exmoor in Devon; the routes featured in this section are inland from the sea and tackle Exmoor's highest moorland and wildest valleys. Also, it would be a crime to side-line the amazing Quantock Hills. Despite being just across the valley from Exmoor, the Quantocks (Britain's first Area of Outstanding Natural Beauty) are completely different; a unique landscape of trails through wooded oak combes leading onto a heathland plateau.

Dunkery Beacon (Route 32)

Tarr Steps

The riverside path.

30 The River Barle

Distance	35km (22 miles)	Ascent	925m (3030ft)
Map	OS Landranger 180, 181 OS Explorer OL9		
Navigation ●●●	Partly following the Two Moors Way		
Terrain ●●●	Rocks, bog, roots, road, meadow		
Wet Feet ●●●	In wet times, this will be unbearable and/or impassable		
Start/Finish	Tarr Steps car park TA22 9QA/SS 872 323		

A challenging adventure following superb riverside and moorland trails

There is something about running alongside water which elevates any trail. This isn't just any bit of water however, and these aren't just any trails. This exceptional outing follows the River Barle as it bubbles freely through a beautiful twisting steep-sided valley, utilising long stretches of entertaining technical trails which will test your foot placement; roots, slabs, rocks, mud, stepping stones.

You start at Tarr Steps. Here is Britain's longest clapper bridge, with stone slabs spanning seventeen arches. It may well originate from prehistoric times! In case you ever wondered, 'Clapper' derives from the Latin *claperius*: 'heap of stones'. In its first half, the route mostly hugs the riverbank upstream, utilising the Two Moors Way long distance footpath. By the time you reach Simonsbath, the Barle is reduced to a moorland stream. On the return route down-valley, you climb high onto the moorland above the river, before finally

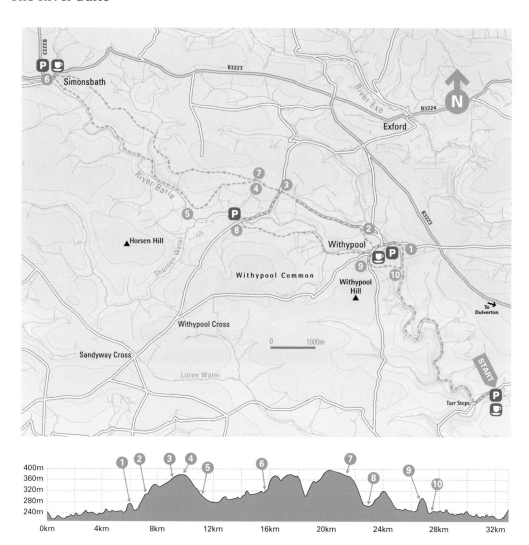

dropping back to water level to enjoy the best of the riverside trails once more. Running across Tarr Steps to the finish point feels like a well-earned victory lap!

This is of course Exmoor, and the weather and ground conditions may conspire to challenge you. Although hugely rewarding, this is a tough outing if taken in one hit. The route is simple to break into smaller chunks sampling edited highlights, if so desired.

Route Description

🏃 START From the car park, follow the path beside the lane downhill to Tarr Steps. Do not cross the river, instead turn right and follow the riverbank upstream (this is signposted as the Two Moors Way). After 6km the TMW climbs away from the river and reaches a road. ❶ Turn left on the road and run downhill into Withypool. After 500m a parallel lane splits off on the right (just before the Post Office), follow this for 50m before turning right (signposted for TMW) up a small lane. Continue past the end of the lane uphill along a footpath, which leads through four fields to reach Kitridge Lane. ❷ Turn left (WNW) onto the lane and follow it for 1.5km to where it becomes a byway, continuing 400m to where it crosses Landacre Lane. ❸ Cross the lane and continue ahead along a bridleway which parallels the stone wall on the left. Ignore a byway leading off on the right opposite an entrance and building. ❹ After 500m along the bridleway, look for a small sign marked 'bridleway only, no vehicles beyond this point' and just afterwards take the bridleway track leading off this track on the right. This quickly becomes more distinct and leads downhill W then SW to reach the river. ❺ Follow the bridleway (TMW) along the valley floor for 4km to where the bridleway splits into two parallel routes. Take the more uphill option and follow it uphill into Simonsbath. ❻ Just before reaching the B3223 road in Simonsbath, look for a bridleway leading off to the right (E) and follow this uphill through the woods for 350m to the forest boundary. Follow the bridleway (marked by blue posts) for 5km to reach ❹ again (along fields, downhill to cross White Water, uphill past Pickedstones Farm and across open moorland). ❼ Continue ahead for 400m to reach Landacre Lane again, this time turn right (downhill) and follow the lane to cross the river at Landacre Bridge. ❽ Shortly after crossing the bridge is a parking

Landacre

Fording a ford

Withypool

area; follow the footpath leading east from this for 3.5km to reach Withypool (across moorland then through farmland along the river). At the bridge in Withypool, don't cross (unless you want the tea shop!), instead turn right and follow Worth Lane (signposted 'Hawkridge') steeply uphill. ❾ After 300m, a bridleway track leads off on the left through a gate marked 'River crossing via ford – no footbridge'. Follow this downhill (including a diversion around buildings) to reach stepping stones across the river. Cross the river. ❿ Turn right and follow the TMW downstream along the riverbank for 4km to a footbridge. Cross the footbridge and follow the river downstream to Tarr Steps. Cross this bridge and head uphill to the car park.

Trip Planning

Tarr Steps car park is found down a lane signposted off the B3223, north of Dulverton. The parking is pay and display, also there is a toilet block. Alternative places to start include the free car parks at Simonsbath ❻ TA24 7SH/SS 774 394, Withypool near ❶ TA24 7RA/SS 844 354 and quiet Landacre Bridge ❽ TA24 7SD/SS 815 360.

Dulverton is the nearest town, with a supermarket and suchlike. Whilst staggering along this route, there are several opportunities to break up the wild sections with food and drink. The upmarket Tarr Farm Inn is directly beside Tarr Steps and serves a fine hot chocolate with marshmallows. In Withypool, the Royal Oak serves food on the route, although it was the Withypool Tea Room (opposite the Post Office) which revived the author when he attempted this route during a heatwave. Simonsbath's Exmoor Forest Inn is directly across the road at ⑥.

The usual moorland planning considerations apply here, even though most of the run is in the valley. Note that the path is directly alongside the river at many sections, and regularly floods over after rain. The stepping stones at ⑩ are only high and dry in low summer levels; with the stones just-covered, the author took off his trail shoes and waded. Exercise extreme caution and if in any doubt, backtrack to the bridge at Withypool.

Other Routes

There are numerous ways to shorten this route, whilst still preserving a great trail running experience. The shortest (3.5km) is to take the first footbridge across the river after Tarr Steps, and head back to the start. Turning back at Withypool (by following the lanes through Withypool from ① to ⑨) gives a 13–14km run. Starting from the top of the valley at Simonsbath TA24 7SH/SS 774 394 and turning back up the valley at ④ gives a superb wild 13km loop.

If you were to continue following the Two Moors Way from Simonsbath ⑥ to its conclusion beside the Bristol Channel at Lynmouth, you'd be looking at a 39km+ adventure. This would make an inspiring long day or overnighter; indeed, the original intention was to feature this route. Exmoor's non-existent public transport links kiboshed that idea, but if you can whistle up a two-vehicle shuttle or a support driver, it is there for the taking. Don't worry though, the route described here is no sorry second.

Events

Simonsbath is the start point for Channel Events' 10K Man vs Moor, which ascends the hills to the north and includes a short cold swim. Despite the name, apparently they allow women.

The Two Moors Way

Also known as the Devon Coast to Coast Route, this waymarked 187km/116-mile trail leads from the English Channel (and South West Coast Path) at Wembury, onto and across Dartmoor, across Devon's rural centre and then over Exmoor to reach the Bristol Channel (and SWCP again) at Lynmouth. The first 24km are actually the Erme-Plym Trail and the Two Moors Way does not officially begin until Ivybridge. The central part includes a fair distance on tarmac, but mostly sticks to footpaths. Perhaps the real interest to trail runners are the crossings of the high moors, which could be tackled as individual expeditions. Public transport links to shuttle these crossings are poor to non-existent, however.

Wild Running have the Two Moors Ultra Marathon, a non-stop 100-mile race from Lynmouth to Ivybridge (with a 50-mile variant to Castle Drogo), while Climb South West offer the Devon Coast to Coast Ultra Race covering it all from Wembury to Lynmouth, with non-stop or 4-day options. Choose your pain.

Dropping into the Doone Valley

31 Doone Valley

Distance	13km (8 miles)	**Ascent**	325m (1070ft)
Map	OS Landranger 180, 181 OS Explorer OL9		
Navigation ●●●	Short sections of open moor, compass recommended		
Terrain ●●●	Plenty of firm trails, but also rough uneven moorland		
Wet Feet ●●●	Plentiful boggy stretches		
Start/Finish	Malmsmead car park, Hookway Hill EX35 6NU/SS 791 477		

A stunning run through the hidden Doone Valley

The Doone Valley is so-dubbed as it was the setting for R D Blackmore's 1869 novel *Lorna Doone*, inspired by the Doune clan of brigands who terrorised the neighbourhood in the sixteenth century. The subtitle to that novel is *A Romance of Exmoor* and fair to say, this route gives you a fair dose of that. Badgworthy Water is the river flowing though this beautiful winding and roadless valley. These are the headwaters of the East Lyn River, infamous for flash-flooding to wreak destruction on Lynmouth, back in 1952. This valley is little-visited and the author confesses that he wasn't aware of it – despite dozens to trips to nearby Watersmeet and Lynmouth – until a recent mountain-biking trip opened his eyes.

The Doone Valley is short but absolutely sweet, and you have to earn it. This route starts with a pleasant bimble along Oare Water, Badgworthy Water's sister stream, before climbing through farmland onto the high moor. Enjoy the views before descending (via some boggy stretches and fiddly navigation) into the

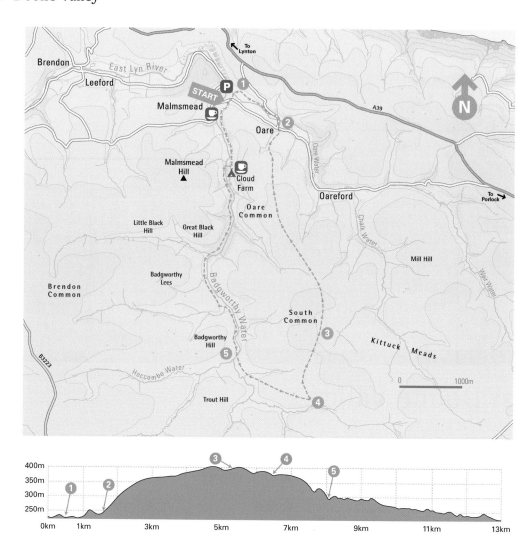

top end of the Doone Valley. Henceforth, the running is simply joyful, following ups and down, never far from the rushing water, with a few side streams to bound across and a handful of technical rocky patches to keep you mindful.

Route Description

START Cross the bridge from the car park and follow the lane. After 200m a bridleway is signposted down a track on the left; take this and follow it downhill to cross Oare Water by a footbridge. ❶ Keep going ahead after the bridge, after 50m turn right to follow a bridleway through Oaremead Farm and through several fields along the river to a lane. Turn right onto the lane, follow it across the river and then turn left at a T-junction. ❷ Follow the lane for 60m and turn right onto a bridleway straight after the church. Follow the bridleway steeply uphill along two fields, then uphill across two more to reach a gate where the ground levels off. Keep following the bridleway along the boundaries of successive large fields. The bridleway follows the edge of the rough moorland for 700m, before crossing several more fields (South Common) for

South Common

1km and entering open moorland. ❸ Care is needed on the moorland as paths are indistinct. Follow the bridleway 80m SSE to cross a wall, then SSW downhill for 280m to a junction with footpaths and a bridleway. ❹ Take the most defined path leading WNW; this leads along Great Tom's Hill and across a wall before descending into the Badgworthy Water valley to reach a footbridge. ❺ Cross Badgworthy Water via the footbridge and turn right (N) to follow the permissive footpath down the valley. This becomes a bridleway; keep following it (crossing the river by footbridge at Cloud Farm after 3.5km) to reach the lane at Malmsmead after 4.5km. The car park is 200m to the left, across the bridge.

Trip Planning

There are two parking areas in tiny Malmsmead, both are free. The route description here refers to the car park beside the bridge. Note that the roads leading here (especially the lane approaching from the east, dropping downhill off the A39) are exceptionally narrow; perhaps leave the minibus at home.

The pub in Malmsmead is the Lorna Doone Inn (of course) and offers lunch beside the river. Tea and

Malmsmead

Badgworthy Water

Oare valley

Doone Valley

sandwiches are available also at Cloud Farm, 1km from the end of your run ... you've made it this far, why not take a break? Cloud Farm is also a campsite.

This route could prove dangerous after heavy rain; some of the side streams will be awkward to cross, and Badgworthy Water itself can flood sections of the path.

Other Routes

It is of course easy enough to cherry-pick and only run the valley, heading upriver and then back again from Malmsmead. This would be easier, but simply not cricket.

Further downstream, the East Lyn River between Brendon and Lynmouth tumbles for 7km through a deep wooded cleft, with the National Trust café at Watersmeet interjecting just after halfway. Excellent trails run along both banks and this makes for a lovely run, however it is a popular weekend spot and (especially in the lower half) the paths will be busy. The early bird, however ...

Events

The Trail Events Company organise the Exmoor Trail Running Challenge, with its 10K, half, marathon and ultra marathon routes incorporating the Doone Valley.

Summit of Dunkery Beacon

32 Dunkery Beacon

Distance	8.5km (5.5 miles)	Ascent	425m (1400ft)
Map	OS Landranger 181 OS Explorer OL9		
Navigation ●●●	Clearly defined bridleways and moorland trails, albeit with little signage		
Terrain ●●●	Stony steep paths		
Wet Feet ●●●	A couple of streams to cross, no problem normally		
Start/Finish	Webber's Post car park TA24 8TB/SS 902 439		

From deep woodland combes to Exmoor's highest point

Dunkery Beacon looms a daunting 519m above the not-too-distant sea, making it the highest point in Exmoor National Park. The northern flanks of this bulky hill are densely covered by the oak trees of Horner Wood, through which clear rivers tinkle downhill. It's all rather nice, but it's also all rather steep. The Beacon is easily and popularly ascended via a short stroll from the nearby road, indeed visiting Exmoor without ascending the Beacon is actually a fineable offence. Trail runners following the route described here arrive at the huge summit cairn deserving a bit more kudos, having slogged at least halfway up the hill's height. This route's ascent is unrelenting, and it'll be a finer runner than me who can knock it off non-stop! Stop, breathe, take in the views. The descent is more varied, taking in moorland, farmland and a quick taste of Horner Wood.

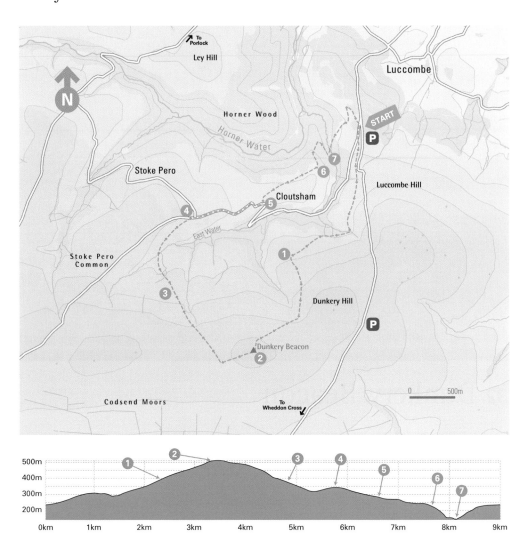

Route Description

START From the car park, start following the lane uphill. Straight away you see a path on the left, take this. Follow the path steeply uphill; after 1km you pass through the woods of Hollow Combe, after 1.8km you reach a crossroads. **1** Turn left (uphill) and follow the path to the summit cairn of Dunkery Beacon. **2** Follow any of the paths leading W from the cairn. After 400m a bridleway path crosses; turn right and follow this downhill. After 900m the bridleway reaches a wide track. **3** Cross the track and continue 200m downhill (bridleway now less distinct) to a gate. Go through the gate and follow the E boundary of the field downhill to a ford at its bottom corner (NOT the ford halfway down the field boundary). Cross the stream and follow the bridleway uphill across fields to a lane. **4** Follow the lane downhill for 800m to Cloutsham Farm. **5** Take the permissive bridleway on the left (opposite the farm buildings) and after 50m, cross a stile to join a bridleway heading ENE along the uphill edge of a field. Keep following the bridleway, ignoring all turn-offs, the correct route marked by blue markers. **6** Follow the bridleway around a left turn where it descends steeply into the trees. Look for and take the first right turn, after about 180m. Follow this downhill (still following blue markers) to East Water. ❼ Cross East Water by the footbridge and then take the rocky path leading steeply uphill on the right after 75m. Ascend until you see paths leading off on the right. All lead back to the car park, but the third (alongside a tarmac path) is the least steep option.

Trip Planning

Webber's Post car park is very pleasantly situated among trees at a great viewpoint overlooking Horner Wood. If approaching from the south (Wheddon Cross), follow signs to Dunkery Beacon; nearly 2km after the road's highest point (and having steeply descended), look for a lane turning off left, the car park is a very short distance along this. Approaching from Porlock, follow signs to Horner and then for Dunkery Beacon; the car park lane is on your right 900m after you start climbing steeply.

The small town of Porlock is a pleasant place in which to refuel afterwards, even better is Porlock Weir where the Ship Inn is perfectly situated to dine outside whilst taking in the view of Porlock Bay and Selworthy Beacon. Fact: the author once witnessed a fight break out in this pub, *about the Harry Potter books*. Dunkery Beacon may not be far from the road, but the weather can change and the visibility can, well, become invisible. Go properly kitted and prepared for moorland conditions and navigation.

Other Routes

As noted above, the easiest ascent of Dunkery Beacon is from the nearby road; park in the layby at TA24 7EE/SS 903 419 for a 3km round trip. This can be extended by following the bridleway further west along the ridge-top, although note that the well-manicured path duly peters out and reverts to traditional Exmoor bogginess. Some will feel that starting halfway up Dunkery Beacon is insufficiently painful; for such folk, a start at the village of Horner TA24 8HY/SS 897 454 might suit, or maybe even further out on the wonderful pebble beach at Porlock Weir TA24 8PB/SS 864 478. The latter option is doable via various possible bridleways ascending the Beacon (note Flora's Ride on the OS map) from Porlock and by following the footpaths and bridleways leading west to Porlock Weir.

Horner Wood is well worth explorations in its own right, see below. To the north, Selworthy Beacon looms over Porlock Bay and has some airy hilltop trails, as well as some brutal descents and ascents to sea level. To the east, the plantation forests around Wootton Common (the ridge stretching to Dunster) offer potential for those wanting to escape the crowds.

Ascending Dunkery Beacon

Horner Wood NNR

View towards Porlock Bay

Dunkery Beacon

Horner Wood NNR

Events

Minehead Running Club offer the Stagger, a 16-mile race ascending Dunkery Beacon from sea level. They also run the nearby Stumble (10K) and the Seaview 17 (miles), which covers the coast path from Minehead to near Lynmouth (ouch). Albion Running despise you and wish to see you suffer, hence they created the Hilly 50; a hilly 50-miler from Minehead to Lynmouth, then inland over Exmoor to Dunkery Beacon and back to Minehead.

Dunkery and Horner Wood National Nature Reserve

This is one of the largest NNRs in England, encompassing a variety of habitats. The high moorland of Dunkery Beacon is buttressed by steep-sided combes covered with grassland and bracken, descending into Horner Wood which is possibly Britain's largest area of ancient oakwood. This magnificent landscape is part of the vast Holnicote Estate which extends east to the Quantock Hills and is owned and managed by the National Trust.

The National Trust maintain permissive paths through Horner Woods which reward exploration. Starting from Webber's Post or perhaps the car park in the village of Horner TA24 8HY/SS 897 454, you can either stick to the valley floors and follow the tumbling rivers of Horner Water and East Water, or you can brave the calf-burning valley sides. Look out for red deer and also the General, an 500-year-old oak tree.

Bagley Combe locals

Wimbleball Lake

33 Wimbleball Lake

Distance	22km (14 miles)	**Ascent**	525m (1700ft)
Map	OS Landranger 181 OS Explorer OL9		
Navigation ●●●	Some care needed at first, idiot-proof around the lake		
Terrain ●●●	Open moor, rugged bridleways and paths, grassy paths, tarmac		
Wet Feet ●●●	A number of squelchy sections along the lake fringes		
Start/Finish	Haddon Hill car park TA4 2DS/SS 969 284		

Eclectic river- and lake-side trails on Exmoor's fringe

Wimbleball Lake is a long, thin reservoir on the south-east fringe of Exmoor. This drowned the upper valley of the River Haddeo in the 1970s, and is one of a depressingly increasing number of features in the landscape which are younger than the author. Today, Wimbleball is used for watersports and harbours several nature reserves. Combining this with the lower valley of the River Haddeo makes for an excellent long-ish outing. This adventure starts high on the moor, with expansive views from Haddon Hill. A breakneck descent down Haddon Lane deposits you at the valley floor, before a long ascent up the banks of the River Haddeo. You finally cross the 49m dam; the long perambulation of the lake shore starts uninspiringly on bland surfaced trails, but gradually accumulates interest with a variety of trail types to negotiate. Finally, the rocky uneven trails along the southern spur of the lake are simply great, runnable but needing constant care to avoid tripping and winding up in a thorny bush … like the author did.

Wimbleball Lake

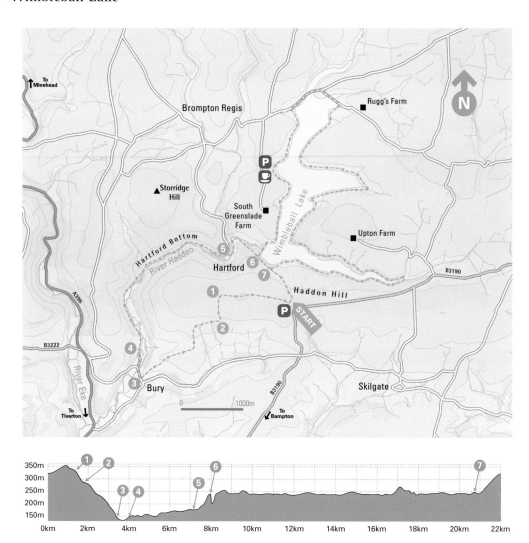

Route Description

START Leave the car park via the NW gate (far corner from the entrance). Follow the right fork of the path 700m uphill to the trig point. Continue ahead 300m (W) on the path until a left turn. **1** Take this footpath and follow it downhill to where it becomes a footpath alongside a forest. Continue downhill until the footpath joins a track leading onto a bridleway (Haddon Lane). **2** Follow the bridleway 350m downhill (W) to Haddon Farm, continue through the farm on the bridleway, which leaves the farm through an overgrown gap just before the last buildings. Follow the bridleway steeply downhill until you reach a lane at the village of Bury. **3** Turn right and follow the lane over the bridge, then turn right and follow the lane up the valley. After 250m it becomes a bridleway track, continue ahead following the River Haddeo. **4** After 3km you reach the small village of Hartford and the bridleway becomes a lane. **5** When it bends left (uphill), leave the lane and continue ahead on the bridleway which passes between houses and reaches a ford. Don't wade the ford, a bridge is hidden a short way upstream! Cross and follow the bridleway uphill to the dam; the final part is on steep tarmac. ⑥ Cross the dam and follow the path around Wimbleball Lake for 13km; 3km after the dam there is a short road section at Bessom Bridge. After 7km is a junction warning that the right path (nearest the lake) is 'rugged' and for summer use only; take this right path! ⑦ When you reach the dam again, turn left onto the tarmac road which ascends directly uphill to the car park entrance.

Haddon Lane

Trip Planning

The large car park at Haddon Hill is free to use, sign-posted off a sharp bend on the B3190. Another possibility is to park lakeside TA22 9NU/SS 965 308 at the Duck Café, open for part of the week in the warmer months. For details of activities and camping at Wimbleball Lake, see the SW Lakes website.

The nearest civilisation is the town of Dulverton, which offers all mod cons.

Haddon Hill in fog

Other Routes

It's obviously easy to split this figure-of-eight route into two smaller parts. For the less hilly lakeside loop (15km), start by simply descending from the car park to the dam ⑥. Haddon Hill is lovely enough in its own right for a few shorts circuits from the car park.

Further lakeside running is possible at nearby Clat-worthy Reservoir, with an 8km trail available around its rim from the public car park TA4 2EJ/ST 042 310, which closes at dusk.

Rugged signage

Events

A triathlon event is based at Wimbleball Lake (including a trail run around it), should spandex-clad monomania be your thing ...

River Haddeo

Wimbleball Lake

West Hill Wood

Exmoor National Park trail running

Exmoor was designated as a National Park in 1954. It comprises 692.8km^2 of moorland and coast, of which 29% is in Devon and 71% is in Somerset. I calculated all of that myself, and definitely didn't use Wikipedia.

Exmoor's high ground is more limited in area than that of Dartmoor, with agricultural land encroaching more noticeably. There are also no tors, on account of Exmoor's different geology of quartzite and sandstone. However, what gives Exmoor its unique flavour is the incredible juxtaposition of high moorland and sea. The result is not just awesome coastal trails, but also deep valleys and gorges incising the hills as they hurry towards the Bristol Channel. Plus, there are the views ...

The National Park have the following to say about trail running;

'With over 1,000km of footpaths and bridleways, trail running on Exmoor is the perfect place to enjoy more than just a stunning backdrop. We have a varied terrain of open moorland, steep woodland combes, and miles of coast path to enjoy, allowing you to revel in the beautiful scenery and test your mettle at the same time. There are paths and routes for all abilities. Whether you are looking to ease your joints with a soft springy track, or sharpen your reactions with a rocky incline.'

View down Weacombe Combe

34 The Quantocks

Distance	17km (11 miles)	Ascent	575m (1900ft)
Map	OS Landranger 181 OS Explorer 140		
Navigation ●●○	A map is recommended to keep track of Quantock's innumerable pathways		
Terrain ●●○	Grassy and stony tracks, narrow rough paths, numerous steep ascents		
Wet Feet ●●○	A few streams to jump across, down in the combes		
Start/Finish	Holford Bowling Green car park TA5 1RZ/ST 154 410		

Demanding doses of Quantock's magnificent high tops and deep combes

The Quantock Hills rise steeply from the surrounding plain to top out at 300m above the nearby sea level. So far, so Exmoor ... but the differences are that the plateau atop the Quantocks is firmer and better drained, covered by heathland and scrub, and that the sides are incised by multiple 'combes'. These remarkable combes are deep winding valleys where streams bubble amongst light woodland. The Quantocks are extremely well-served by footpaths and bridleways giving access to all areas. Running these trails is an absolute delight, except for the fact that there is an awful lot of upping and downing. The route featured here is at the challenging end of the spectrum and offers plenty of said upping and downing; it will almost certainly see you reduced to wobbly-legged walking on some of the ascents. At such trying times, console yourself by mentally focusing on both the expansive views and the wonderful flowing descent to inevitably follow ...

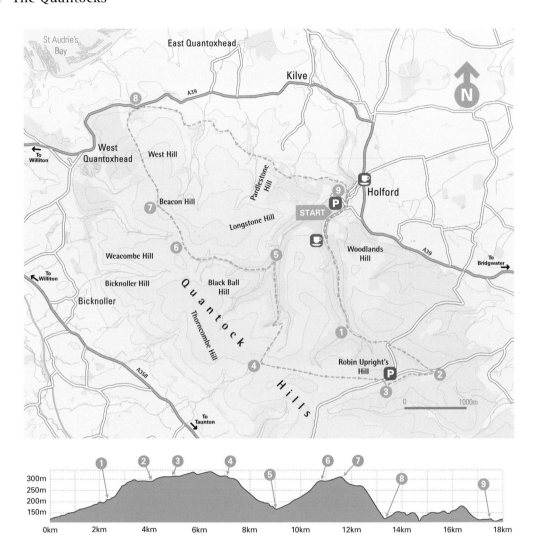

Route Description

START From the car park, follow the road back toward Holford village for 80m until you reach a junction with a white signpost. Turn right following the sign's direction for Holford Combe. The lane passes a hotel and becomes a bridleway leading up the floor of the combe (valley), keep going ahead ignoring any turn-offs. **1** 1.5km after the hotel, the valley splits in two directions; take the bridleway leading up the left-hand split (SW) to climb steeply up Lady's Combe. When this reaches a T-junction with a bridleway, turn right and follow this for 60m to a lane. Cross the lane and follow the bridleway ahead for 900m to another lane. **2** Cross the lane and turn right (W). Follow the bridleway along the lane for 700m to Dead Woman's Ditch car park. **3** Cross the lane and follow the bridleway leading W. Pass across the top of the first valley on the right (Frog Combe) and then across the top of the second (Stert Combe); take the bridleway leading right (NE) into Stert Combe, after 2km (if unsure, continue until you see Halsway Post (see Trip Planning) and then backtrack 100m to the junction). **4** Descend the bridleway along Stert Combe and then Somerton Combe. **5** After 2km you reach a junction with a bridleway and combe (Lady's Edge) on the left; turn left and follow this uphill for 1.8km to Bicknoller Post on the ridgetop. ⑥ Turn right (N) and follow the bridleway leading N. After passing across the top of Weacombe Combe, bear left off the bridleway to reach the summit of Beacon Hill. ⑦ Descend N to rejoin the bridleway and follow it steeply downhill into Perry Combe (be careful not to be drawn into following the edge of the woods). ⑧ At the bottom of the Combe (just before the A39), take the bridleway on the right (signposted 'Quantock Greenway'). Follow this ahead following signs for Holford, ignoring any paths turning off. After 3.4km a disused hotel is passed on the right and the bridleway is now tarmac; continue 800m to a footpath signposted downhill on the left. ⑨ Follow the footpath downhill into a ravine, across a bridge and then uphill into Holford village. Turn right onto the lane and follow it 200m to the car park.

Trip Planning

Holford Bowling Green car park is free, reached by driving through the village having left the A39 and following signs for 'Hodder's Combe'. Another possible start point is Dead Woman's Ditch car park TA4 4AP/ ST 161 381 ③, up on the heath ... if you don't mind finishing with an uphill stretch!

Navigation atop the Quantocks can be confusing, on account of the sheer number of trails (not all mapped). The 'posts' (Halsway Post, Bicknoller Post) on the summit heath are a useful feature to help with this, and they are exactly what they sound like: wooden posts which have their names clearly marked.

The Quantocks are one of the most popular mountain-biking destinations in the UK; the combe paths which make for great trail running also serve as great singletrack, so stay alert for bikers hurtling downhill.

Holford offers a choice of ways to refresh oneself; the unfussy Plough Inn is passed just towards the end of this route, and the staff do not blink at serving sweaty runners caked in lycra and mud. You might need to

Somerton Combe

Beacon Hill summit.
Photo: Andy Levick

Stert Combe

Lady's Edge
Photo: Andy Levick

scrub up (and save up) a bit more for the Combe House Hotel which is passed just up Holford Combe, but it is a pleasant place for civilised tea and cakes. For a shop, you will have to head 4km east along the A39 to Castle Stores in Nether Stowey.

Other Routes

To shorten this route to a still-very-satisfying 10km, ignore the left turning up Lady's Edge at ⑤ and simply continue down Hodder's Combe back to Holford. Of course, you can try an alternative loop of similar distance by starting your run up Hodder's Combe and picking up from ⑤.

If you have someone to pick you up at the end, a run of around 15km enjoying the fantastic Quantock views but relatively free of grinding climbs can be enjoyed, starting at Lydeard Hill car park TA4 3DY/ST 180 338 and simply following the bridleway north-west along the main ridge, before descending to Holford or West Quantoxhead.

As for other routes ... where to start? The density of possible trails around and atop the Quantocks is quite remarkable, and this compact region will reward many repeat explorations. The southern summits and combes of the Quantocks are not even touched upon here; go see.

Events

Quantock Harriers' Quantock Beast is a 6-mile race exploring the south-east end of the Quantocks. The Inov8 Original Somerset Race (distances of 8km, 17km and 22km) organised by Maverick Race starts at Kilve before heading up into the Quantocks, covering some of the ground of this route.

The Quantock Hills Area of Outstanding Natural Beauty

The Quantock Hills were the first place in Britain to be designated as an AONB. This took place in 1956, only five years after the first National Park was created. John Dower, secretary of the National Parks Committee, recommended that protection be offered to beautiful areas that were insufficiently wild or too small to become National Parks ... hence, AONB's were created.

The Quantocks were certainly an apt choice. The range of hills is barely 20km from end to end, but pack a wealth of wonderful and distinctive scenery within this small area. The AONB neatly sum up the area's appeal in their promotional bumf: 'Coast, Heath, Combe'. The coast is notable for Jurassic cliffs and reefs (see Route 35), whilst 200–300m above, the heath covers a broad summit plateau criss-crossed by trails. Combes are the steep-sided valleys covered with sessile oak woodland which incise the main Quantock ridge. For trail runners, they are the stand-out feature of the AONB; running along the rocky and rooty trails that weave along their sides and floors is nothing short of sublime.

The Quantocks were home to Samuel Taylor Coleridge in 1797, hence the 82km/51-mile Coleridge Way linking Lynmouth with his home at Nether Stowey. The Quantock scenery (augmented by industrial quantities of opium) inspired him to write some of his greatest poetry, including *The Rime of the Ancient Mariner* and *Kubla Khan*.

Kilve Pill

35 The Quantock Coast

Distance	15km (9.5 miles)	Ascent	350m (1150ft)
Map	OS Landranger 181 OS Explorer 140		
Navigation ●●○	Multiple signed junctions to negotiate		
Terrain ●●○	Grassy and stony paths. One section of heavy-going field boundaries.		
Wet Feet ●●○	The field boundaries are pretty muddy after ploughing		
Start/Finish	Kilve Pill Beach car park TA5 1EG/ST 144 442		

Solitude above Quantock's Jurassic reefs

This route explores the quiet woods and farmland where the Quantocks slope down to meet the sea. This longish run is rolling and hilly but without the severe gradients of the main Quantock range. You won't find many folk in your way whilst running these trails; this area is less frequented and visited than the summits to the south. However, it's not hard to see why it is included in the Quantock Hills Area of Outstanding Natural Beauty. There are expansive views across the Bristol Channel to the Welsh hills and the islands of Flat Holm and Steep Holm, as well as along the coast to Exmoor (we'll overlook Hinkley Point Power Station to the east). The real scenic highlight is the dark cliffs of oil-rich shale that you run atop, and the reefs that lay at their feet. Try to run here around low tide, when long fingers of rock strata snake far out from the base of the cliffs towards the waves. These are remnants of a Jurassic sea floor (195 to 200 million-years old). When you reach Kilve Pill at the end of your run, step down onto the beach and marvel at the huge fossilised ammonites visible all around.

The Quantock Coast

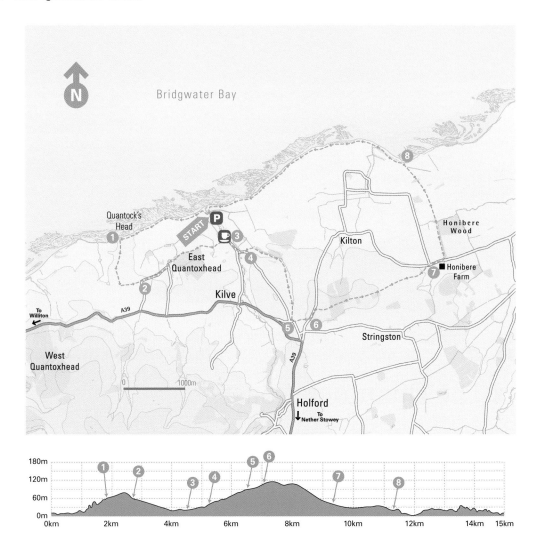

Route Description

🚶 START From the car park, follow the coast path W. After 900m a footpath leads inland signposted for East Quantockhead: ignore this and continue 850m to the next junction. ❶ Turn left (inland) and follow this permissive footpath along three fields to a crossroads with another footpath. Turn left (E) and follow this footpath along a track to meet a lane after 400m. ❷ Follow the lane straight ahead into the village of East Quantockhead. When you reach the junction at the village centre, turn left and head to the duckpond, then turn right to follow the footpath track beside the duckpond. Continue ahead through three fields (ignoring footpaths turning off N and S) to St Mary's Church in Kilve village. ❸ Turn right (SE) onto the lane beside the church. After 280m the lane splits, take the left fork. After 100m take the footpath track leading off on the left. ❹ Follow this footpath for 1.8km; after 200m it bends right to follow the edge of a wood uphill, then after 900m it crosses a lane at Lower Hill Farm, and after a further 1.5km it passes Higher Hill Farm on a short section of lane. Eventually it emerges on Hilltop Lane between houses. ❺ Take the track immediately to your left and follow this E onto the bridleway at the end. After 270m you

emerge onto a lane beside the gates to Oakley Lodge.
❻ Turn left (uphill) and after 175m, take the footpath
signposted on the right. Follow this footpath 2km ENE
through a wood (Waltham's Copse) and along several
field boundaries to a lane junction beside a signpost.
❼ Follow the lane heading ENE (signposted Burton)
and after 260m, turn left onto a footpath track. Follow
this 1.7km to the coast. ❽ Turn left and follow the
coast path 4km back to the car park.

Kilve Beach

Trip Planning

The car park is pay and display, located at the far end of
Sea Lane, reached by turning off the A39 at Kilve. The
peculiar tall red brick building at the car park is a retort,
built in 1924 and used to process oil from the cliffs;
thankfully this industrial venture was short-lived.

The fenced-off military installation that you pass on
the coast approaching Kilve is a lookout for Lilstock
Gunnery Range. This live firing range is offshore, used
for helicopter training, and there are no restrictions to
access on the coast path.

The Chantry Tea Gardens are passed on Sea Lane,
shortly before the car park. Their rather pleasant light
lunches are recommended, and customers could base
their run here, using their parking area.

Knap Plantation

Other Routes

For a quick and simple run, turn left at ❸ to bring you
back to the car park, reducing the distance to 5km.

It's simple enough to extend further along the coast
in either direction, but eastwards brings you into proximity with the nuclear power station, and westwards
towards Watchet is more developed, with holiday parks
to negotiate.

Near Kilve Pill

Events

Albion Running's West Country Ultra Flat 50 Miler slogs
from Taunton down the River Parrett to the sea, before
following the Somerset coast west to Minehead.

Lilstock from the Quantocks

The Quantock Coast

Near Lilstock

The England Coast Path

The England Coast Path is well underway! Given that coastal trail running is along the greatest experiences available to humankind, this is something worth us getting excited about. When completed in 2020, the ECP will measure 4500km, making it the longest coastal trail on earth. Add in the 1400km of the already-completed Wales Coast Path, and you are unlikely to run out of coastal trail runs any time soon.

Quantock's Head

Eleven coastal trails already exist in England, of which the longest is of course the South West Coast Path. These will have their signage 'upgraded' but the real challenge is of course in creating the new trails linking them all up; this is being done by Natural England. In 2009 the Marine and Coastal Access Act opened up the Right of Coastal Access to pretty much all parts other than private houses and MOD land.

Within the region of this book, the ECP will lead continuously from the Hampshire border to the Severn Bridge at Aust. The most exciting development so far has been the opening in 2016 of 93km of trail from Minehead to Brean Down in Somerset, hugely expanding on the 42km West Somerset Coastal Trail. The following 80km(?) to Aust will be open by 2020.

North and East Somerset

These parts of Somerset offer trail runners a truly diverse variety of landscapes. Along the southern rim irregular high ground arcs between Yeovil and Taunton, including the heavily wooded Blackdown Hills Area of Outstanding Natural Beauty. Runners hereabouts are unlikely to suffer overcrowded trails. Centrally, the fenlands of the Somerset Levels have plenty to offer those who dislike gradient, but are punctuated by occasional surprises such as Glastonbury Tor. Somerset's northern reaches are walled off by the impressive barrier of the Mendip Hills. Long-vanished rivers have incised deep gorges into the Mendips, most spectacularly at Cheddar.

Mendip descent (Route 39)

Staple Park Wood

View from Staple Hill

36 The Herepath Trail

Distance	22km (14 miles)	**Ascent**	500m (1640ft)
Map	OS Landranger 193 OS Explorer 128		
Navigation ●●●	Well signposted throughout		
Terrain ●●●	Mostly even-surfaced paths, one or two steep climbs		
Wet Feet ●●●	A few short sections reduce to quagmires in the wet		
Start/Finish	Castle Neroche car park TA20 3JZ/ST 273 156		

Easy trails through big forested hills and quiet farmland

Herepath is a ninth-century word approximately meaning 'people's path'. The Staple Fitzpaine Herepath Trail is a waymarked loop around the highest section of the Blackdown Hills. A Forestry Commission ranger told the author that it was specifically created to add visitor infrastructure to the quiet and little-known Blackdown Hills Area of Outstanding Natural Beauty, but that the hills were still mainly frequented (infrequently) by locals from Taunton.

This route is a great option for those wanting to cover distance without much navigational and terrain challenge. The trail follows bridleways through the entire loop, with several short lane sections. The running surface is often compacted and level gravel (slightly tedious) but there is also plenty of rougher going. The route starts beside the overgrown Motte and Bailey earthworks at Castle Neroche and heads north to thread numerous forest enclosures, passing the summit of Staple Hill (315m, highest point in the

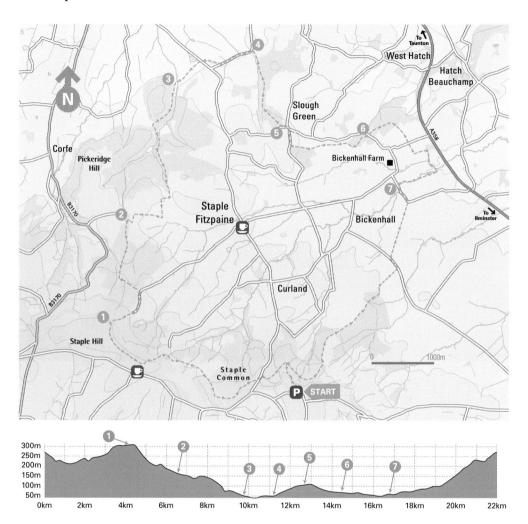

Blackdown Hills) en route. After descending to the valley floor at Thurlbear, you turn back south, again largely through forest enclosures. The final 200m ascent to Castle Neroche is made bearable by mild gradient and attractive surrounds; you might even have energy left to climb the Motte mound!

Route Description

This route is waymarked almost throughout: look for the blue arrows and the vertical carved 'HEREPATH' signs topped by a leaf insignia. This description just outlines the main features of the route. The part marked *** is the only unmarked route section.

START The first part of the trail descends from the car park to meet the Herepath bridleway. Turn left if you plan to follow the Herepath Trail clockwise. Tracks contour along the hillside until a steep ascent onto Staple Hill. ❶ A long descent from Staple Hill (including 400m of lane) brings you to Lawns Farm. ❷ The route leaves the forests to follow field boundaries (marked route is different to that shown on older OS maps) before re-entering forest and descending N to join Netherclay Lane. ❸ Netherclay Lane leads to a short field boundary section and then another lane into Thurlbear. ❹ In Thurlbear, the turning is on the right just before the church and is ***unmarked*****; take the track to the left of the Church Farm buildings. This leads S through Thurlbear Wood to another lane. ❺ A short section of lanes leads S to a left turn-off into woods, along fields and through another wood (Ben's Copse). ❻ When you reach the road, turn left onto it and follow it for 80m to where the Herepath Trail turns off on the right into Birkenhall Wood. Follow the trail markers for 2.5km through Birkenhall Wood, across Bickenhall Lane and then winding along a stream to reach a lane opposite Bridge House. Turn left (SE) onto the lane. ❼ The lane is followed for 340m to a left bend, where Curry Mallet Drove track is taken on the right. This leads S to a short lane section, before the long climb back to Castle Neroche, mostly through forest. When you rejoin the very first junction, you have the option of following the main track uphill to the car park, or of a steep detour to the right onto the castle motte (mound).

Trip Planning

The start car park belongs to the Forestry Commission, and is free. Turn off the A303 beside the Eagle Tavern and then take the third turning on your right, reached after 2km. The car park is less than 1km along this lane. An alternative start point is the nearby FC car park at Staple Hill TA20 3RA/ST 246 159, ❶.

The nearest refreshment after running is the above-mentioned Eagle Tavern, which caters to hordes of carvery-seeking A303 travellers. Alternatively, head into the village of Staple Fitzpaine (you have after all just expended considerable effort running around it) and try the rustic Greyhound Inn.

The Neroche Scheme created the Herepath Trail. A map of the route and useful updates can be downloaded from their website.

Herepath Trail signage

Blackdown Hills resident

Other Routes

Cutting this loop short doesn't really work, however consider an out-and-back run along the Herepath Trail from Castle Neroche. The numerous individual forests linked by this route all invite short runs; indeed there is practically a lifetime's worth of further exploring within this area. The Neroche Scheme website also suggests alternative shorter routes in the region. See page 146 for more information about the AONB.

Thurlbear Wood

The Herepath Trail

Middleroom Wood

Events

Running Forever Running Club (based in Taunton) are the organisers of the Herepath Half, which as the name suggests, is a half marathon largely following this route.

Forestry Commission trail running

Forestry Commission land is one of the best resources available to English trail runners. Their forests are criss-crossed by unsurfaced access roads and smaller paths which you can explore freely; visitors enjoy open access to all of the FC's freehold land. There are some wonderful trails hidden away awaiting discovery, but don't get too lost (conifers are hard to distinguish from one another!) and take note of signs warning about forestry work.

The FC manages over a quarter of a million hectares of forest in England and they estimate that over 85% of people in England live within 30 minutes of their forests. Their website outlines only a handful of selected forests and obtaining location details of their thousands(?) of sites is tricky; scanning your OS map for the FC symbol seems to be the best bet.

The FC actively promote trail running, noting that it is *'proven to generate greater feelings of revitalisation, increased energy and positivity, and fewer feelings of confusion, anger and depression'*. Yep, we agree with that. Their website also offers training, technique and meditation tips for runners. 'Run Forest Run' is a free six-week email fitness programme. The FC are creating a network of 1/2/3km marked running trails, but at time of writing (2018) none exist in the South West. If this wasn't enough, they also offer a rather cheesy Spotify playlist of motivational tunes (Queen's 'We are the Champions' on loop, anyone?).

Ham Hill Country Park

37 Ham Hill and Montacute House

Distance	10km (6 miles)	**Ascent**	300m (1000ft)
Map	OS Landranger 183, 193 OS Explorer 129		
Navigation ●●○	Partly on unsigned open land		
Terrain ●●○	Watch out for roots, rocks and badger setts!		
Wet Feet ●●○	A few unavoidable mud splodges		
Start/Finish	Ham Hill Viewpoint car park TA14 6RW/ST 477 167		

Rooty and rocky woodland trails, with a stately home interlude

Just west of Yeovil is a small range of hills that just cry out to be run around. Delightfully, there is lots to see along these trails. Ham Hill Country Park occupies the overgrown site of an Iron Age hillfort, perched atop a plateau with steep scarps surrounding. This run begins and ends by following these scarps. Within the park are various sculptures, monuments and even a vast faux-prehistoric stone circle! Not far away is the Montacute Estate, which you access via the Ladies Walk; this hidden pathway takes you down to open parkland right in front of Montacute House, an impressive Elizabethan stately home. After the woodland trails atop the hill, it's a bit of a culture shock to run through the 700m long Lime Avenue fronting the house. Leaving Montacute village, it's back onto the scarp which leads back to the park ... but not before the thigh burning ascent of St Michael's Hill, which is topped by the eighteenth-century Prospect Tower. Climb this and gaze far across Somerset, Dorset and Wiltshire.

Ham Hill and Montacute House

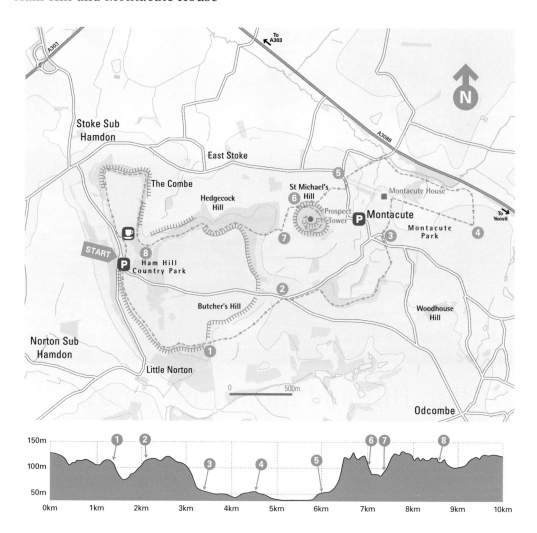

Route Description

START From the viewpoint, head S along the lane and take the first footpath on the right. Follow this ahead through the woods, ignoring any paths diverging off up or downhill. ❶ After 1.4km you reach a T-junction with a bridleway (the Liberty Trail); go straight ahead through a gate into a wide open valley. Descend to the valley floor, then follow the path leading left up to the head of the valley. This brings you out onto a junction of two lanes (Hollow Lane and Park Lane). Head to the field gate between the two lanes (with a sign about horses), and take the tiny path squeezed to the left of this gate. ❷ Follow this narrow path (watch out for badger setts) for 250m, take the path leading off to the right, up steps. After 1km this reaches the road in Montacute village. ❸ Cross the road and take the lane opposite (Back Lane). Straight away there is a gate on the right signposted 'Montacute Park'. Pass through and follow the boundary of the park to your left for about 300m to Montacute House. From Montacute House, follow the avenue of lime trees for 700m to its end. ❹ At the end of the lime avenue, turn left (N), after 250m you reach the park boundary. Turn left again, follow the boundary for 750m to a lane. Do not leave the park and enter the lane, instead turn left and follow a path to the left uphill to reach a road after 300m. ❺ Cross the road and follow it for 100m to the left. Pass a play area and turn right (uphill) onto the path beside it. After 120m, take the footpath signposted off to the left through a gap in the hedge. Ascend to the treeline on St Michael's Hill and turn right on the path along this. After 160m a track leads off to the left (uphill): follow this up to the summit tower and back. ⑥ Back at the treeline, follow the path leading downhill (W) to a small pond and then head 160m uphill to the head of this valley. ⑦ Take the footpath leading uphill (W) into the woods, signed for the Monarch's Way. Follow this for 1.4km (ignoring offshoots) until it ascends rocky steps leading to a trio of stone sculptures. ⑧ Turn right (N) at the sculptures and follow the path (not the bridleway signposted for Montacute) to a car park, then head a short distance along a lane to the right, to the Prince of Wales Pub. Pass this and follow the path N along the earthworks to the war memorial (an obelisk), then back S to the viewpoint.

St Michael's Hill

Prospect Tower

Trip Planning

Ham Hill viewpoint is alongside Ham Hill Road. If there is no space here, there are various other parking areas dotted around the park. The Prince of Wales pub is a short distance from the viewpoint (it is also passed on the route) and conveniently serves ice cream.

Montacute House is an alternative start point for this run. The car park (TA15 6UZ/ST 498 170) is free, as is access to the surrounding parkland. If you have time after running, the Elizabethan house and surrounding gardens are definitely worth a visit, free to National Trust members.

Final note: avoid Ham Hill Viewpoint car park after dark. Things happen there that once accidentally witnessed, can never be un-seen ...

Monarch's Way

War Memorial

Other Routes

Runners can enjoy shorter loops of just the Montacute or Ham Hill sections, by cutting the loop short between ❷ and ❼. At ❷, take the footpath on the far (N) side of Hollow Lane and then turn left onto another footpath after 150m; this leads to ❼. If just doing the Montacute section, start from the Montacute Park car park and at ❷ take the footpath leading straight ahead.

Ham Hill and Montacute House

Montacute House

Events

Montacute Park hosts a parkrun every Saturday, heading up and down the Lime Avenue. The Ham and Lyme Race is a 50km/100km trail ultramarathon along the Liberty Trail. The 100km option goes from Lyme Regis north to Ham Hill Country Park. Ham Hill is also the start of their 70-mile Conquest of Albion race to Glastonbury.

National Trust trail running

You will find yourself running on National Trust land sooner rather than later, as they own huge tracts of land in the South West e.g. 327km of the South West Coast Path in Cornwall. The NT have been working to encourage trail running on their land and properties, with many such places now having waymarked trails and/or recommended routes. They organise Trust10 events, monthly 10K trail runs at selected properties. Weekly 5km parkruns are currently held at eight properties in the South West. The NT also partners with England Athletics' RunTogether scheme to organise group and guided runs. Their website has further details.

Glastonbury Tor

38 Glastonbury Tor

Distance	9km (5.5 miles)	**Ascent**	225m (740ft)
Map	OS Landranger 183 OS Explorer 141		
Navigation ●●●	Route fairly obvious, a few signposts missing		
Terrain ●●●	One steep climb, some potentially heavy-going farmland		
Wet Feet ●●●	One potentially muddy section of farmland		
Start/Finish	Chilkwell Street, Glastonbury BA6 8DJ/ST 503 388		

Viewpoints of, and from, the mystical Isle of Avalon

Glastonbury, perched on the Isle of Avalon above surrounding fenland, is of course associated with New Age mysticism, hippies and King Arthur. When you see Glastonbury Tor rising abruptly from the surrounding Avalon Marshes, it's not hard to grasp why some folk regard this as a special or sacred place.

This run starts in the town, heads downhill into the surrounding reclaimed farmland, then loops around and then finally ascends the Tor itself. The paths scaling the Tor are tediously concreted over, but you won't care as you'll be too busy finding the effort to ascend them. The views are wonderful, accentuated by the flat surrounds. You won't be alone up there, even on a dawn run; the author had company from a silent meditation group who were not impressed by his phone going off!

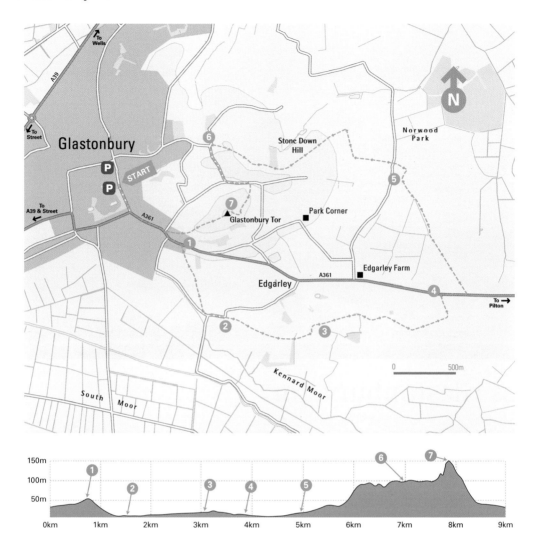

Route Description

START Follow Chilkwell Street S and then E (ascending house numbers) for 750m. 130m after passing the junction for Cinnamon Lane (on your R), look for an entrance on your left marked 'Claremont'. Hidden across the road beside a red-brick building is a gateway to a footpath. ❶ Follow the footpath diagonally downhill to the opposite corner of the meadow. Continue ahead on the footpath through two small fields and then cross a large field (path leads through the crops) to Cinnamon Lane. Turn left (E) and follow the lane for 150m to a left bend. ❷ At the bend, continue ahead on the footpath. This leads E through three fields to Bere Wall Farm (pass left of the white buildings) and then through two more fields to Middle Edgarley Farm; pass between the buildings onto a track to a parking area. ❸ Pass through the parking area and continue E on the footpath past school playing fields. 800m from the farm you cross a field diagonally to reach a track (Edgarley Field Lane). Follow the track around a left bend to the A361. ❹ Cross the A361, turn right (E) and follow the pavement for 220m to gates beside a sign for 'Havyatt'. Pass through the kissing gate to the left of the gates, and follow the footpath NW. After 500m it joins a track leading to

On Glastonbury Tor

Norwood Park Farm. ❺ Pass the farm buildings on your left to reach Wick Lane. Follow this to the left (W) for 20m and turn right onto the track (Stone Down Lane) leading uphill. After 320m, turn right at a crossroads onto a footpath. Follow the footpath for 230m and then take the footpath stile on the left. Follow this footpath uphill towards Glastonbury Tor and then through trees along the hillside to join a track (Paradise

Stone Down Hill

Lane). ❻ When you reach a crossroads, turn left (S) and follow Stone Down Lane towards the Tor. Turn left at a T-junction and after 200m go through a gate to the footpath ascending Glastonbury Tor. Climb! ❼ From the summit, descend on the path towards Glastonbury. When you reach Chilkwell Street, turn right and head back to the start.

Trip Planning

There is no parking near the Tor (except for a few disabled spaces on Stone Down Lane BA6 8JZ/ST 513 388), so it's necessary to run from the centre of town. If there is no space beside the Abbey House gate on Chilkwell Street (BA6 8DJ/ST 503 388), you'll have to run 350m further each way, starting from Butt Close car park (BA6 9HY/ST501390). This latter option is pay and display.

There are numerous food and drink options within Glastonbury; vegetarians and vegans will find themselves with an unusual degree of choice. Whilst in the centre, Glastonbury Abbey is well worth a visit, a peaceful and sane enclave in a town where the shops only sell wind chimes, healing crystals and books about 'magick'.

Glastonbury Tor

Other Routes

It is possible to extend this route further out to the River Brue in the Avalon Marshes, although some road time will be involved. The river is followed by a footpath, although this gets overgrown in summer.

Events

The rather demanding Conquest of Albion finishes at Glastonbury Tor after 70 miles from Ham Hill (Route 37). There are also 50 and 30-mile options, for the weak.

The Avalon Marshes

There are numerous options for trail running the Avalon Marshes, which stretch in all directions around Glastonbury's Isle of Avalon. The numerous National Nature Reserves are criss-crossed by drove lanes, which can be monotonously straight (and of course flat), but this is a truly beguiling landscape. The Avalon Marshes Centre BA6 9TU/ST 425 414 is 7km west of Glastonbury and is the best place to head first. The Centre will give advice and their website also suggests trails to follow. Nearby Shapwick Heath National Nature Reserve has the lovely Sweet Track path which winds through humid fen woodland following the course of the remarkable Sweet Track, a 6,000-year-old raised wooden pathway discovered in the 1970s.

Avalon Marshes

Descending to Cheddar

39 Wells to Cheddar

Distance	17km (10.5 miles)	**Ascent**	525m (1700ft)
Map	OS Landranger 182 OS Explorer 141		
Navigation ●●○	Mostly waymarked		
Terrain ●●○	Fields, rocky paths, one easy scramble		
Wet Feet ●●○	Some paths can become rather 'quaggy'		
Start	Wells Cathedral, Cathedral Green BA5 2UQ/ST 550 458		
Finish	Tweentown, Cheddar BS27 3JF/ST 460 536		

Through a claustrophobic gorge onto a high Mendip plateau

This cherry-picked section of the West Mendip Way (incorporating detours) showcases the best of Mendip trail running. Woodland trails lead to Wookey Hole, famous for its limestone caves. You evade the Wookey crowds by venturing into Ebbor Gorge, an amazing National Nature Reserve where the path steepens and narrows ... until it is barely two metres wide and you are forced to scramble uphill for a short distance. Emerging blinking into sunshine from Ebbor's dark folds, you discover that you're now high up on the Mendip plateau. Running across Mendip fields, you'll notice two things; that there are no streams or groundwater due to the porous limestone beneath, and that Mendip stiles are made from wearyingly tall limestone slabs. The final reach of this run is along the Mendip scarp, perched 250m above the Somerset Levels, followed by a fantastic rocky descent towards Cheddar. The views stretch past the Quantock Hills to Exmoor and across the Bristol Channel to Wales. Enjoy!

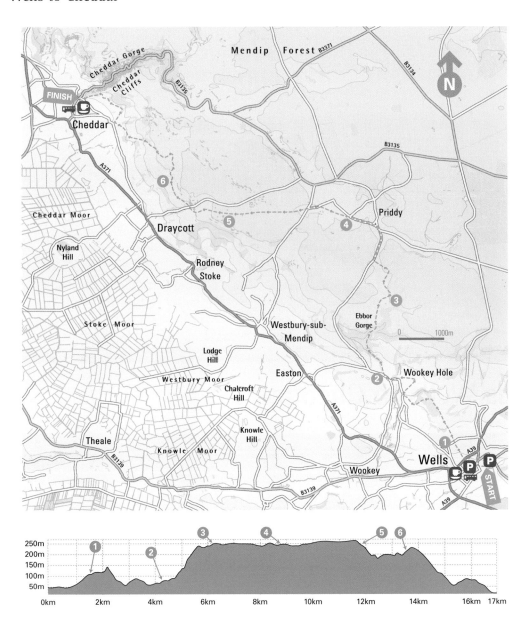

Route Description

This route is waymarked almost throughout: look for the blue circular markers with arrows and the text 'WEST MENDIP WAY'. This description outlines the main features of the WMW route. The parts marked *** describe deviations from the marked route.

START The first 1.5km stretch leads you out of town; across the green in front of the cathedral, along a couple of streets then through a school grounds and a steep climb through a housing estate. ❶ The WMW follows tracks and paths around Milton Hill before descending to Wookey Hole, where there are short lane sections. ❷ After leaving the village, you turn off right from the road onto a bridleway. ***When you reach the sign for Ebbor Gorge National Nature Reserve, ignore the WMW signage and follow the

'Main Gorge Route' marked red on signs. Ascend on this 'red' path uphill through a narrow gorge (with a short scramble). When you reach a T-junction, turn left (uphill) out of the gorge. Follow the footpath N through three fields until you reach a byway track (Dursdon Grove) and turn right onto this. After 200m take the footpath on the left: you are now back on the WMW.*** ❸ The WMW follows field boundaries to a lane (Pelting Drove) leading into Priddy, then leaves Priddy via another lane. ❹ You follow footpaths across fields (with one short lane interlude) for 3.5km. ❺ ***When the footpath starts descending, the WMW splits. This route follows the shorter route, not marked on all OS maps. At the bottom of the third field leading downhill, do not cross the stile to continue downhill; instead take the path heading right and slightly uphill to the road. Cross the road and enter Draycott Sleights National Nature Reserve. Follow the bridleway ahead around the hillside and then uphill to where the two WMW routes reconverge.*** ❻ The WMW now descends steeply to Bradley Cross before climbing again and contouring along the hillside, followed by a final steep descent into Cheddar. The bus stop is reached by following roads straight ahead when the town is reached.

Trip Planning

After running, a variety of refuelling options are available in Cheddar Gorge's touristy area, mostly based around chips, chocolate and ice cream.

As an 'A to B' run, this requires a little forethought. You can park free all day outside Wells Cathedral on Cathedral Green on Sundays, otherwise you'll need to ditch a car further afield, for example at the nearby (fee paying) Waitrose car park BA5 2PJ/ST 546 458. To return after the run, you'll need to use the 126 bus service which leaves every hour ... except for Sundays, when it runs every three hours; check timetables beforehand! The journey takes about 25 minutes. Of course, it is possible to park in Cheddar and then take the bus to Wells before running, but parking around the gorge entrance (where this run finishes) is expensive and ... well, competitive.

Other Routes

A great option for the keen is to finish off this route with a victory lap around magnificent Cheddar Gorge (Route 40).

Events

Albion Running's Mendip Marauder is two side by side ultramarathons: the full 30 miles of the West Mendip Way from Wells to Uphill, or the same again with the East Mendip Way from Frome tacked on for good measure, making 50 miles. An easier alternative is Prostate Cancer UK's Uphill to Wells Relay which, as the name suggests, is tackled as a team. The 49-mile Butcombe Trail Ultra includes parts of the WMW.

Approaching Wookey Hole

Ebbor Gorge

Mendip plateau

The West Mendip Way and East Mendip Way

The West Mendip Way continues west from Cheddar following the Mendip ridge, to finish at the sea at Uphill. The total distance (including Wells to Cheddar) is 48km. Completing this without a shuttle driver would require an additional few kilometres into Weston-super-Mare to catch a bus back to Wells.

WMW

The East Mendip Way extends 32km east from Wells to Frome, following a less defined part of the Mendips at a generally lower elevation.

There seems to be no 'official' information source for either the East or West Mendip Ways, which is odd: presumably someone must be putting the signs up? There are a few guidebooks, but they are out of print. Older OS maps will show just one route, whilst up-to-date maps show alternative routes such as at ⑤ in the description above. Confusingly however, there are other variant routes which are not even on recent maps; for example some of the paths on the west side of Cheddar Gorge (Route 40) have WMW signs, whereas the Ordnance Survey has it passing to the east. The good news is that between Wells and Cheddar at least, the route choices are pretty clear. The best bet for information on the WMW and EMW is the Long Distance Walkers Association website.

South rim of Cheddar Gorge
Photo: Chris Eden

40 Cheddar Gorge

Distance	11km (7 miles)	Ascent	450m (1500ft)
Map	OS Landranger 182 OS Explorer 141		
Navigation ●●●	Not too many route choices		
Terrain ●●●	Several severe ascents, rocky paths		
Wet Feet ●●●	Well-draining limestone terrain		
Start/Finish	Velvet Bottom Nature Reserve entrance BA5 3BT/ST 502 555		

Airy trails around the rim of a natural wonder

Google reveals that Cheddar Gorge was voted Britain's second favourite natural wonder (Dan yr Ogof Caves in Wales were Number 1). The 140m-deep limestone gorge is indeed a wonder, but the heavily touristified entrance at Cheddar somewhat distracts from nature's visual feast. This route manages to (mostly) steer clear of the tackiness and crowds, starting high up on the Mendip plateau and descending to the gorge via two successive nature reserves. These stunning dry valleys reveal clues that they were once an industrial landscape; you will run over glistening lead shards past quarried cliffs and over small dams which once created settling beds. You then reach the gorge itself, and the route is not complicated! A murderous climb onto the south rim, a descent to the gorge entrance, an even more murderous climb onto the north rim. The reward is the opportunity to run along exposed cliff tops enjoying truly epic views of this 1.2 million year-old landform, far above the ant-like tourist crowds.

Cheddar Gorge

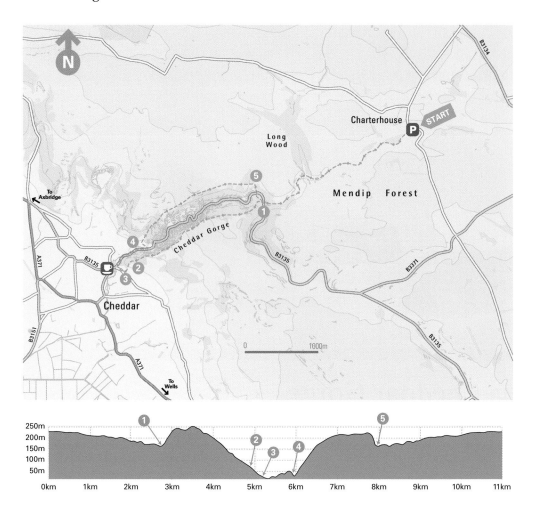

Route Description

START Pass through the Nature Reserve entrance gate and follow the footpath track downhill for 2.6km to the B3135 road. **1** Cross the road and ascend steeply on the bridleway path. When the gradient eases and the path begins to descend, various paths lead ahead along the south rim of the gorge; follow those nearest the edge, with care! **2** 2km after the road you reach an observation tower. Turn left onto a small bridleway path leading steeply downhill. After 200m you reach Lynch Lane which leads downhill to another lane, The Lippiatt. **3** Follow The Lippiatt 160m downhill to a junction; turn right along the road up the gorge, past the shops. After 550m, take a left turning up Cufic Lane (opposite 'The Original Cheddar Cheese Co' and 'Café Gorge'). Head 120m up Cufic Lane, then take the signposted 'permissive path' on the right. **4** Ascend very steeply up the path. When the path levels out, continue ahead following the path which follows the N rim of the gorge. After 1km, you descend to a junction. Take the path leading right (steeply downhill) towards the road, cross the road and ascend on the bridleway ahead. Look for a trail on the left descending back to the road, follow this to cross the road and reach the track you originally took from the parking area. **5** Follow this footpath track 2.5km back to the start. When the valley splits two ways after a quarry, take the righthand (E) fork signposted for Velvet Bottom Nature Reserve.

Cheddar Gorge

Trip Planning

Parking is free outside Velvet Bottom Nature Reserve; it's simply a layby on a quiet lane, reached by driving up the gorge along the Cliff Road/B3135, turning left onto the B3371 and then left again at the first crossroads. This route follows the top of tall cliffs, take care! Those with vertigo will be pleased to know that there is always an alternative path further away from the edge.

Food and drink can be acquired in Cheddar, and of course in the tourist cafés along the gorge; note that parking down here is expensive and also fills up on busy days.

Other Routes

Just the gorge itself makes for a 7km run. You could start from the layby at Black Rock ❶ BA5 3BT/ST 482 545 or down in tourist town.

Longer routes could combine sections of the West Mendip Way, either east towards Wells (Route 39) or west towards Uphill. Beacon Batch (highest point in the Mendips) is 2.5km NW and is a straightforward ascent from the start of this route.

Events

Several gruelling trail races take place hereabouts, utilising parts of this route. The Big Cheese is a 16-mile fell race organised by Cheddar Running Club and the Cheddar Gorge Challenge is part of the South West Outdoor Festival, with numerous distance choices from 3km to full marathon.

Feral goat

Cheddar Gorge

North rim of Cheddar Gorge

Cheddar Gorge and the Mendip Hills

Cheddar Gorge is the crown jewel of the Mendip Hills Area of Outstanding Natural Beauty. The AONB is effectively a limestone plateau with steep sides, incised with several deep gorges. Mendip's carboniferous limestone consists of remnants of living organisms, laid down in stages on the bottom of shallow tropical seas, between the Devonian and Jurassic eras (385-161 million years ago). If that timescale is too mindboggling to compute, Cheddar Gorge's 140m sheer cliffs helpfully offer a cross-section through this geology, giving some insight as to what 200+ million years of sea-bed detritus looks like.

Cheddar Gorge is relatively youthful compared to the limestone it incises. Water tends to flow into limestone and dissolve out underground passages, however from around 1.2 million years ago ice blocked these passages, forcing glacial torrents to flow along the surface and (in due course) slice savagely down into the plateau.

'Cheddar Man', the UK's most ancient intact skeleton, occupied caves in the Gorge around 9,000 years ago; an extremely recent blink in the timescale of the Mendips. Should you venture into the tourist trap around the modern gorge entrance, the National Trust Office is a sane place to start your exploring and the museums and show caves are actually quite pleasant and interesting.

Cheddar Gorge

Goblin Combe

41 Goblin Combe

Distance	12km (7.5 miles)	**Ascent**	375m (1230ft)
Map	OS Landranger 172 OS Explorer 154		
Navigation ●●○	Map and compass helpful, multiple unmarked junctions		
Terrain ●●○	Several steep climbs, one precarious descent on steps		
Wet Feet ●●○	Mendip mud galore, especially at the top end of the Combe		
Start/Finish	Goblin Combe car park, Cleeve Hill Road BS49 4PH/ST 459 653		

Winding forest trails around a secret limestone gorge

It was tempting to squeeze another run on the main Mendip range into this section; however this route was chosen instead for its great Mendip-style limestone landscape and woodland trails in an area which is much less frequented, despite being just a short distance from the M5 and Bristol. Well hidden beneath the tree cover in this small range of hills are several limestone gorges, with the deepest splendidly known as Goblin Combe.

This route starts with an exploration of King's Wood, where an eye on the map will be needed to prevent becoming lost in this beautiful forest of mixed deciduous and coniferous trees. The author can (almost certainly probably) guarantee that you'll have these woods to yourself. Full disclosure: you are directly beneath Bristol Airport's flightpath, so the solitude might not be accompanied by silence. Emerging from the trees, a few paths and tracks across farmland deposit you at the top end of Goblin Combe. This

Goblin Combe

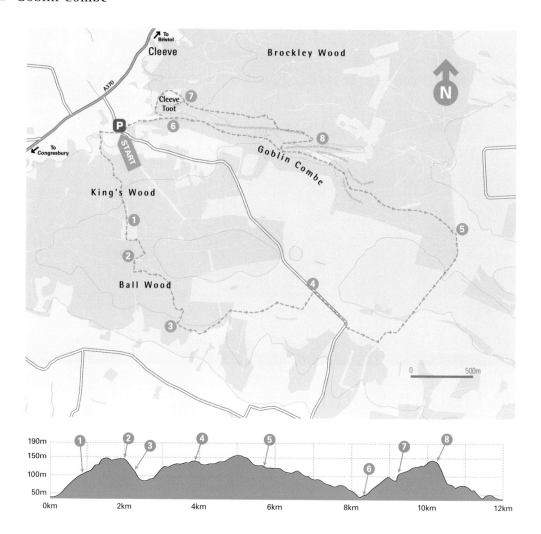

descent starts as an overgrown mire and you'll wonder if you've made a mistake. Soon however, the path widens and you glimpse hefty boulders and tall cliffs through the leaves. This run ends with the best bit; a modest scramble above the cliffs to Cleeve Toot, a rather surprising summit and viewpoint from which the landscape around will suddenly make sense!

Route Description

START Follow the lane downhill from the car park for 50m and turn left (E) onto a footpath. After 150m this bends left and splits, take the left (uphill) path. Climb across a meadow and into King's Wood. Follow the footpath uphill (S, look for signs at junctions) for 600m to a cleared area with houses. ❶ Follow the footpath ahead past the houses to a tarmac drive. Turn left onto this footpath drive and follow it for 100m past the houses, then turn right onto the footpath leading steeply uphill and follow this for 130m to a footpath track. Turn right (SW); after 80m you reach a junction with around six exits. Continue ahead at this junction and you will be presented by the track splitting two ways. Take the left split, leading downhill (S). ❷ Follow this footpath downhill for 100m, then take the footpath leading off on the left (E). Follow this

Goblin Combe from Cleeve Toot

for 600m to where it bends sharp right and follow it another 200m steeply downhill before taking the footpath heading off left (ESE). ❸ Follow this footpath for 600m to where it leaves the woods, then another 600m across three fields to join a bridleway. Turn left onto the bridleway and follow it 175m to a lane. ❹ Turn right onto the lane and follow it 400m to a right bend; just after the bend take the footpath on the left. Follow this 300m across a field to a bridleway track and turn left (NE). Follow the bridleway for 1.2km,

ignoring all footpaths turning off. ❺ Just after descending into a valley, take the footpath on the left beside a 'PRIVATE WOODLAND NO HORSE RIDING' sign. Follow this footpath down the valley (this is Goblin Combe) for 2.7km. ❻ Where the valley starts to open out, look for a footpath leading uphill to the right (beside an information board) and take this. You are following the orange marker arrows for 'Cox's Loop' for 3.5km to the end; bear right at all major junctions. ❼ After 500m, look for a clearing around a lone tree; take the path leading steeply uphill out of the back of this clearing; this leads 100m to the summit of Cleeve Toot, ascend this and then return to the main trail. ❽ 2km after joining Cox's Loop, the trail follows steep steps to the floor of Goblin Combe. When you reach the bottom, turn right (downhill) and retrace your previous route, this time continuing ahead to the road. The car park is 50m away on the left.

King's Wood

Goblin Combe

Brean Down from Cleeve Toot

Trip Planning

The car park on Cleeve Hill Road is free. Facilities in nearby Cleeve Village are rather limited, amounting to a newsagents and the Sun Hall Chinese Takeaway (I went with the House Special Chow Mein). The prominent Lord Nelson pub, near the turning for Cleeve Hill Road, is currently closed with demolition being mooted.

Goblin Combe Environment Centre is located at the entrance to the Combe and offers various outdoor activities as well as accommodation options. Goblin Combe is a nature reserve managed by Avon Wildlife Trust, more information about its limestone grassland and woodland ecology can be found at their website.

Other Routes

Three short waymarked routes lead from the car park around Goblin Combe and Cleeve Wood; Knapp's Loop (3km), Cox's Loop (3.5km) and Warren Walk (5km).

5km south and part of the main Mendip range is Dolebury Warren, a long hill topped by a hillfort. A wide network of trails covers this and links with other Mendip summits such as Beacon Batch, the highest point in the Mendips. Start your exploration from Dolebury Bottom, just off the A38.

West Dorset

The landscape of West Dorset is, depending upon your perspective, either a blessing or a curse for trail runners. There are steep hills everywhere! Whatever your feelings about the hills, the scenery is undeniably stunning. The majority of this area is within the Dorset Area of Outstanding Natural Beauty, which encompasses chalk stream valleys, high exposed ridges, crumbling sea cliffs and also a wealth of prehistoric remains. One local quirk is sunken roads, known as 'holloways'. Running these eroded trackways, hidden below the surrounding farmland, can be a joy. With no motorways and few major roads, much of West Dorset is little-frequented and it can be surprising how few people you encounter on the trails.

South Dorset Ridgeway

Golden Cap from Thorncombe Beacon

Hell Lane
Photo: Claire Pinder

42 Golden Cap

Distance	13km (8 miles)	**Ascent**	600m (1970ft)
Map	OS Landranger 193 OS Explorer 116		
Navigation ●●○	Some care needed, OS map helpful		
Terrain ●●●	Some very steep ascents and descents		
Wet Feet ●●○	Regularly in muddy and slippery condition!		
Start/Finish	Langdon Hill National Trust car park DT6 6JW/SY 412 930		

Tough-going trails through sunken lanes and above crumbling cliffs

This run explores one of the hillier areas of hilly West Dorset! North of the A35 is a complex of sunken roads, known as Holloways. These are ancient farm tracks which have been gradually eroded into the sandstone landscape by human activity. This route passes through the finest of all, Hell Lane. Running through this greenery-draped six metre deep gorge is an amazing experience. If this sounds claustrophobic, don't worry as you soon emerge on the coast, high above the waves. A steep and often slippery climb up Thorncombe Beacon is followed by a similar grind from sea level all the way to the top of Golden Cap. At 190 metres, this is the highest point on the south coast. Naturally the views are magnificent. Golden Cap's name comes from the band of pale yellow-green sand which forms the top part of its cliffs.

Golden Cap

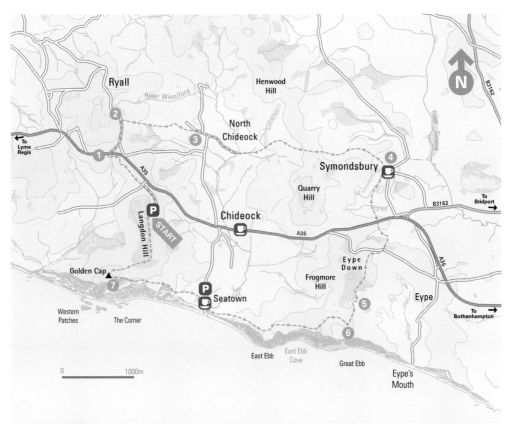

Route Description

START Follow the downhill track from the car park and turn left onto Langdon Lane, back the way you drove in. At the T-junction with Muddyford Lane, take the footpath ahead. Follow this through three fields and up a lane to the A35. ❶ Cross the A35 at the lights and take Sun Lane which is 30m to the right. After 120m turn left at the junction onto Ryall Lane. Follow this for 320m to a bridleway sign on the right. ❷ Follow the bridleway downhill and through four fields to Butt Lane. Turn right onto this and follow it to the junction with Hell Lane which continues ahead. ❸ Follow Hell Lane. After 360m keep right, don't turn onto Brighthay Lane. Follow Hell Lane uphill. At the summit is Quarry Cross junction: turn right and then left again directly after to stay on Hell Lane. Follow the lane (now a gorge) downhill to the junction with Shute's Lane and ahead into Symondsbury. ❹ At the school, turn right onto a footpath and follow this for 1km to the A35. Cross to the footpath sign and follow this. In the second field, don't miss a right turn after 50m. Climb steeply uphill to a lane and cross this. Continue on the footpath to a junction with bridleways at Down-House Farm. ⑤ Follow the bridleway on the right (farm signs ask you to consider following a short diversion) to the coast. ⑥ Turn right onto the SWCP and follow it up Thorncombe Beacon, down to Seatown, and up Golden Cap. ⑦ From the summit of Golden Cap, retrace your route down the final steps. Go through a gate and head inland across two fields to Langdon Woods. At the woods, take the path to your left leading uphill to a track. Turn right onto the track, follow it for 900m to the car park.

Trip Planning

Langdon Hill National Trust car park is free to members, otherwise pay and display. Other possible start points could be the villages of North Chideock or Symondsbury. There is a pay car park at Seatown DT6 6JU/SY 420 917, however tackling the 190m climb of Golden Cap as a warm-up seems a bit perverse.

The most convenient shop is Chideock Post Office and Stores on the A35. There are pubs in Chideock and also Symondsbury, but surely the best place to eat after your adventure is down on the seafront at Seatown, where there is a great view of Golden Cap. The Anchor Inn dauntingly divides its dishes into Sea, Land and Field (fished, farmed, shot?); cheaper food is available from the pizza takeaway 200m up the road at Golden Cap Holiday Park or you could carb up on ice cream: van usually present.

Other Routes

An extension to this run is to follow the bridleways looping north of North Chideock ③ over Coppet Hill and south again via Henwood Hill. This joins Hell Lane halfway, but includes some more Holloways.

Thorncombe Beacon from Golden Cap

Sunken lane

Golden Cap from West Bay

A short run can be enjoyed from the car park by simply following the track which loops around Langdon Woods and back, with the option to climb Golden Cap.

The Golden Cap Estate extends several kilometres to the west with numerous paths to explore; there are suggested routes on the National Trust website.

Golden Cap

Morcombelake from Golden Cap

The c30km of the South West Coast Path from Charmouth to Abbotsbury starts challengingly with the high hills described here, then follows lower cliffs past West Bay and Burton Bradstock, before descending to follow a pebbly track behind Chesil Beach; a shuttle is possible using the X53 bus, although this author got a telling off from the driver for not cleaning his trainers first.

Events

The Charmouth Challenge is a 13km run including Golden Cap, with an accompanying 3km Fun Run. Beyond Events organise the Jurassic Trail (half marathon near Bridport) and the Three Peaks Trail (5km, 16km, 25km from Symondsbury). The Colmer's Hill Challenge is a 10K hill slog. The LDWA's Doddle West passes through here, heading 26 miles between Charmouth and Dorchester.

Ascending Lewesdon Hill

43 Lewesdon Hill

Distance	12km (7.5 miles)	Ascent	400m (1300ft)
Map	OS Landranger 193 OS Explorer 116		
Navigation ●●○	Numerous paths to choose from		
Terrain ●●●	Heavy going underfoot, lots of ups and downs, steep ascent of Lewesdon Hill		
Wet Feet ●●●	Nightmarish when wet		
Start/Finish	St Mary's Church Beaminster DT8 3BA/ST 479 012		

Via secret sunken lanes to Dorset's highest point

Beaminster is a pleasant market town surrounded by hills in the deepest darkest corner of West Dorset. This run begins in Beaminster, yet you are out in the wilds within ninety seconds. Lewesdon Hill is Dorset's highest point (279m), crushing the opposition (nearby Pilsdon Pen) by a full two metres. The summit boasts an Iron Age hillfort (pretty much *de rigueur* in Dorset) but is shrouded by trees. What makes this run so enjoyable is not necessarily reaching the high point, but the maze of quiet rural tracks around it, including some hidden sunken lanes. The author did not meet a single soul outside Beaminster on his last circuit! The running can be heavy-going with a distinct 'cross-country' feel to it; there are countless ups and downs and muddy stretches. The final climb up Lewesdon Hill is hard, but mitigated by the wonderful surrounding woodland. Gerrard's Hill near the end offers great views to reward you for all you've survived.

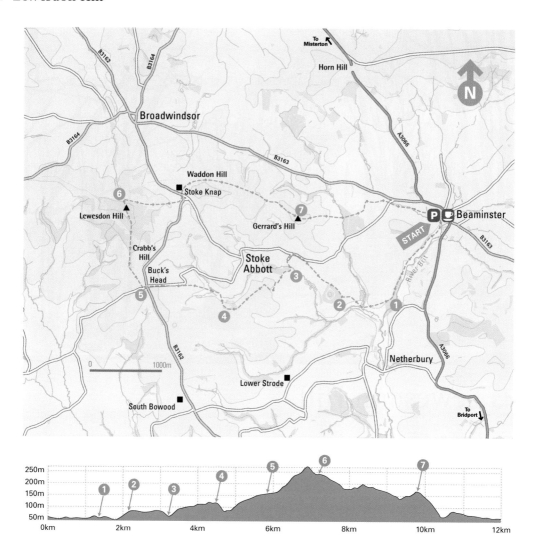

Route Description

START Turn off Church Street onto St Mary Well Street. Follow this to the end and continue on the bridleway following the River Brit. 300m past a junction with track leading downhill to the left, take the footpath signposted to the right. ❶ Follow the footpath across a lane, and then across a field to a stile at the far downhill corner. The footpath winds through the woods beside a stream (bear right at junctions), emerging after 100m at a large field with two isolated trees. Cross this uphill to a bridleway at the far corner. ❷ Follow the bridleway (Long Barrow Lane) to a lane after 700m, turn left and follow this 200m to a junction, turn left again into Horsehill Lane. ❸ When Horsehill Lane ends after 150m at a stream, don't cross the footbridge – the bridleway leads downstream (through the stream!) for 50m, then steeply uphill on the far bank. Follow this bridleway (Beech Lane), ignoring the footpaths leading off at corners. ❹ A power cable passes over the bridleway after 1km, go through the gate on the right to join a bridleway leading steeply downhill to mill buildings. Follow the footpath through the mill buildings and uphill to a lane. Continue 500m ahead on the lane to a crossroads, cross the B3162 and continue ahead, take the footpath on the right after 50m. ❺ Follow the footpath across two fields uphill to a track, cross this to a bridleway leading steeply uphill, via steps at first. At the summit of Lewesdon Hill, follow the right-hand (E) edge of the hillfort; this leads to a 300m footpath descending to a bridleway. ❻ Turn right on the bridleway (Lewesdon Hill Lane) and follow this to the B3162. Cross this and continue ahead on the footpath signposted for Chart Knolle. After 1.2km pass in front of buildings (Chart Knolle), then look for a stile to a footpath on the right. Follow this to the top of Gerrard's Hill. ❼ Descend Gerrard's Hill following the line of stiles. At the bottom a footbridge is crossed, then follow the path uphill into Beaminster. The footpath leads E through Beaminster to Church Street.

Trip Planning

It's possible to park in Church Street beside St Mary's Church. Alternatively, Yarn Barton car park DT8 3EQ/ST 481 014 is a short distance away. Beaminster of course has a choice of shops, pubs and cafés to choose from. The quirky Art Deco café is recommended if you like to take your coffee surrounded by vintage tat.

Should you fancy a bit of culture afterwards, Mapperton House and Gardens are close to Beaminster; this is home to the Earl of Sandwich and has been the location for many films, including the 2015 *Far from the Madding Crowd*.

Other Routes

A gentler ascent of Lewesdon Hill can be had by following the bridleways after ❺ out to the B3164 and back, although this is partly surfaced and misses the lovely direct path. Hill baggers may want to stretch that extension further by also conquering 277m Pilsdon Pen; this also has a hillfort on top and enjoys unobscured views. Some road running on the B3164 would be necessary. The bridleway heading east over Coombe Down Hill to Mapperton House passes through a fine sunken road.

Lewesdon Hill

Wet bridleway near Stoke Abbott

Gerrard's Hill

Pilsdon Pen and Lewesdon Hill

A tree

The Wessex Ridgeway

Not to be confused with either the Ridgeway National Trail (page 306), the Wessex Ridgeway in Wiltshire or the South Dorset Ridgeway (see Route 45), this is a 100km/63 mile trail leading across West and North Dorset between Tollard Royal and Lyme Regis. The signs are a distinctive 'Wyvern' design, but carry maps as the signage tends to disappear around large farms. A full route guide can be downloaded from the Dorset County Council website.

Despite the name, there is no continuous ridge along the route and whilst the trail mostly keeps to the high ground, there are a painful number of descents and ascents. Tackling this non-stop would require super-human endurance (the author struggled to mountain-bike it over two days), but taken in sections or as a multi-day challenge (with some discreet bivvying?), a great adventure could be had. The reward is a tour of inland Dorset's finest scenery, taking in parts of Routes 43, 46 and 49, with truly epic vistas from the hilltops. The Dorset Doddlers Running Club lay on the Wessex Ridgeway Relay which breaks the trail into twelve digestible chunks.

Wessex Ridgeway signage

Eggardon Hill

44 Eggardon Hill

Distance	10km (6 miles)	**Ascent**	325m (1075ft)
Map	OS Landranger 194 OS Explorer 117		
Navigation ●●○	Easier once you're out of Powerstock!		
Terrain ●●○	One big runnable climb		
Wet Feet ●●○	Muddy farmland		
Start/Finish	Powerstock Church DT6 3TD/SY 517 962		

Quiet farmlands and a hillfort with commanding views

This route explores a little-trodden area of rural West Dorset that, whilst pleasant enough in itself, happens to be well-placed to give great vistas of the surrounding hills and coast, encompassing Pilsdon Pen and Lewesdon Hill (Dorset's highest summits), Golden Cap (highest point on the south coast), the Cerne Abbas Hills and the South Dorset Ridgeway; all of which feature in this book! Eggardon Hill is of course the best viewpoint, but the tracks along Knowle Hill and the Eggardon Farms also offer wide horizons. Eggardon hillfort is divided by a boundary fence running down the centre, with this route necessarily following the footpath to the north of the fence. However, a small diversion to run along the exposed ramparts on the National Trust land to the south of the fence is recommended; you'll have to backtrack afterwards, but you'll feel like you are running on air!

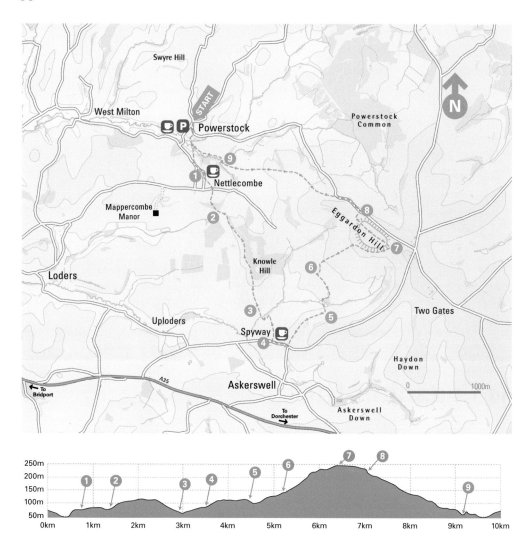

Route Description

🏃 START ▸ Follow King's Lane past the Three Horseshoes Inn to a footpath on the right, leading downhill. Cross the footbridge and follow the footpath through another gate and over another bridge. The footpath leads uphill (stay right when it forks) to a lane. Follow the lane left for 150m until a junction and turn right. ❶ After 50m on the lane, cross the stile on the left to a footpath and follow this across two fields into woodland. ❷ When the footpath joins a crossroads of tracks, take the footpath track heading uphill (E) and follow it for 1.5km along the edge of the woods and then downhill to Loderstand Farm. ❸ Follow the footpath past Loderstand Farm and then follow the footpath track across the stream and around a left and then right bend leading to Spyway Road. ❹ Follow Spyway Road 200m uphill past the Spyway Inn to a crossroads. Turn left onto the bridleway drive signposted for South Eggardon Farm. ❺ After 700m on the bridleway drive you reach the farm entrance, go through the gate on the left and follow this bridleway past the pond and uphill to North Eggardon Farm. Passing the farm, take the bridleway track on the right. ❻ Follow the bridleway 500m uphill to the edge of the hillfort. Cross the gate and turn right

Eggardon Hill

and follow the bridleway beneath the ramparts. **7** When you reach a stile on the left beside a NT sign, cross it and follow the footpath along the fence leading through the hillfort. At the far (NW) end, follow the walls to find a gate leading onto King's Lane. **8** Descend on King's Lane for 400m until it bends right, take the track on the left. After 900m the track bends left, take the footpath continuing ahead and follow this through several fields to cross a disused railway. Cross the following field and exit via the stile hidden on the right near the bottom. **9** When you reach houses, take the footpath alongside the stream and follow it along the stream for 450m back to the footbridge you crossed at the start. Cross this and head uphill to the village.

Trip Planning

Park beside the road in front of the church tower on King's Lane, or wherever you can find in this small village.

Refreshment and food is available from the Three Horseshoes Inn in Powerstock, the Marquis of Lorne in nearby Nettlecombe or at the Spyway Inn along the route.

Other Routes

A longer circuit is possible by diverting at Spyway **4** to follow (rather muddy) footpaths through Askerswell to Stancombe Farm and up onto Haydon Down.

Eggardon Hill

Hardy Monument and
South Dorset Ridgeway

45 The Hardy Monument

Distance	15km (9.5 miles)	**Ascent**	375m (1230ft)
Map	OS Landranger 194 OS Explorer OL15		
Navigation ●●●	Some care needed in the first half		
Terrain ●●●	Some heavy-going agricultural land		
Wet Feet ●●●	A few muddy stretches		
Start/Finish	Elwell Street, Upwey DT3 5QG/SY 669 849		

Airy ridge running amidst Bronze Age burial mounds

The South Dorset Ridgeway stretches for about 30km between West Bexington and Osmington, several kilometres north from the sea. The run described here starts by taking in the little-trodden smaller ridge to the south of the Ridgeway, before climbing gradually to the highest point at the Hardy Monument. This unsettlingly phallic tower commemorates Thomas Hardy, not the famous Dorset writer but actually the Admiral made famous by Nelson's dying words, "Kiss me Hardy." After this viewpoint is enjoyed, the route back to the start is along a fine road-free section of the Ridgeway, winding between countless Prehistoric burial mounds.

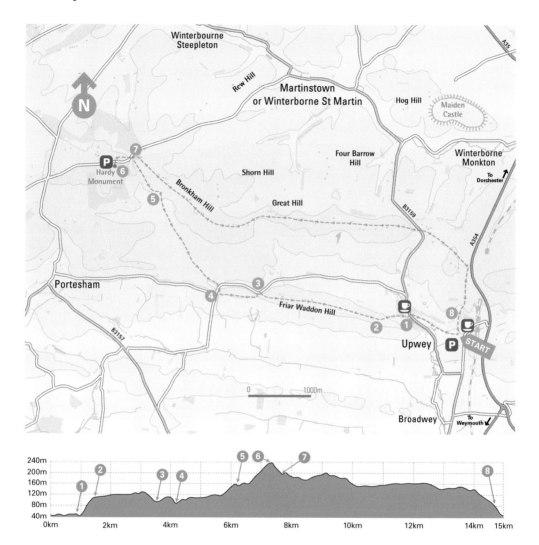

Route Description

🏃 START Follow the Little Hill lane off Elwell Street, take the footpath on the left after 20m. Follow this behind the houses for 850m to the B3159. ❶ Cross the B3159 and follow the pavement left for 50m. Turn right onto the footpath track beside the Wishing Well Tea Rooms, follow this steeply uphill to the ridgetop. ❷ Follow the footpath along the ridgetop W for 2km, before passing beneath power cables and descending to a lane. ❸ Take the track to the left signposted 'Corton' and then take the footpath immediately on the right. Descend on the footpath past the chapel but keep to the right-hand (uphill) edge of the field. The footpath leads along the right-hand edge of a fence, marked by posts. When you reach a lane, turn right (uphill). ❹ 100m along the lane, take the track on the left. After 80m, take the bridleway signposted on the left. ❺ Follow the bridleway for 1400m into a large field; after crossing and leaving this field, turn left onto a bridleway leading downhill. Follow this down and up to a parking area. Cross the road and take the footpath leading steeply uphill to the Hardy monument. ❻ Take selfies, then descend from the monument by the same footpath back to the parking area. Turn left on the lane, after 40m take the bridleway on the right. ❼ Follow the bridleways and permissive paths E along the ridgetop. After 5km the B3159 is crossed, after another 500m is a crossroads of tracks, continue ahead. 500m further another crossroads is reached just before the A354, turn right (downhill). ❽ Follow this track for 800m to a footpath on the right; follow this back to the start point.

Trip Planning

There is plenty of parking space near the start, along Elwell Street in Upwey.

The Hardy Monument is in the care of the National Trust; after inexplicably and annoyingly closing off the parking area DT2 9HY/SY 612 875 by barrier for a number of years, it opened again from March 2018. They have also re-opened the tower, enabling visitors to climb to the top. There is also a small parking area DT2 9HY/SY 615 877 just down the hill from the monument, on the route; handy if you just wish to run sections of the South Dorset Ridgeway.

The Old Ship Inn in Upwey is a few hundred metres from the start point, serving food and drink. The Wishing Well Tea Rooms in Upwey are along the route and will attempt to deviate you from your exertions with the offer of Dorset apple cake.

Hardy Monument

South Dorset Ridgeway

Other Routes

The last climb to the monument can of course be bypassed! There are also a number of paths which allow you to short-cut this loop, e.g. just after ❸ and ❹. Those wishing to avoid big climbs may wish to start from the parking area below the monument and run out and back along the South Dorset Ridgeway, perhaps also exploring the trails in the woods and heath around the summit.

It is possible to extend the loop to and past Portesham, but note that the footpath along the lower ridge is blocked and pretty impassable; you'll have to take Winter's Lane from ❹.

An excellent long route would be to run the whole South Dorset Ridgeway from West Bexington to Osmington (about 27km), using the X53 bus as a shuttle.

A great short run in the vicinity is to explore the vast earthworks of Maiden Castle, just outside Dorchester; looping around and around the multiple (multivallate, in archaeologist speak) walls and ditches is to be recommended.

The Hardy Monument

Isle of Portland from the
South Dorset Ridgeway

Burial Mounds

Around a thousand ancient monuments have been identified on the South Dorset Ridgeway; this is possibly the densest concentration of prehistoric sites in the country! Most recognisable today are the four hundred-ish burial mounds, also known as 'barrows'. These populate the high ground, being visible from miles around. They mostly date from the Bronze Age (2500BC–700BC), when it seems that a huge cultural shift took place. Abandoning the standing stones and mass community

South Dorset Ridgeway

tombs of the Neolithic era (e.g. West Kennet Long Barrow, Route 63), our ancestors shifted to smaller individual burials, with the bodies cremated before burial. They didn't completely ditch the past, as these mounds are usually erected in already sacred places; for example, the hundreds of mounds that surround Stonehenge (Route 59) are thousands of years younger than the stones.

The Cerne Abbas Giant

46 The Cerne Abbas Giant

Distance	12km (7.5 miles)	Ascent	225m (740ft)
Map	OS Landranger 194 OS Explorer 117		
Navigation ●●●	Few opportunities to become lost		
Terrain ●●●	Some running across churned up agricultural land		
Wet Feet ●●●	Plenty of muddy stretches in the first half, some cow poo		
Start/Finish	Cerne Abbas Giant Viewpoint DT2 7JX/ST 662 016		

Mild running along a bubbling river and a chalk ridge

Cerne Abbas nestles in a long straight valley, in a part of Dorset characterised by parallel chalk ridges running north-south. What makes Cerne Abbas special is the Giant; carved into the turf and chalk on the hillside behind is a 55m high naked man with an impressive erection, waving a club. Ladies, preserve your modesty and look away!

This run starts by following the valley of the River Cerne downstream, often close alongside this shallow and clear chalk stream. You cross farmland, so expect to accumulate some cow manure on your soles! After crossing the river, a mild climb onto the ridge allows an easier return to Cerne Abbas with wide views of the surrounding ridges and finally the 'angry' Giant.

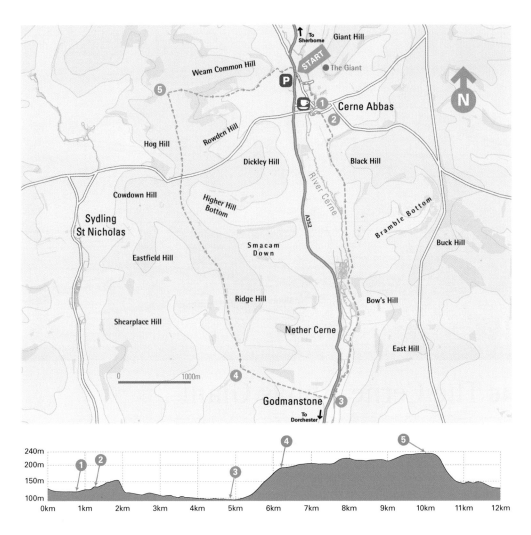

Route Description

🏃 **START** From the Viewpoint, follow Duck Lane for 100m and turn left onto a lane. Pass the car park and village hall, then turn right onto a footpath along the stream, into the village. Turn right onto Long Street. ❶ 100m along Long Street, turn left onto Back Lane. Follow this 200m and turn right into Chescombe Close. Follow this ahead to a footpath entrance. ❷ Follow the footpath 200m to the edge of the hill and then turn right onto another footpath. Follow this ahead for 4.5km, passing through Pound Farm and the hamlet of Nether Cerne. After Nether Cerne the River Cerne is joined; a footbridge signposted to Reynard's Copse is reached, ignore this and continue 550m to the footbridge signposted for Godmanstone. ❸ Cross the footbridge to the A352, cross to the bridleway 70m to your left. Follow this 1.3km to the ridgetop. ❹ Turn right onto the ridgetop bridleway. After 200m there is a junction, take the left-hand bridleway. Continue along the ridge for 3.5km (passing Higher City Farm and crossing a lane) until you reach a radio mast. ❺ Take the footpath on the right just after the radio mast. Follow this to the treeline, then downhill through the woods to the valley bottom and ahead for a further kilometre. Take the second footpath on the right back to the A352 and the Viewpoint.

Cerne valley

Trip Planning

There is a small parking area beside the Cerne Abbas Giant Viewpoint, on Duck Street, just off the A352. Alternatively there is a larger car park DT2 7LA/ST 663 014 200m away. Both are free.

Cerne Abbas has three pubs and various eating places; Abbot's Tearoom does a nice line in homemade scones. Provisions including local produce can be acquired from the village store. More information about Cerne Abbas and the River Cerne valley can be found at the Cerne Valley community website.

Hog Hill

The National Trust look after the Giant, and a number of paths behind Cerne allow you to examine it closer.

Other Routes

This loop can easily be extended by following the ridge and valley further north from ⑤ or south from ③. Going further north will involve some road time.

A more strenuous option is to widen the loop into the valleys to the east, ascending the bridleway below the Giant from the start, going via Piddletrenthide, and rejoining at ③.

Cerne Abbas

Cerne Abbas

Events

The Giant's Head Marathon by White Star Running is a highly rated, well established and murderously hard event, starting from Sydling St. Nicholas in the next valley to the west. Completing the event earns you a t-shirt which you can never wear in public. On the same weekend, the 10K Sydling Hill Race and 5km Sydling Bell Race are held; the latter involves running wearing a cow bell!

The Cerne Abbas Giant

The origins of the Giant are a complete mystery. It may well be truly ancient, representing some kind of prehistoric fertility god. Indeed, local tradition has it that alfresco sex* atop the turgid part of the giant's anatomy will help couples to conceive. However, there is no record of the Giant before the late 1600s and many believe that the giant is actually a seventeenth-century practical joke, making fun of the joyless Puritanism of the era. It has even been suggested that the Giant represents Oliver Cromwell!

*Presumably the National Trust would take a dim view of this.

Portland Bill Lighthouse

47 The Isle of Portland

Distance	14km (8.5 miles)	Ascent	350m (1150ft)
Map	OS Landranger 194 OS Explorer OL15		
Navigation ●●●	Wholly follows the South West Coast Path		
Terrain ●●●	Plenty of rough/rocky ground through quarries		
Wet Feet ●●●	Gets pretty muddy on the west side		
Start/Finish	New Ground car park DT5 1LQ/SY 689 730		

A spectacular and technical coastal run through abandoned quarries

The Isle of Portland is effectively a Brobdingnagian slab of limestone, towering above nearby Weymouth and tilted downhill towards its southern tip at Portland Bill. This heavily-quarried isle almost seems purpose-built for trail running, supplying a variety of landscapes and running surfaces to keep you constantly entertained, all the while with an expansive backdrop of lively seas and distant cliffs.

In truth Portland isn't quite an island; it is attached to the mainland by the pebbles of Chesil Beach, alongside a road causeway from Weymouth. The start point of this run gives a tremendous view back over this. On the west coast, sheer cliffs tower 100m above the waves. The path diverts inland through amazing Tout Quarry, where the limestone waste has been used to produce dozens of sculptures. Portland Bill is Dorset's southernmost point. Here, a lighthouse overlooks the Portland Race, where extremely powerful tidal flows can be whipped into a frenzy by wind. The east coast offers even more entertaining running, through abandoned quarries and amongst rough limestone waste, closer to sea level.

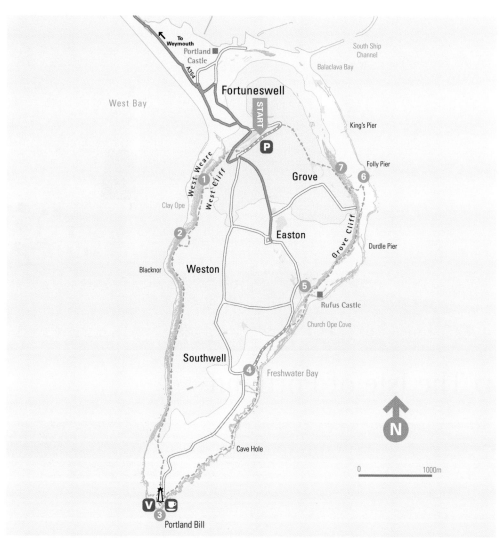

Portland Bill

Route Description

This route follows the South West Coast Path, the description here outlines features along the route.

START Follow the road W past the War Memorial. Follow SWCP signs downhill to a crossing point across the A354, or cross with care at the roundabout. Follow the track along the top of the western cliffs S to a diversion barrier. ❶ Since 2013, the SWCP has been diverted inland due to unstable cliffs: follow the signage through (wonderful) Tout Quarry and back to the cliffs. ❷ A second diversion briefly leads inland. After rejoining the cliff top, negotiate a rough section around an old fort. Continue for 3km downhill on the SWCP to Portland Bill Lighthouse. ❸ Round the lighthouse and turn onto the E coast, follow the track N through beach huts into a series of abandoned quarries. Mind the gaping holes! ❹ When the SWCP reaches a road, cross and follow it for 700m then cross again and follow SWCP signs back into the quarries. At Church Ope Cove, descend behind the beach huts and climb a steep section of steps. ❺ At the castle, take the right-hand path which eventually joins a disused tramway leading gradually downhill. ❻ Look out for the stone marker indicating a left turn off the tramway. Take this turn to climb zigzagging steps to the Young Offender's Institute at the top of the cliffs, then follow the road N beside the YOI. ❼ Follow SWCP signs inland along tracks between quarries. At the Verne Fort, take the left-hand (uphill) road back to your start point.

West side of the Isle of Portland

Tout Quarry

Trip Planning

New Ground car park is free. Access it by driving the steep A354 road up through Fortuneswell to the round-about at the top of the hill, where you turn left past the War Memorial.

A good place to head after running is Portland Bill itself, the southern tip of Dorset; there is the Lobster

Chesil Beach from the Isle of Portland

Pot Restaurant where you can eat inside, or better, chomp on burgers and chips outside, watching the tide rush past. The lighthouse can be visited.

You will have briefly experienced the sculptures of Tout Quarry during your run; many will want to revisit afterwards (simply walk across from the route's start point) and further explore this magnificently un-kempt and little-known Dorset wonder.

Other Routes

Starting from the Chesil Beach Centre on Portland Beach Road DT4 9XE/SY 668 756 (where there is also a pleasant café) will extend this route to half marathon distance, as well as adding a punishing 125m climb onto the island! Parking charges apply here.

To the north-west of the Chesil Beach Centre, the SWCP leads behind Chesil Beach along the Fleet Lagoon to Langton Herring and is a beautiful and quiet trail; note that parts occasionally flood after heavy rain or big tides.

Chesil Beach is common land over which there is a right of public access on foot. However running on its surface of loose pebbles is near-impossible; utter masochists only need apply!

The Isle of Portland

Isle of Portland

Events

The Isle of Portland Coastal Marathon involves two circuits of the island, going around in both directions. A half marathon and 10K are also included in this event. The Round the Rock 10K follows a route incorporating some of the coast and the inland quarries.

Portland Stone

Portland's 140 million year-old limestone has sustained a quarrying industry for at least a thousand years. Large sections of Portland's surface are simply gone, loaded from the cliffs onto ships to leave a sparse landscape of quarry pits, hewn plateaus and waste heaps. Much of Portland's stone now adorns London's public buildings. After the 1666 Great Fire, Sir Christopher Wren utilised 6,000,000 tons to rebuild St Paul's and fifty other churches. The nineteenth century saw Portland stone used for constructing the Portland Harbour breakwaters. The industry peaked in 1904 when 100,000 tons were quarried. Portland stone is still quarried and employed for significant projects such as the Commonwealth War Graves Commission's headstones and memorials.

East side of the Isle of Portland

Running through the abandoned and overgrown quarries along the coast, you'll appreciate how this post-industrial wasteland is now returning to nature, forming a beguiling landscape.

East Dorset

East Dorset's complex geology means that it is blessed with some of the finest and most spectacular scenery in Britain. Two Areas of Outstanding Natural Beauty (Cranborne Chase and Dorset) are characterised by steep-sided ridges, making for some tough climbs rewarded by expansive views, often out across the English Channel. The highlight is the Isle of Purbeck where the geology is densely varied, meaning that a short run can encompass a wide range of differing landscapes. Where this diversity intersects with the coast path, the inevitable result is some truly brutal climbs and descents.

Swyre Head (Route 50)

Ascending Swyre Head

Bat's Hole

48 Durdle Door

Distance	13km (8 miles)	Ascent	425m (1400ft)
Map	OS Landranger 194 OS Explorer OL15		
Navigation ●●●	Well-signposted, partly following the South West Coast Path		
Terrain ●●●	Several agonisingly steep ascents and descents		
Wet Feet ●●●	Can be muddy after rainy periods		
Start/Finish	Ringstead Bay car park (National Trust) DT2 8NQ/SY 757 825		

Steep climbs back-dropped by breath-taking chalk cliff scenery

The spectacular chalk arch of Durdle Door, near Lulworth Cove, is one of the UK's most recognisable natural landmarks. The near-vertical white cliffs to the west which this route traverses are no less impressive, especially at Bat Head where an isolated stack rises from the sea beside the cave of Bat Hole which pierces this headland. This may be the finest scenery of the Jurassic Coast World Heritage Site, if not the entire South West Coast Path. Crowds throng to Durdle Door; however this route approaches from the 'quiet' western end and even in summer an early start will ensure that you get to enjoy this iconic landmark by yourself.

Durdle Door

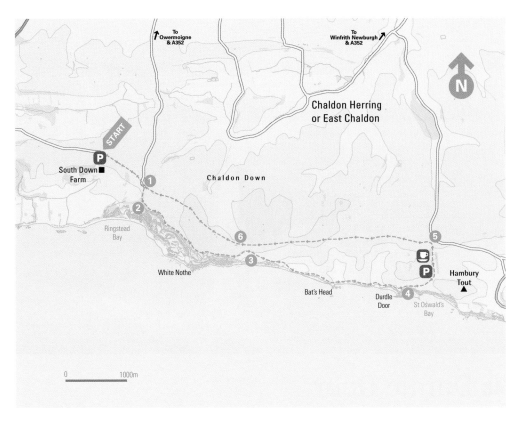

Route Description

🏃 START Follow the bridleway track out of the E end of the car park, past a gate. ❶ The bridleway track bends right and leads downhill. ❷ When you reach the signs for the South West Coast Path, turn left up the hill following the SWCP, onto the cliff edge. Follow the obvious footpath along the cliff for 2km past White Nothe Cottages until you reach a stone obelisk. ❸ At the obelisk, take the right-hand footpath contouring downhill until you can descend no further at Middle Bottom. Continue E on the footpath over two successive steep climbs and descents atop the cliffs. The third climb from Scratchy Bottom(!) is less steep and leads to Durdle Door. ❹ Just past Durdle Door, take the wide footpath track forking left off the SWCP and leading steeply uphill to a car park and caravan park. Continue N through the caravan park to the entrance (or follow the path signposted around the E side of the park). ❺ Continue 100m past the caravan park entrance to Newlands Farm; take the footpath on the left that leads through this. Follow this footpath leading W through farmland. After 3km you reach a junction where the footpath leads downhill and there is a bridleway on the right accessed by a gate. ❻ Take the bridleway. After 2km this merges with the original track leaving the car park, leading you back to the start.

Durdle Door

Trip Planning

Ringstead Bay car park is free and belongs to the National Trust; it is not to be confused with the village of Ringstead (some distance downhill). Access it by a sharp turn off the A353 Weymouth-Poole Road, signposted for Ringstead; follow this lane right to its end.

Durdle Door Holiday Park (which this route passes through) has a restaurant and supermarket. Ice cream and tea is often sold at the car park above Durdle Door BH20 5PU/SY 810 804, an alternative and much busier start point. Further east, Lulworth Cove is well worth a visit. This is another possible start point, but parking BH20 5RQ/SY 821 800 is expensive.

White Nothe cliffs

Durdle Door, used as an art installation!

Other Routes

The highlights of this route could be included in a loop from the village of East Chaldon.

An extension west from ❷ following the SWCP will take you past Ringstead beach to Osmington, enjoying some fairly muddy paths en route. If the steep climbs here have only whetted your appetite, follow the SWCP further east from ❹ past Lulworth Cove via two outrageous climbs to the abandoned village of Tyneham, and back along the ridgetop. Note that this is military land which can be closed to the public; Google 'Lulworth Ranges' for firing times.

Above Bat's Hole

Events

A short distance north, the Lulworth Castle 10K follows trails around the Weld Estate. Endurance Life's popular Dorset CTS is usually based from Lulworth Cove, and incorporates much of this route. The choice of distance ranges from 10K to 'Ultra Plus', whatever horror that is; the author has survived the 'Ultra' course which involves c1800m of numbingly steep ascent!

The Jurassic Coast World Heritage Site

In 2001, the 154km of coast between Exmouth in Devon and Studland Beach in Dorset became England's first natural UNESCO World Heritage Site. This recognition came as a result of the amazing diversity of geology on display; the cliffs time-travel through 185 million years of the Earth's history, spanning the entire Mesozoic Era. This was the Era when dinosaurs roamed the earth, and is divided into three 'Periods': the dark red sandstone of Ladram Bay's stacks (Route 27) hails from the Triassic Period (252–201 million years ago). The landslips forming The Undercliffs (Route 29) and cliffs and quarries of Portland Stone (Routes 47 and 51) reveal the Jurassic Period (201–145 mya). The stunning chalk scenery around Durdle Door (Route 48) was formed during the Cretaceous Period (145–66 mya) by remnants of marine algae known as coccoliths, six billion per cubic centimetre of chalk!

What all this Geology stuff means on the ground for trail runners is, basically, phenomenal scenery, numerous tough climbs and truly remarkable diversity along sections of the coast. Those taking on events which traverse most of the World Heritage Site, such as Endurance Life's 46-mile Jurassic Quarter, Votwo's three-day Jurassic Coast Challenge* and Brutal Events' hideous non-stop 'Oner', should prepare to have their legs battered and more pertinently, their minds blown.

In the last few kilometres of the JCC, the author actually hallucinated that Studland Beach was curling uphill.

Hambledon Hill

49 Blandford Forest and Hambledon Hill

Distance	16km (10 miles)	**Ascent**	450m (1500ft)
Map	OS Landranger 194 OS Explorer 117, 118, 129		
Navigation ●●●	Plenty of route choices to figure out!		
Terrain ●●●	Easy going … but you 'will' crawl up Hambledon Hill		
Wet Feet ●●●	Muddy patches crossing farmland		
Start/Finish	Hod Hill parking area DT11 8PS/ST 853 112		

Quiet woodland trails and an Iron Age hillfort

This part of North Dorset sees relatively few visitors, which is surprising as it is quite beautiful. Small villages line the River Stour, Dorset's largest river, as it winds between two ridges of hills. To the south is a long high ridge, covered at its east end by Blandford Forest, which is refreshingly free of 'plantation' feel. To the north, Hambledon Hill rises sharply on all sides, topped by a truly amazing Iron Age hillfort: a great finale to this run. This route offers constantly engaging running along on a variety of surfaces and landscapes. If you get lost in the forest, don't worry – all routes lead to the summit, eventually …

Blandford Forest and Hambledon Hill

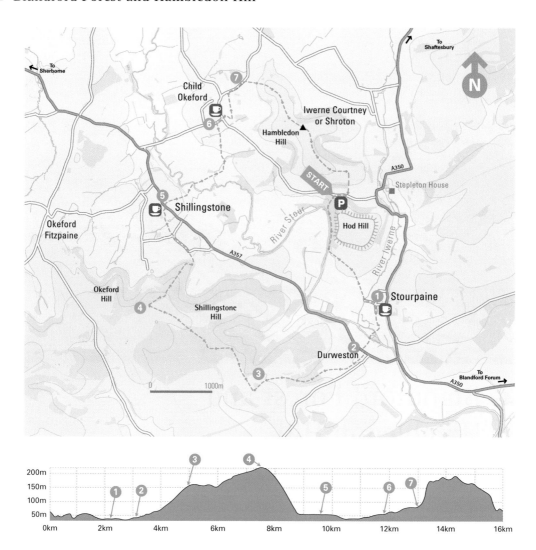

Route Description

🏃 **START** Follow the bridleway downhill from the car park and along the riverbank. This becomes Hod Drive, a bridleway track into Stourpaine village. **1** Turn right at the crossroads in the village, towards the church. Follow the footpath ahead after the church and pass under the disused railway. Cross the River Stour via two bridges to Durweston village. **2** Turn left onto the A357, then turn right after 50m into a lane. After 50m this bends left; take the bridleway leading right and uphill. After 2km the bridleway joins a lane. **3** After 200m on the lane take the footpath on the right. Follow this footpath for 750m until it begins to descend steeply, then take the bridleway leading uphill on the left. When this reaches a T-junction, turn right and after 125m, turn left onto a bridleway. After 1km this leads to a trig point. **4** Turn right (NE) at the trig point, and after 350m, follow the bridleway steeply downhill to Shillingstone village. This merges into a lane, follow ahead until a fork; take the left fork and immediately cross the lane to a footpath into the village centre. **5** Cross the A357 and take the footpath 50m to the left. Follow this to the River Stour. Cross the bridge, follow the obvious footpath NE across the field and through a gate to join a bridleway leading N into Child Okeford village. ❻ When the bridleway reaches a lane, turn right and cross the main road after 100m. Follow the footpath ahead and turn right (SE) when it splits two ways. After 150m take the left turn, follow this footpath for 750m behind the village and then alongside a lane to a right (uphill) turn. ❼ Climb Hambledon Hill! Follow the ridge to the earthworks barring the SE end; passing left of these is easiest. The path merges with a bridleway. When this reaches a junction, turn right (S) along the Stour Valley Way. Follow this bridleway along the ridgetop until you reach a barn, then turn right and descend to the road. The car park is 200m to the right.

Trip Planning

The start car park is free, found by turning west off the A350 onto a lane signposted for Hanford.

The four villages which this route passes through (Stourpaine, Durweston, Shillingstone and Child Oke-ford) are all quiet with limited facilities. All, other than Durweston, have pubs; only Child Okeford has a village shop, Cross Stores. The Willow Tea Rooms in Shilling-stone are pleasant, and the garage in Shillingstone is another source of refreshment.

Hambledon Hill is a National Nature Reserve (due to its wild flowers) administered by the National Trust. If this fix of Iron Age Dorset isn't enough, directly adjacent is Hod Hill with another hillfort, later converted into a Roman camp.

Blandford Forest

Shillingstone Hill

Other Routes

Either of the two hills here can be tackled in isolation, but where is the fun in that? Deviants may wish to start this route by directly ascending Hod Hill from the car park to rejoin at ❶, rather than circumventing it along the river.

The ridge leading south-west from Blandford Forest ❹ has a road along it; however there are various trail options leading off (or up onto) it. The bridleway leading west from Rawlsbury Camp hillfort is blocked in places by hedge-to-hedge ploughing.

Events

The Stickler is a 16km trail race around the same hills (also including Hod Hill, for good measure). White Star Running's Dorset Invader Marathon is a trail race in the River Stour valley. There is also a half marathon event.

Crossing the River Stour

National Trails in the South West

Cotswold Way – Chipping Campden to Bath, 164km/102 miles (see page 328)

England Coast Path – under construction, completion in 2020 (see page 176)

South West Coast Path – Minehead to Poole, 1014km/630 miles (see page 32)

Thames Path – Thameshead to Thames Barrier, 296km/184 miles (see page 316)

The Ridgeway – Avebury to Ivinghoe Beacon, 140km/87 miles (see page 306)

Other selected long-distance trails in the South West

Coleridge Way – Nether Stowey to Lynmouth, 82km/51 miles

Copper Trail – Loop around Bodmin Moor, 97km/60 miles

Devonshire Heartland Way – Okehampton to Exe Valley, 60km/43 miles

Dorset Jubilee Trail – Forde Abbey to Bokerley Dyke, 142km/88 miles

East Devon Way – Lyme Regis to Exmouth, 64km/40 miles

Exe Valley Way – Exford to South West Coast Path, 72km/45 miles

Macmillan Way West – Castle Cary to Barnstable, 164km/102 miles

Mid Wilts Way – Ham to Warminster, 110km/68 miles

River Parrett Trail – Cheddington to Stert Point, 77km/48 miles

Two Moors Way/Devon Coast to Coast – Wembury/Ivybridge to Lynmouth, 187km/116 miles (see page 156)

Wessex Ridgeway – Tollard Royal to Lyme Regis, 100km/63 miles (see page 212)

White Horse Trail – Loop around Wiltshire, 145km/90 miles

More info and additional trails from *www.ldwa.org.uk*

Worbarrow Bay

50 Corfe Castle

Distance	24km (15 miles)	Ascent	675m (2200ft)
Map	OS Landranger 195 OS Explorer OL15		
Navigation ●●●	Partly along the South West Coast Path, easy to follow ridge lines		
Terrain ●●●	Many climbs including one long steep slog from sea level		
Wet Feet ●●●	Slippery when wet		
Start/Finish	Quarry car park, Kimmeridge BH20 5PH/SY 918 800		

Airy overhanging cliffs, sublime ridge-running and an epic ruin

This might just be the greatest trail run on earth; the author is biased however, having lived on the route for over a decade. Serious runners can no doubt beat his sub-8 minute mile personal best from Corfe Castle up Swyre Head and back, but he's proud of it.

This route takes in some of the best of the Isle of Purbeck's celebrated scenery. For most of the run you are high above the surrounding sea and land, with views in all directions. The western half of this circuit is on military land, including a traverse atop the incredible overhanging Gad Cliff. Below is the ruined village of Tyneham, cleared for military use during World War II and (despite promises) never returned. A descent to the brilliant white chalk of Worbarrow Bay is followed by a steep climb onto a long straight ridge leading all the way east to Corfe Castle, taking in Flower's Barrow hillfort and Grange Arch folly en route. Huge ruined Corfe Castle dominates the route for several kilometres, before a climb to the summit of Swyre Head. This is the highest point in Purbeck and an outstanding viewpoint.

Corfe Castle

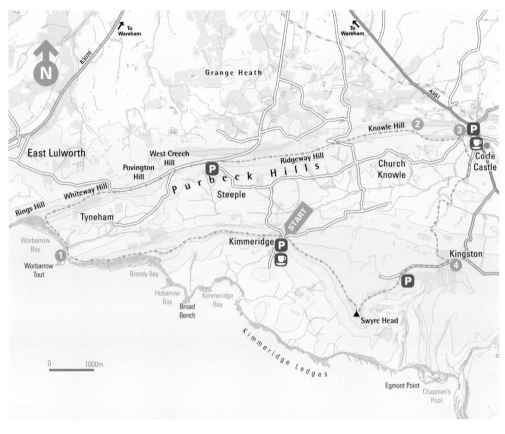

Route Description

🚶 **START** From the car park, follow the lane 50m N (away from the sea) past a junction; cross the stile on your left onto a bridleway. Follow the bridleway W along the ridgetop onto military land. The SWCP is joined, follow this along the top of the Gad Cliff and then descend steeply to Worbarrow Bay. **1** Climb steeply from Worbarrow Bay on the SWCP; at the top (Flowers Barrow hillfort) turn right and follow the permissive path along the ridgetop all the way E to Corfe Castle. When road sections are encountered, follow the paths marked out to the right of the road. 800m after Grange Arch, don't miss a gate on the left leading to the permissive path. **2** About 8.5km from Flowers Barrow, the permissive path descends steeply down a track on the right-hand (S) side of the ridge; take this and follow the bridleway at the bottom towards Corfe Castle. **3** At the lane, cross and take the footpath 50m to the right. Follow this for 500m across a footbridge to a car park. Follow the lane S (away from the castle) to reach West Street, turn right and follow this to a cattle grid. Continue on the permissive surfaced track which follows. After 1.5km pass through Blashenwell Farm and follow the bridleway track uphill to a gate. Through the gate, follow the bridleway track to a lane. ❹ Follow the lane to the right for 1km to a parking area. Pass through a gate and follow the bridleway leading up to the summit of Swyre Head. Continue along the ridge following a permissive path until you descend to a lane. Turn left and left again to the start car park.

View from Swyre Head

Trip Planning

Follow signs to Kimmeridge. The start car park is a disused quarry to the left of the road, just after the sea comes into view. There is no charge. It's also possible to start in Corfe Castle village (usually busy). The car park BH20 5HH/SY 958 818 on this route ❸ belongs to the National Trust, free to members. There is also a NT car park on the other side of the castle beside the A350 at BH20 5DR/SY 959 824. Free non-NT options can be found halfway up Swyre Head at BH20 5LP/SY 943 792 and atop Grange Hill at BH20 5PA/SY 904 816 ... both mean a climb at the end of this long run!

Descending to Corfe Castle

Provisions can be bought in Corfe Castle village; there's no shop in Kimmeridge, although it has a café, but it pales next to the Model Village Tea Rooms in Corfe Castle and their monolithic cake slices. Corfe Castle itself of course deserves a visit (free to NT members), also consider visiting Kimmeridge Bay (toll road) and ruined Tyneham village. Indeed it's all good – this is one of the most beautiful places in Britain.

The Gad Cliff

The western part of this route is on military land which can be closed to the public; Google 'Lulworth Ranges' for firing times. Firing is common Monday to Friday, but only takes place on a few weekends annually.

Corfe Common

Other Routes

If firing is taking place, or if you want a shorter run, reduce the route to 10km by following the bridleways and roads via Steeple Leaze Farm, turning north off this route 1km after the start.

A possible extension or alternative is to explore the ridge continuing east of Corfe Castle ❸, which has various bridleways and paths offering great trail running. Or consider the SWCP continuing further west to Lulworth Cove from ❶, which is outrageously hilly. Enjoy, if this is your sort of thing.

Whiteway Hill

Events

Much of this route is shared with the Purbeck Marathon. This exceptional trail event is one of the top-rated marathons in the world, beginning and ending in Swanage. The author is a local and has currently survived it four times. There is also a concurrent 16-mile event. Corfe Castle is the base for Maverick Race's Inov8 Original Dorset Race, with 9km, 16km and 23km distances.

Corfe Castle

The castle dominates the landscape around, as of course it was meant to do; a 'corfe' is a gap between hills, and William the Conqueror chose this location in order to control travel and trade in the area. The castle's amazing shattered appearance and profile of tottering towers is not due to natural wear and tear. The castle survived the Middle Ages intact, but was besieged by Parliament during the English Civil War. After it was finally captured (the formidable Lady Bankes was betrayed by one of her

Corfe Castle

men), Oliver Cromwell ordered for it to be blown up. The vast quantities of gunpowder used failed to destroy Corfe Castle, and cost so much that plans to demolish all of England's castles were abandoned.

View from St Alban's Head

51 St Alban's Head

Distance	13km (8 miles)	Ascent	425m (1400ft)
Map	OS Landranger 195 OS Explorer OL15		
Navigation ●●●	Well-signposted, partly following the South West Coast Path		
Terrain ●●●	Uneven ground, one extremely steep descent and ascent		
Wet Feet ●●●	Usually slippery and muddy around St Alban's Head		
Start/Finish	Dancing Ledge National Trust car park BH19 3HG/SY 997 782		

A traverse of limestone sea cliffs and abandoned quarries

This run traverses the limestone cliffs of the Isle of Purbeck. These cliffs were extensively quarried well into the twentieth century, with limestone blocks loaded onto ships. Today, the quarries are eerie open spaces hewn out of the vertical cliffs. St Alban's Head is a wonderful isolated viewpoint, occupied by a Norman chapel, a Coastwatch lookout and a sculpture commemorating the local role in the WWII development of radar. The paths on this peninsula tend to get muddy, and the insane steps on the west side (you'll know them when you see them) are a challenge; but this is an outstanding coastal run. The return is along the Priest's Way, an ancient road used by a priest (unsurprisingly) but also by local quarry workers.

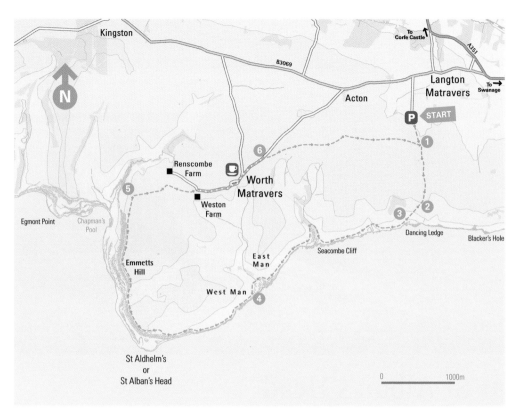

Route Description

START Follow the footpath track S from the car park. **1** At a junction with a bridleway, continue ahead on the footpath following signs for Dancing Ledge. Continue past Spyway Barn and across two fields. **2** When you reach the steep slope down to the clifftop, descend with care following signage – the first path encountered is closed (2018) due to landslips. **3** At the clifftop, turn right onto the SWCP, follow this W. At Seacombe Quarry, descend steps before heading 200m inland to steps back onto the cliffs. Winspit Quarry soon follows, another descent and climb. **4** After Winspit, you are above a precipice: don't turn left! The SWCP ascends to the Coastwatch Station on St Alban's Head, then swings N and steeply descends and ascends 50m via steps. **5** A stone tablet on the path marks where to leave the SWCP and turn right following a footpath towards Worth Matravers. Cross the wall and two fields to a car park. Follow the footpath through Weston Farm to a road and follow the road through Worth Matravers village for 1km. **6** After the last houses are passed, a footpath on the right is signposted for Swanage. This crosses several fields before reaching a gate where the Priest's Way track begins. After 1.6km, the footpath track to the car park crosses the Priest's way, turn left back to the start.

Trip Planning

Dancing Ledge car park is free and belongs to the National Trust; access it by turning off the B3069 in the village of Langton Matravers, onto Durnford Drove; follow this lane past its end onto a stony track.

If you divert to explore any of the quarries along this route, note that the huge caverns extending into the cliffs are unstable and decaying.

There is a tea shop along the route in the village of Worth Matravers, however the big draw is the Square and Compass Pub, internationally famous among bearded real ale enthusiasts. Surrounded by lumps of quarried limestone and serving infinite varieties of beer (along with pasties), this may tempt you into an extended 'rest' stop.

Further east, Durlston Country Park is a great viewpoint and has exhibits giving insight into local geology and industry.

Other Routes

A shorter circuit of St Alban's Head can be completed from Worth Matravers.

This route could be extended by following the Priest's Way from ① down into Swanage and the seafront, and then returning along the SWCP through Durlston Country Park to rejoin at ③; much of this is surfaced, however.

Events

Poole Athletic Club's Beast is a popular and painfully hilly 19km trail race. It starts in Corfe Castle and loops out to St Alban's Head.

Chapel on St Alban's Head

Approaching St Alban's Head

Radar memorial on St Alban's Head

St Alban's Head

Winspit Quarry

Steps near St Alban's Head

Godlingston Heath

52 Studland Beach

Distance	13km (8 miles)	Ascent	150m (500ft)
Map	OS Landranger 195 OS Explorer OL15		
Navigation ●●○	Some care needed at junctions		
Terrain ●●●	All runnable, but numerous different surfaces		
Wet Feet ●●●	You cross several bogs!		
Start/Finish	Knoll Beach car park (National Trust) BH19 3AH/SZ 034 836		

Outstanding rough trails on every surface imaginable

Studland Beach is a glorious arc of sand, facing east ... an incredible place to be running at sunrise! Less well known and frequented is the stunning landscape behind it. Studland Heath National Nature Reserve will see you running through dunes, heath, bog and forest alongside a beautiful lake (the Little Sea). Godlingston Heath National Nature Reserve is similar terrain, rising in height to give stunning views of the beach, Poole Harbour and even the Isle of Wight. The Agglestone is encountered hereabouts, a prominent and solitary lump of sandstone; perhaps interrupt your run to climb it! The dash through the golf course is a real highlight, a narrow path winding through dense gorse over rough and constantly changing terrain ... you'll probably want to go back and do it again.

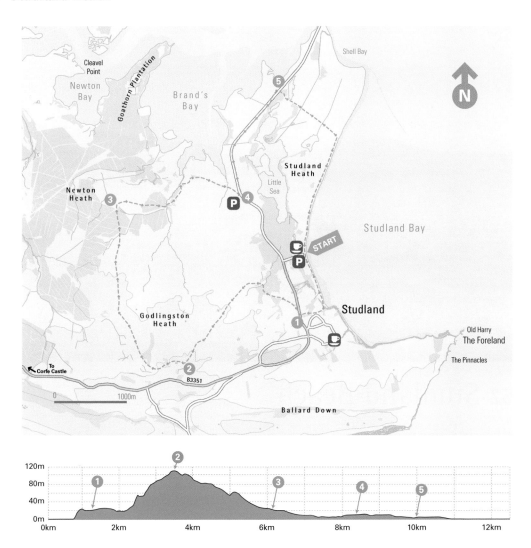

Route Description

🏃 START Turn right at the beach and run S on the sand for 700m until it ends. Follow the road uphill until a junction, then follow the footpath leading off right to the B3351. ❶ Cross the B3351, follow it right for 100m and take the track leading inland. Follow this to the end, then follow the bridleway ahead. After crossing a bridge, look for the Agglestone (large rock!) to your left. Take the next footpath leading left, follow it to the Agglestone. Continue uphill following a bridleway path past a crossroads to a golf course. ❷ Turn right on the first track reached in the golf course, after 100m a stone marker on the right is signposted 'Rempstone'; follow this small bridleway. After 100m it splits, stay left. Keep going ahead. After a descent across sandstone slabs, take the footpath off to the right (N), downhill towards the forest. Reaching the forest, continue ahead at two crossroads of tracks. ❸ At the third crossroads, turn right onto a bridleway and follow this for 650m to a bridge and ford. Cross the bridge, follow the left-hand track past a large barn. After 1.5km the B3351 is reached. ❹ Cross the B3351 and turn left along the bridleway. After 1.5km, a track joins from the right and the bridleway deteriorates. Cross the B3351 and

Studland Beach

follow the gravel pavement for 200m to a bus stop. ⑤ At the bus stop, cross the B3351 and follow the track through the woods. At the beach, turn right and run 1.5km back to the start.

Trip Planning

Studland Beach is hugely popular in summer, and mid-day on a hot weekend may not be the best time for this run. The early bird gets the worm, however …

The start car park belongs to the National Trust, membership or payment is required. Follow signs for 'Knoll Beach' off the B3351, which connects the Sandbanks Ferry to Corfe Castle. The ferry crosses the entrance to Poole Harbour and is cheap and regular. A cheapskate parking alternative is the gate entrance at BH19 3AH/SZ 025 843, ④ on the route.

The National Trust café at Knoll Beach serves good food, as does the Bankes Arms in Studland village. An ice cream van is seemingly permanently on station at the viewpoint at BH19 3AA/SZ 006 818, and this is a great place to survey the landscape you have just traversed.

Studland NNR

The Agglestone

Rempstone Forest

Other Routes

A diversion to Old Harry Rocks from ❶ and back will reward you with some wonderful chalk cliff scenery. It's also possible to continue up onto and along the ridge, if you need more of a hill fix. Rempstone Forest is briefly entered on this route – there are numerous trails to explore if you continue west to explore further (you *will* get lost).

Need more sand? Take the chain ferry across Poole Harbour's mouth and run Bournemouth Beach, 16km with groynes to Hengistbury Head.

Events

The 12km Studland Stampede covers similar ground to this route. Purbeck Runners organise the 5km Studland Fun Run on local trails. The 'Rempstone Roast' is a mountain bike/trail running duathlon in Rempstone Forest.

Pentridge Down

53 Pentridge Hill

Distance	10km (6 miles)	Ascent	175m (575ft)
Map	OS Landranger 184 OS Explorer 118		
Navigation ●●●	Numerous junctions, mostly signposted		
Terrain ●●●	Easy running surfaces, mild gradients		
Wet Feet ●●●	Can get muddy in places		
Start/Finish	Martin Down National Nature Reserve car park SP5 5RH/SU 037 201		

A mild run through prehistory, pristine meadows and rolling downland

A great little trail run on Dorset chalk hills which (for once) aren't near-vertical! The first part of this route passes a huge high earthwork which was actually a WWII-era firing range, before following Bokerley Ditch, a Bronze Age earthwork which was built up higher during the Dark Ages. This follows the county boundary and you're actually several metres into Hampshire at this point. You run along the edge of Martin Down National Nature Reserve; these wide meadows haven't been ploughed for 2,000 years and form a haven for wild flowers, insects and birds. The ridge along Pentridge Hill isn't too dramatic, but has wide views. Running behind the village of Pentridge at the base of the hill are traces of the remarkable Dorset Cursus, a 10km-long line of parallel earthen banks from the Neolithic era. What was it for? No one really has a clue.

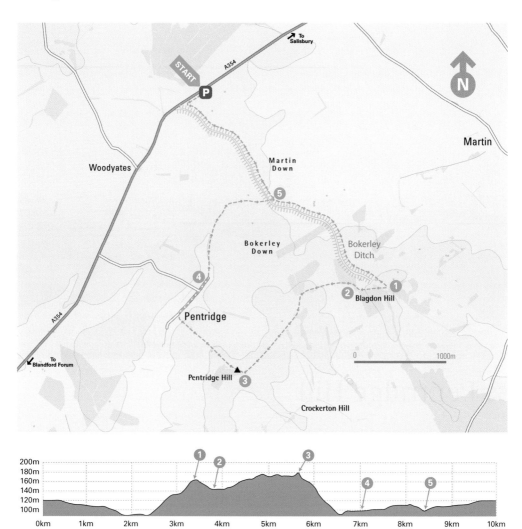

Route Description

START Take the path leading SW out of the far end of the car park. This joins the bridleway alongside Bokerley Ditch, turn left and follow this for 3km. ❶ When this bridleway reaches the top of the ridge, take the bridleway on the right into the woods. After 300m a T-junction is reached, turn right and then immediately turn left twice, through gates. ❷ Follow the bridleway for 500m W along the edge of a field, then turn left (SSW) onto the bridleway signposted left across the field. Follow this to the summit trig point after 1km. ❸ Take the footpath from the trig point leading NW steeply downhill into the village of Pentridge. Turn right and follow the road for 500m until it ends, then take the left-hand of the two bridleways it splits into. ❹ Follow the bridleway for 800m to a crossroads: turn right and follow this bridleway across Bokerley Ditch. ❺ Turn left and follow Bokerley Ditch back to the start.

Penbury Knoll

Trip Planning

The car park is located on the south side of the A354 Blandford-Salisbury road, 1km past Woodyates if heading towards Salisbury, 1.6km past Martin Drove End if heading towards Blandford. There is a height barrier. The car park is free and features information boards about Martin Down National Nature Reserve.

There are no facilities nearby. The village of Cranborne has the nearest shops and The Inn at Cranborne, as the pretentious name implies, is an expensive gastropub. Cheaper food is available from Cranborne Garden Centre's café.

Pentridge Hill

Other Routes

This run could be extended by starting from Cranborne, although this would involve some road time. You may also wish to divert away from Bokerley Ditch in the first stretch, to further explore the meadows of Martin Down NNR.

Pentridge

Pentridge Down

Bournemouth and Poole trail running

Poole runners are well served; just across the Poole Harbour chain ferry is Studland Beach (Route 52) and there is also Upton Country Park bordering Holes Bay in Poole Harbour. The latter is connected to the rough trails of Upton Heath by a surfaced track. Canford Heath is similar but larger, located on the northern edge of Poole.

Bournemouth's main draw is possibly the beach; 16km of sand running is a bracing way to start to any day, if you don't mind jumping or dodging a few groynes. At the

Bournemouth Pier

eastern extremity, Hengistbury Head has some interesting trails (many surfaced) with great views.

Around the two towns, there are some decent spots to visit. To the west, Wareham Forest sprawls over a huge area of trees, heath and bog, criss-crossed by bridleways and paths. To the north, the National Trust's Kingston Lacy estate (including Badbury Rings) offers a fine escape from the conurbation and The Stour Valley Way is mostly unsurfaced along the river down to Christchurch Harbour.

Heading up the River Avon Valley, both Avon Heath Country Park and Moors Valley Country Park have marked trails to follow through forestry plantation.

South Wiltshire

The northern half of this area is Salisbury Plain, a vast expanse of gently rolling downs with the occasional steep scarp. The military presence on the Plain since the nineteenth century has on the one hand restricted public access, but on the other ensured that there are plenty of undeveloped open spaces. The southern half of this area is the Cranborne Chase and West Wiltshire Downs Area of Outstanding Natural Beauty, characterised by a range of long steep-sided ridges. Both halves are criss-crossed by long die-straight chalky byways and bridleways ... ideal for trail runners looking to cover ground and clock up mileage!

View over Cranborne Chase (Route 57)

Beech Clump

White Sheet Down

54 Stourhead

Distance		20km (12.5 miles)	Ascent	400m (1300ft)
Map		OS Landranger 183 OS Explorer 142/143		
Navigation	●●○	Inconveniently spread across two OS Explorer maps		
Terrain	●●○	Chalk tracks, sunken byways, forestry roads and parkland		
Wet Feet	●●○	Muddy byway lanes, best when dry or frozen		
Start/Finish		White Sheet Lane car park BA12 6QQ/ST 797 350		

Chalk downs, sunken lanes, forest and a stately home

Stourhead is a popular attraction run by the National Trust, comprising a Palladian mansion built in the 1740s and stunning landscaped gardens. This run explores the landscapes around the 1072 hectare Stourhead Estate, negotiating a wide enough variety of terrain to keep you from boredom.

White Sheet Hill rises sharply above the vale, giving you a panoramic overview of the Stourhead Estate. The round earthwork encountered at the top of the climb is a Neolithic causewayed enclosure, a very early religious site; it is truly ancient, having been dated to 3595 BC! The way back across the vale follows a series of sunken tracks, which make for wonderful secluded running ... as long as it isn't really wet, because then they flood. The latter portion of this run drops over a ridge into the woodlands lining the Somerset border, looping behind Stourhead. You eventually run right past the front door of Stourhead's grand mansion.

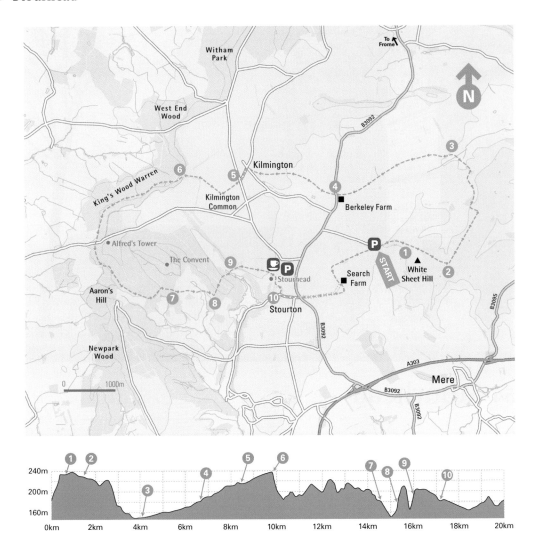

Route Description

🏃 START ▸ Cross the stile at the end of the car park and follow the path up the ridge. At the top, cross the field to join the bridleway track. ❶ Follow the bridleway track E for 800m until you see gates either side. ❷ Turn left to follow the bridleway along a field beside a fence. After 1km, take the track to the left leading downhill towards the woods. At the bottom of the hill, pass through Rodmead Farm and then take the bridleway signposted left through a gate. ❸ Follow the bridleway across two fields to a lane. When this lane bends right after 250m, take the byway track (Field Lane) branching off left. Take the right-hand branch when it forks after 1km, cross the B3092 shortly after onto another byway (Harepit Lane). ❹ Follow the byway for 850m to a lane, turn right onto it and then left at a crossroads. In 300m the lane reaches a T-junction: cross the road and take the bridleway track ahead. ❺ Follow the bridleway track to a field, cross this and then take the footpath to the right along the hedge line. This joins a line of trees leading you to King's Wood. ❻ Follow the footpath track downhill into the forest and stay on it, ignoring any side branches. Cross the road after 2.5km and keep going ahead, passing a crossroads after 1km and turning right at a T-junction after another

Stourhead Estate

kilometre. **7** When the footpath leaves the forest, follow it to the footpath track at the valley bottom and turn right onto it. Take a footpath on the left, just before a gate. **8** Follow the footpath up through woods, then down again to a causeway between ponds. Cross the fence opposite onto a track. **9** Take the footpath leading left (uphill), 30m along the track. When you reach the parkland at the top, follow the track going right. Pass in front of the mansion and follow the track to High Street in Stourton. **10** Turn left and follow High Street for 400m to the B3092. Cross and continue ahead along the farm road. When this bends left into Search Farm, keep going ahead on the bridleway. After 200m turn left and follow this bridleway through the farm until you reach a T-junction. Turn right and follow this back to the start.

Alfred's Tower

Lake at Stourhead

Trip Planning

The suggested car park is located at the end of White Sheet Lane and is free. Another alternative is to use the National Trust Stourhead car park BA12 6QF/ST 779 340 off the High Street in Stourton, but this is busy and will require membership.

Refreshments are available on the Stourhead Estate at the café beside the Stourhead car park, and also at the Spread Eagle Inn on High Street, in front of the gardens. Both are close to the route, should you fancy a break.

White Sheet Down

Other Routes

With a little inclusion of road running using the lane at ❺, it is possible to tackle the east and west halves of this route as two separate runs. It's also possible to extend the loop northwards by carrying on ahead at ❸ to take in the shapely hill Long Knoll; the track leading up to this is disappointingly now tarmac.

If you enjoyed the woodland parts, similar footpaths continue for many kilometres north, partly following the Macmillan Way. The woods closer to Stourhead have many more footpaths to explore; a loop through the woods up to Alfred's Tower is a popular short run. See the National Trust website for a map and suggestions.

Stourhead Gardens

Although this run passes through the estate, it does not take in the celebrated landscaped gardens. A short diversion to the front gates in Stourton during your run will give you a good view, but direct access is for ticket-holders only. It's recommended to visit after your run and take a proper stroll around; free to National Trust members, of course.

Stourhead Gardens

Bratton Camp

55 The Imber Range Perimeter Path

Distance	48km (30 miles)	Ascent	800m (2625ft)
Map	OS Landranger 173, 183, 184 OS Explorer 143, 130		
Navigation ●●●	Fully signposted		
Terrain ●●●	Steep climbs in the latter half. A wide variety of surfaces		
Wet Feet ●●●	Some parts heavy going when wet, pick a dry day!		
Start/Finish	White Horse car park BA13 4TA/ST 899 513		

An epic and varied circuit of a military firing range

The Imber Range Perimeter Path is a way-marked long-distance trail route which (the name gives the game away) literally follows the perimeter of the Imber Live Firing Range. This huge undulating swathe of Salisbury Plain is closed to and hidden from the public. The IRPP mostly follows high ground and scarps with extensive views. This bucolic scenery is occasionally tempered by the distant sound of machine gun fire, or low-flying Chinook helicopters, but it all adds interest.

The IRPP starts off by heading east from the Westbury White Horse along wide chalk roads (some tarmac interludes) which are fast but borderline tedious. Variety kicks in when you turn south, with narrower paths and occasional heavy going (due to the poor synergy between wet chalk and tank tracks). A quirky highlight is the 'Bosnian' village, a full size replica built for urban warfare training. The author ran up to the entrance for a closer look, but backtracked slowly after he noticed the sniper monitoring us from a high window ...

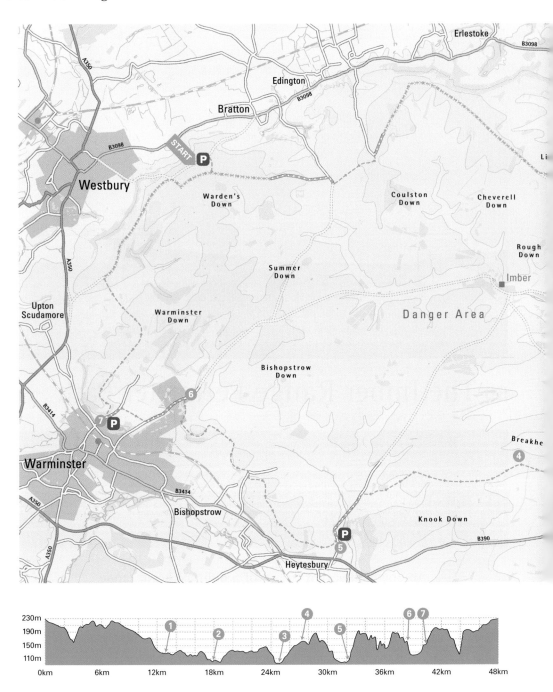

From Chitterne, the IRPP's second half bends back north following the rim of Salisbury Plain. This is the hilliest section, with at least three hillforts to ascend ... hopefully you kept something in reserve.
Running/staggering the IRPP in one day is a hefty challenge for any runner, but there are regular road intersections where you can meet a support crew or bail out, or divide your run into more than one day.

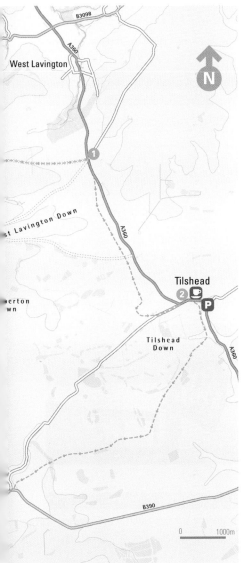

West Lavington

B3098

A360

st Lavington Down

A360

erton wn

Tilshead

Tilshead Down

A360

B390

0   1000m

Route Description

This route is waymarked throughout: look for the white square signs with a cannon insignia and the words 'Imber Range Path'. This description simply outlines the main features of the route. START Run 13km E along wide tracks to Gore Cross, a small village. ❶ Turn right onto the A360 and follow it 160m to a byway leading off right. Follow this byway S for 5km to Tilshead (the route has changed from older OS maps). ❷ Join the A360 in Tilshead and turn off right onto a byway after just 150m. Follow signs S and then W for 4km to the Bosnian village, continue another 3km W to Chitterne. ❸ Follow the B390 for 450m through Chitterne, turn off on the right just before a left bend, follow this byway up Breakheart Hill(!). ❹ When you reach the perimeter fence, follow it W for 2.3km to a footpath on the left which descends steeply downhill (there is also the option of taking the adjacent track). Turn left onto the lane at East Hill Farm and follow this 1.3km downhill to where a footpath leads uphill on the right. ❺ Follow the path for 6km N, climbing and descending five hilltops. ❻ When you descend to reach a lane (Sack Hill), follow this downhill for 1km and turn right onto Elm Hill, follow this to a T-junction and turn left (downhill) for 400m to a lane on the right signposted for West Wilts Golf Club. The path is hidden to the left of the first house reached up this lane. ❼ Run the final 8km N to the White Horse car park! After 4km and just after Field Barn you have the choice of turning off right to steeply ascend Upton Cow Down (do it!) or of a longer ascent by continuing ahead.

Trip Planning

White Horse car park is free and is located off Port Way, the lane leading steeply uphill from Bratton. Directly alongside is the Westbury White Horse, carved below the ramparts of Bratton Camp hillfort. Other points (not an exhaustive list) to begin or finish are Gore Cross SN10 4NE/SU 008 509 at 13km ❶, Tilshead SP3 4RY/SU 030 479 at 18km ❷, Chitterne BA12 0LJ/ST 990 438 at 25km ❸, Heytesbury BA12 0HG/ST 929 431 at 33km ❺ and Warminster BA12 0AU/ST 878 458 at 41km ❼.

Near Chitterne

Along the IRPP, there is only one option for refuelling; the Rose and Crown Pub in Tilshead at 18km. There is also a Londis supermarket in Tilshead, 200m off-route on the A360. The King's Head in Chitterne at 25km is currently closed, this may change.

A 1:20,000 hand-drawn map of the IRPP is available (ISBN 0993505716). We found this confusing; easier (for runners, at least) to just follow the signage and keep track of overall progress using an OS map. OS Explorer maps have the route marked. A detailed route description (anti-clockwise) can also be downloaded from the MOD website.

A bivvy en route to break up this epic is an appealing possibility, but you would have to be very discreet and bed down well clear of the military perimeter!

Other Routes

Above are suggestions for start/finish points to tackle shorter sections of the IRPP. If cherry-picking, the author's suggestion for finest section (best scenery, best trails) is the c17km from Heytesbury ⑤ back to White Horse car park. By happy coincidence, this is the only section where public transport makes shuttling easy; the 265 bus takes half an hour to go from Westbury back to Heytesbury, naturally you'd have to run downhill into Westbury first.

Events

The Imber Ultra starts and finishes in Westbury, organised by the Westbury Rotary Club. It faithfully follows the IRPP and totals at 53km. The White Horse Gallop is an 8-mile race from Westbury including parts of the IRPP. Easier again is the Hilly Helmet Challenge, a 4-mile loop out of Westbury.

Imber Range Perimeter Path signage

The Army and Salisbury Plain

The Army have been training on Salisbury Plain since 1898. The 'Defence Training Estate' encompasses about half of Salisbury Plain's 780 square kilometres of chalk downlands, with about a quarter of this permanently closed to the public. Live firing takes place on the vast majority of days, yet ironically the low population and limited farming mean that the DTE has excellent biodiversity and that the flora and fauna are in good health. The DTE stretches about 40km west to east, with three distinct training areas, outlined on OS maps by red Danger Area text and red arrows;

* **Imber Ranges** are westernmost. They are permanently closed off to the public but are surrounded by the Imber Range Perimeter Path.

* **Larkhill Ranges** are central. They are criss-crossed by bridleways and byways which are freely accessible when firing is not taking place.

* **Bulford Ranges** are east of the River Avon and are smaller than the other two, with the same access situation as Larkhill Range. However, there is a large area around Bulford marked as 'Managed Access' on OS maps (the red Danger Area arrows are not filled in), where access is open even while exercises are underway. Stay on the paths, and don't pick *anything* up! Flags and signs warn when firing is taking place. Firing dates and times can be obtained from a recorded message service; 01980 674763.

New Wardour Castle

56 The Wardour Castles

Distance	5.5km (3.5 miles)	Ascent	100m (330ft)
Map	OS Landranger 184 OS Explorer 118		
Navigation ●●●	Clearly signposted		
Terrain ●●●	Gentle undulations around farm tracks, forestry roads and fields		
Wet Feet ●●●	Some mucky farmyards		
Start/Finish	Old Wardour Castle car park SP3 6RR/ST 938 264		

Easy circuit via two very different castles

This is a lovely short run around the old estate of Wardour Castle with a mix of farmland tracks and grassy fields underfoot. Actually there are two castles; Old Wardour Castle and Wardour Castle. Old Wardour Castle is the impressive medieval ruin where you start your run, and Wardour Castle isn't really a castle, actually it's a huge Palladian mansion built when Old Wardour Castle became a bit too draughty. Amusingly, you can run right past the front door of this very exclusive private residence. This run is perfect in mid-week when you will have the valley to yourself. It also makes a nice combination with a family visit to explore the castle ruins. Is the distance too short for your taste? No problem, knock off a second lap and try to beat your first time around.

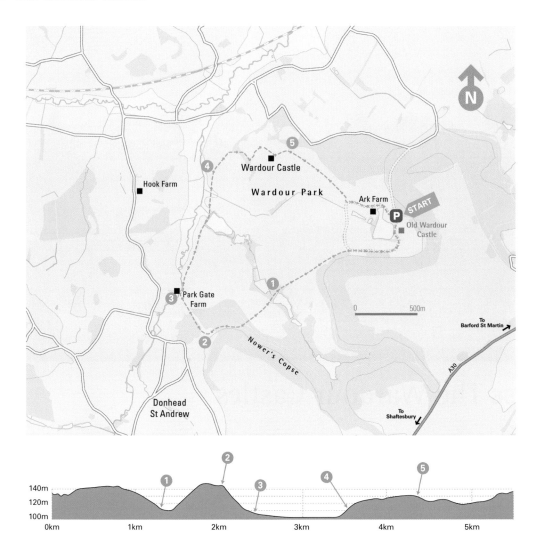

Route Description

START From the car park, follow the footpath track between the ruined castle and the lake. Continue ahead following footpath signs, through woods and then across fields. **1** Pass between two ponds, then ascend ahead to a forest and at a crossroads take the footpath track leading ahead. **2** After passing a house on your right, take the path on the right leading downhill into woods. Continue ahead on the footpath to Park Gate Farm. **3** Pass through Park Gate Farm and follow the signed footpath. When you see Westfield Farm ahead, aim left of the buildings to a stile and cross the road. **4** Ascend to the treeline and then follow the yellow markers around the large house to Wardour Castle (a larger house). The correct footpath follows the drive crossing directly in front of the house to a gate. **5** Follow the footpath track SE for 600m and then bear left into Ark Farm. Pass through the farm to the car park.

Old Wardour Castle

Trip Planning

The start car park is located at the end of a track leading off Nightingale Lane, with clear English Heritage signposts for Old Wardour Castle. The car park is free, even if you are not entering the castle. It is also possible to access this route from the village of Donhead St Andrew, adding 1.6km to your run. The only good parking is at The Forester Pub SP7 9EX/ST 916 248 (seek permission).

The entrance shop at Old Wardour Castle has a tea/coffee machine (eurgh) otherwise the nearest food and drink is available at The Forester Pub in Donhead St Andrew, which has a Michelin Bib Gourmand Award, so probably doesn't do cheesy chips. Shaftesbury is just over ten minutes away and has many shops, pubs and cafés.

You get a reasonable view of Old Wardour Castle on this route, but is it still recommended to have a proper look around it afterwards. English Heritage members enter free, otherwise there is a charge. The ruins are much larger and more complex than you might guess from outside, with numerous floors and staircases to investigate.

Other Routes

A longer loop, with some road time, can be completed by taking one of the footpaths from Wardour Castle ❹ out to Nightingale Lane, and returning across the hill behind Old Wardour Castle along Park Pale, to descend to Old Wardour Castle. You can also extend by starting from Donhead St Andrew (above).

Along the trail

Old Wardour Castle interior

Ascending Win Green

57 Win Green

Distance	17km (10.5 miles)	Ascent	350m (1150ft)
Map	OS Landranger 184 OS Explorer 118		
Navigation ●●●	Well-signposted throughout, easy to follow trails but numerous junctions		
Terrain ●●●	Grassy fields, wide estate tracks, rutted byways, several steep descents		
Wet Feet ●●●	Well drained tracks, muddy patches aren't too hard to avoid		
Start/Finish	Tollard Royal SP5 5PP/ST 944 178		

Through Cranborne Chase's forests to a lofty viewpoint

Win Green is the highest point in Cranborne Chase at 277m, offering epic views across Wiltshire, Dorset, Hampshire and beyond. The running around Win Green can be a bit 'safe' following wide and firm estate tracks, but there are enough intermittent patches of winding or rough pathway to keep you awake.

This route starts in the quiet village of Tollard Royal (the 'Royal' appellation refers to the former presence of a hunting lodge nearby) and leads through the forests of the Rushmore Estate, before turning uphill for a long climb onto the summit plateau. A little bit of tarmac time is unavoidable (although – whisper it – there are unofficial paths in the woods alongside) before you join the byway leading to Win Green itself. The descent back to Tollard Royal is rapid and direct, with a hurtling descent into a dry chalk valley.

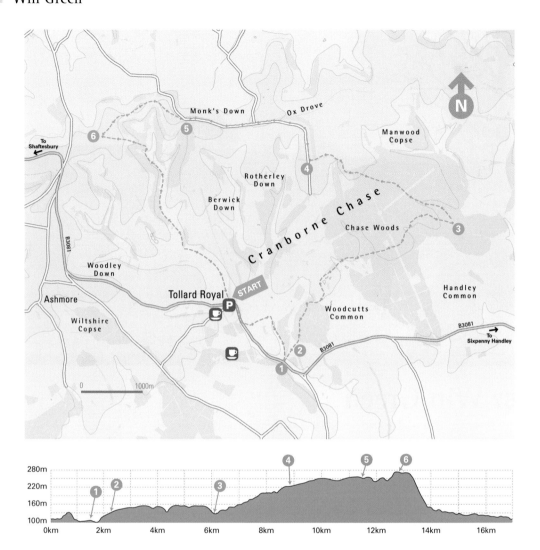

Route Description

🚶 **START** Follow the road downhill from the village centre for 350m to a gate on the left which is the start of a footpath. Follow this uphill and then downhill into the next valley (Tinkley Bottom). Turn right and follow the footpath track downhill to the road. **1** Cross the estate drive (not the road) and take the footpath opposite. Follow it uphill across an estate track to another track along the edge of the woods. Cross the track and take the footpath track leading ahead into the woods (there are three tracks in close proximity, make sure you take the one signposted as a footpath). **2** Follow the footpath ahead for 4km, keeping to the footpath signage and ignoring any turn-offs (after 1km it reaches a golf course and follows the edge of this before entering the woods again). When the footpath descends steeply to cross a bridleway track (not to be confused with the bridleway crossed 1km before), turn left (uphill) onto this bridleway. **3** Follow the bridleway track (Longcroft Road) uphill for 2.8km to meet a lane. **4** Turn right and follow the lane for 2.5km along the ridgetop until it begins to turn downhill; on the left is a byway track (Ox Drove) continuing along the ridge. ❺ Follow the byway track 1.2km until a gate on the left signposted 'Win Green' and go through this to ascend the last 300m to the summit. ❻ From the summit trig point, cross the green to the parking area. Turn left (E) to follow the footpath over a stile and then steeply downhill to the valley floor. At the bottom turn right and follow the footpath down the valley (Ashcombe Bottom) back to Tollard Royal. When the valley splits two ways, be careful to stay on the footpath and follow the valley to the left, rather than the byway track along the valley to the right.

Trip Planning

In Tollard Royal, there are various roadside parking options but the most convenient is the small area right in front of a pond where the B3081 bends south. Another possibility is to start up high at Win Green car park SP5 5QG/ST 923 204 ❻, although this would mean ending your run with a long climb.

Tollard Royal is not the sort of place where you're likely to find a Spar. The very upmarket King John Inn prides itself on catering to Shooting Parties and even offers to supply you with a 'dedicated Shoot Butler'. However, just south of the village are the Larmer Tree Gardens, a popular attraction with a café open for part of the week; you don't need to enter the gardens to visit the café. The Larmer Tree Races, a running festival, are hosted here annually.

Other Routes

If you just want to ascend and descend Win Green (9km), follow the byway track which leads directly north out of Win Green (at the same point this route ends) for a 3km grinding ascent to reach Ox Grove at ❺.

Extending this route is possible by continuing further E from ❸ and taking one of the numerous later left turns to ascend the hill. Those looking to run major distance may wish to head 10km east along the ridge (Ox Drove byway) to link up with Route 58.

Ox Drove

Descending Win Green

Leaving Tollard Royal

Rotherley Bottom

Longcroft Road

Chase Woods

Events

White Star Running organise the Larmer Tree Races, ranging from 10K to marathon distance around the nearby Larmer Tree estate grounds.

Cranborne Chase Area of Outstanding Natural Beauty

Routes 53, 54, 56, 57 and 58 are all within Cranborne Chase AONB. The Chase is a thousand square kilometres of rolling and often steep-sided chalk downs extending into Dorset, Wiltshire, Hampshire and Somerset, protected as an Area of Outstanding Natural Beauty. Much of the Chase is a huge plateau incised with deep valleys, with remnants of ancient forest clinging to the sides.

A 'Chase' is a Royal hunting ground; following the Norman Conquest, these lands were requisitioned by William the Conqueror for his wife Matilda. The area is rich in prehistoric remains, and it was here that nineteenth-century estate owner Augustus Pitt Rivers originated the methodology of modern archaeology through excavating sites on his own lands.

Fovant Down

58 The Fovant Badges

Distance	28km (17.5 miles)	**Ascent**	450m (1475ft)
Map	OS Landranger 184 OS Explorer 130		
Navigation ●●●	Clear tracks, but a distinct lack of signage		
Terrain ●●●	Easy underfoot on stony byways and firm bridleways, some mild climbs		
Wet Feet ●●●	Avoid in the wet, when the byways flood		
Start/Finish	Fovant Badges Viewpoint SP3 5JF/SU 011 288		

Solitude and fast running on endless drove roads

A series of long chalk ridges and valleys radiate westwards from Salisbury, topped by ancient 'drove roads' used to herd cattle to market. This hinterland where Cranborne Chase and Salisbury Plain blur together sees few visitors; in trips to explore and run this route, the author did not meet a single person away from the roads.

This run begins and ends beneath the Fovant Badges, regimental insignia carved from the chalk hillside during the First World War. You climb up and traverse the firm and level byway atop the memorials, as well as the rather less firm and level byway topping the ridge opposite across the River Ebble valley. The hills are green, the views expansive, the going is easy (as long as the byways are dry!), and you will likely have the place to yourself. What's not to like?

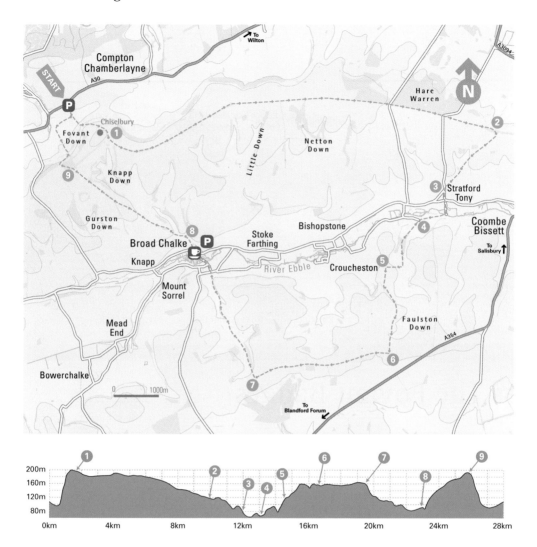

Route Description

🏃 START Cross the A31 to the pavement, go 150m W to a crossroads with a bridleway. Turn left and follow the bridleway track 550m uphill to an old quarry. Take the footpath leading left up the hillside. At the top, follow the earthworks to a byway track and turn left onto it. ❶ Follow the byway for 8km E, going ahead at all junctions. After you cross the second surfaced road, the tarmac byway passes Salisbury Racecourse. A muddy section follows, and (1.1km from the road crossing) a track leads off to the right. ❷ Follow the track – which becomes a lane – for 150m and take the bridleway on the right. Follow this downhill for 1.6km to a lane. ❸ Turn left onto the lane and follow it downhill and straight ahead at a crossroad. When the lane splits three ways, take the right-hand branch signposted for the church. Cross the River Ebble and take the signposted footpath opposite the church entrance. This leads 50m to a bridleway, turn right onto this and follow it to some houses. ❹ Pass the houses and turn left (uphill) on a concreted byway. After 350m go ahead at a crossroads, and then directly after take the byway to the left (the concreted track becomes a private drive). After 750m the byway turns right at Throope Bottom Cottages; follow it uphill to a bridleway. **5** Turn left (uphill) onto the bridleway and follow it 400m uphill to the junction with a bridleway track (Faulston Drove). Turn left onto this bridleway track and follow it to a T-junction at Faulstone Down Farm. **6** Turn right (W) onto the byway track. After 2km, you reach a T-junction. Turn right onto a farm track and then immediately left again to keep on the byway. After another kilometre, turn right at a crossroads with a bridleway track. **7** Follow the bridleway track downhill through the valley of Church Bottom to Broad Chalke village. Continue ahead on the road through the village to the Queen's Head pub, where you turn left and then immediately right following North Street. At a left bend, take the track ahead signposted for Chalk Pyt Farm. At the farm, take the left-hand of two bridleways, leading W. **8** Follow the bridleway path uphill. After 3km you reach a crossroads with a byway road. Cross the byway and take the byway path signposted as 'farm vehicles only'. **9** Head downhill on the byway path and take the bridleway on the right after 270m. This leads to the bottom of the hill and beside fields to Fovant. When you reach buildings, turn right onto a bridleway leading back to the start of your run.

Knowle Hill

Gurston Down

Throope Bottom

Trip Planning

Fovant Badges Viewpoint is simply a layby along the A30. Should this not suit, limited roadside parking is possible around the corner in Fovant, or consider starting from the village of Broad Chalke; this latter option means missing the Badges, however.

Fovant has a village shop, but the pub is currently boarded up. However, the Queen's Head in Broad Chalke is open for business and rather pleasant.

Other Routes

This loop can be easily truncated by following any of the bridleways descending to the right (south) off the byway after **1** and then following them through to the opposite ridge. On the other hand, it can be extended by up to 20km by simply heading along the ridgetop byways to the west. The southerly ridge culminates at 277m Win Green, highest point on Cranborne Chase (Route 57).

The Fovant Badges

Gurston Down

The Fovant Badges

The Fovant Badges were created by locally garrisoned soldiers waiting to be sent to France during the First World War, each representing a distinct regimental badge. The first was carved out of the chalk in 1916 and around twenty followed, although only five of the original badges survive at Fovant today, alongside several later additions. Lest you imagine that the badges were just lazy graffiti, bear in mind that each needed around fifty tons of chalk transported uphill to fill their outlines in!

The Fovant Badges are now listed as both official war memorials and Scheduled Ancient Monuments. They are maintained by the Fovant Badges Society. In 2016 the 'poppy' badge was newly added to commemorate the centenary of the Battle of the Somme.

Fovant Badges

Stonehenge

59 Stonehenge

Distance	19km (12 miles)	Ascent	225m (740ft)
Map	OS Landranger 184 OS Explorer 130		
Navigation ●●●	Route mostly obvious and signposted		
Terrain ●●●	Mild gradients on chalk tracks and grasslands, some tarmac		
Wet Feet ●●●	Salisbury Plain mud		
Start/Finish	Bonnymead Park, Amesbury SP4 7BB/SU 149 411		

Immersion in prehistory via chalk tracks and a sacred river

Stonehenge! Few of the crowds pre-booking an expensive visit realise that you can get really close to the stones on the adjacent National Trust land, for free, at any time. The iconic standing stones are just the central component of a vast landscape of prehistoric monuments, which have been given World Heritage Site status. This route starts by following the River Avon downstream; archaeologists have recently discovered that this modest chalk stream was used as a ceremonial approach route to Stonehenge. After crossing the river, a gradual ascent onto Salisbury Plain passes between rows of Bronze Age burial mounds (thousands of years younger than Stonehenge!) before reaching the stones themselves. The route then follows The Avenue, the ancient approach to Stonehenge from the river. The final kilometre is on roads through Amesbury, but you won't mind by then.

A dawn run will allow you to experience the stones in solitude ... unless it happens to be the Summer Solstice.

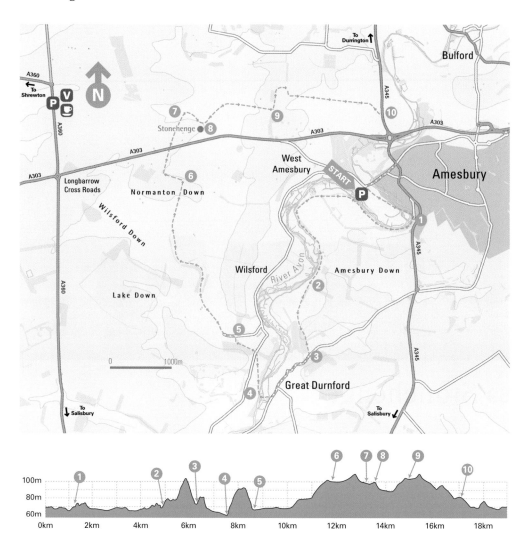

Route Description

START Follow Recreation Road out of the car park to the junction with Church Street, take the track leading off immediately to your right. Follow this footpath ahead and cross a footbridge after 900m. **1** Turn right onto the footpath along the riverbank. After 500m a bridleway leads uphill, but stay on the footpath and keep going ahead at junctions. **2** After 2.5km, the footpath leaves the river and heads uphill, shortly joining a bridleway; follow this for 1.1km to a lane. **3** Turn right onto the lane and follow it into Great Durnford. 80m after passing the Great Horse Inn, take the bridleway on your right across the river. **4** Follow the bridleway on the right uphill to a road. Cross the road and follow the footpath ahead, which leads downhill to a crossroad of tracks. **5** Turn left at the crossroads and follow the byway track up the valley. After 1.5km pass through Springbottom Farm and keep right at a junction, to stay on the byway. Continue uphill and after passing between burial mounds after 1.5km, leave the byway on the left via a National Trust gateway. **6** Cross the field along a path and turn right onto another byway track. After 400m cross the A303 (Careful!) and continue another 400m ahead to the entrance to Stonehenge.

7 Continue ahead for 80m past the entrance to Stonehenge and pass through the National Trust gateway on the right. Follow the fence to Stonehenge – enjoy!
8 Follow the path leading downhill from Stonehenge ('The Avenue'). After 500m, turn right at an information board and follow the path through a gate and 770m uphill to a gate between two clumps of trees. **9** Turn left onto the bridleway and follow it around a corner to a T-junction. Turn right here and continue 1.6km to Countess Road. **10** Cross Countess Road and follow it downhill, take the underpass beneath the A303 and continue uphill to the traffic lights. Turn right onto High Street and continue ahead 300m onto Church Street to reach Recreation Road.

Trip Planning

The car park in Bonnymead Park is free to use. There aren't any other public car parks on the route, although there is plenty of roadside space in Great Durnford if you need an alternative.

Amesbury is well equipped with shops and eating places. Another option is the pleasant but busy café at the Stonehenge Visitor Centre (nice pasties) which is open to those without entrance tickets.

A 'proper' visit to Stonehenge is arguably unnecessary after running this route, however you will get a slightly better perspective on the stones from the other side of the fence and the new Visitor Centre gives an excellent introduction to the significance of this landscape. It is located 2.5km west at SP4 7DE/SU 098 428. Shuttle buses take you to the stones at your allotted time. English Heritage and (pre-booked) National Trust members go free, everyone else pays a hefty sum.

Ham Wood

The Stonehenge Avenue

Stonehenge

Other Routes

Continuing north along the byway at Stonehenge **7** will take you through Larkhill barracks and out onto Salisbury Plain, where numerous byways criss-cross the open landscape, allowing an extension loop before returning via Durrington to rejoin the route just after **9**. About 3km north of Larkhill is a firing range, note the warning signs!

Normanton Down

Events

The LDWA and Amesbury Walkers organise the 10km Woodhenge Womble and the 10km/20km/30km/40km Stonehenge Stomp, and the 5km/10km/20km/30km/42km Amesbury Amble; many runners (including the author) participate. The Neolithic Marathon starts at Avebury stone circle (Route 63) and crosses Salisbury Plain to end at Stonehenge. There is also an accompanying half marathon. These are run by Wiltshire Wildlife Trust.

Restoring the Stonehenge landscape

Notable changes have taken place around Stonehenge in recent times, and your OS map may well be out of date. The old car park and the A344 beside the stones have been completely removed, part of ongoing efforts to restore the ancient landscape. Interminable debates and public enquiries about what to do about the far-too-close A303 road seem (at time of writing) to have decided upon diverting the road underground past the stones. Check up-to-date online sources of OS mapping like Bing Maps to see if any changes have occurred impacting upon this route.

North Wiltshire

Much of Wiltshire's northern half is green and rolling downland like its southern counterpart; however there are key differences. The Vale of Pewsey separates South Wiltshire's Salisbury Plain from the North Wessex Downs which are also chalk hills but generally higher and steeper. Most of Wiltshire's quirky white horses are found here. The landscape is peppered with prehistoric earthworks, with the truly ancient Ridgeway track snaking through. Variation is offered by the glades of huge Savernake Forest, whilst across the River Avon to the west, the limestone Cotswold Hills begin to announce their presence.

On the Ridgeway (Route 65)

By Brook valley

Castle Combe

60 Castle Combe

Distance	9.5km (6 miles)	Ascent	275m (900ft)
Map	OS Landranger 173 OS Explorer 156		
Navigation ●●●	Few junctions to negotiate, well signposted		
Terrain ●●●	Road, dirt paths, firm tracks, grass, stony bridleways, sometimes steep		
Wet Feet ●●●	Pretty muddy for much of the year		
Start/Finish	Castle Combe car park SN14 7HH/ST 845 777		

Secluded Cotswold valleys around a picture-postcard village

Castle Combe is a tiny village which often wins 'Prettiest Village in England' contests and is basically a default location for film directors wanting a quaint backdrop; recent productions include *Stardust* and Steven Spielberg's *War Horse.* This run differs markedly from the others in North Wiltshire because these are the fringes of the Cotswold Hills, the first clue being the honey-brown colouring of the limestone buildings. What is on offer here is a lovely outing along and around the wooded valley of By Brook, a bubbling clear stream with mills dotted along its length. The trails are often a delight to run; gradual ascents or descents, lined by pollarded trees either side. The hills are modest in size, certainly compared to the Cotswold giants you'll find lurking in the Gloucestershire section of this book. There are a few steep bits to boost your heart rate, but mostly this route offers just enough masochism to justify the leisurely cream tea or pub lunch that you are going to enjoy back in the village afterwards.

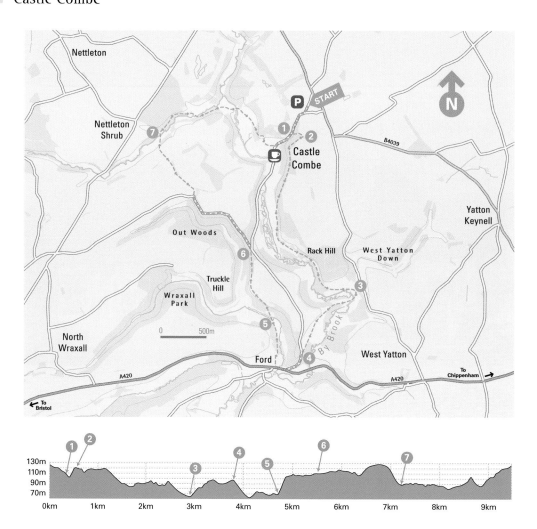

Route Description

START Turn right (downhill) on the road out of the car park. Bear right at the first junction and continue 275m downhill on the road until you see a bridleway signposted on the left. ❶ Ascend this bridleway steeply, ignoring the first footpath on the right. Take the second footpath leading off right, found at the top of the hill. ❷ Follow this footpath ahead. After 900m it descends and merges with another footpath, continue ahead. After another 500m the footpath goes right but the trail continues ahead as a bridleway, stay on this and go ahead for another 800m until a junction is reached among houses. ❸ Turn right, following the bridleway past a house on the left, and then uphill. After 500m the path splits in a field, take the left footpath (R is the bridleway, continuing uphill) which contours along the field to a lane. ❹ Turn left and follow the lane downhill to the A420. Turn right and follow this 100m to a track between houses on your right. Take this and follow it to the end, where it becomes a footpath leading up the valley. ❺ After crossing the stream via a bridge, ascend following the footpath through the woods to emerge at the rim of a hill. Follow the footpath along this until you reach a lane. ❻ Turn left onto the lane and follow it for 1km to a sharp left bend. Take the bridleway on the right and follow this across the hill and steeply downhill to a stone

Parsonage Wood

slab bridge. **7** Cross the stone slab bridge and turn right to follow the footpath leading along the stream. Follow this through a golf course and into Castle Combe village. When you see a footpath on the right leading down steps, descend these into the village centre or continue ahead to join the road close to the car park.

By Brook valley

Trip Planning

The car park is free (at the request of villagers, who suffered illegal parking problems when it charged) although Wiltshire Council are discussing reintroducing charges. The car park and indeed the whole village can get busy at weekends, although the trails remain quiet. Consider an early or late arrival at such times. There is also limited roadside parking just downhill along the road into the village.

Bridge over Broadmead Brook

Castle Combe is famed for the stalls that villagers put out or run in their front rooms, but lacks a shop actually selling anything useful. Neighbouring Yatton Keynell (2km towards Chippenham) helpfully has a combined Post Office and grocer's. There are two main choices for refreshments within the village; the White Hart Inn is quite pleasant and welcoming, or alternately try the Castle Combe Tea Rooms for a slightly surreal experience of English village life (the tea rooms are in a private home); booking is needed.

Castle Combe

Bridleway above Castle Combe

Other Routes

An extension loop of about 7km can be made by crossing the A420 just after ❹ and following the Macmillan Way to Slaughterford and plotting a course via footpaths and bridleways to North Wraxall.

Events

Chippenham Harriers' Slaughterford 9 is a 9-mile trail race following a loop, located a short distance down the By Brook valley.

The Cotswolds Area of Outstanding Natural Beauty

Routes 60, 68, 69 and 70 (but not Route 67, Cotswold Water Park!) are all within the Cotswolds AONB. Its 2050 square kilometres make it the largest AONB outside Scotland and the second largest protected area in England (behind the Lake District). The landscape is unmistakeable; gently rolling hills and ever-so-slightly-twee villages. The underlying geology is oolitic limestone formed through the Jurassic Period, 201–145 million years ago. Oolites are small 'eggs' of calcium carbonate that precipitated on the margins of the shallow, tropical Tethys Ocean. This honey-coloured building stone is seen everywhere, in bridges, houses and walls.

Trail runners will find no shortage of undulating footpaths to explore in the region, but the highlight in terms of both scenery and trail running is the scarp along the north-west rim of the AONB, traversed by the Cotswold Way National Trail (see page 328).

Ascending Cherhill Down

61 Cherhill Down

Distance		11km (7 miles)	**Ascent**	250m (820ft)
Map		OS Landranger 173 OS Explorer 157		
Navigation	●●●	Some care needed on the open access land		
Terrain	●●●	Occasional ruts, stones and roots and one long climb		
Wet Feet	●●●	A few sections seem permanently muddy!		
Start/Finish		Smallgrain Picnic Area SN10 2LP/SU 019 671		

A splendid fix of chalk scarps and prehistoric earthworks

Easy navigation, straight paths and byways and inspiring views will enable you to positively belt around this route! After picking a route through the hamlet of Calstone Wellington, take a big breath for the long ascent up Cherhill Down. The National Trust manage the Down, whose summit is crowded by a hillfort, a white horse, various mounds and the Lansdowne Monument, a 38m obelisk erected in 1845 and which alarmingly looks ready to topple at any moment. A short descent and ascent around the valley head brings you onto the White Horse Trail. This was a Roman Road and we all know what they are famous for ... you'll be back at the start in no time at all.

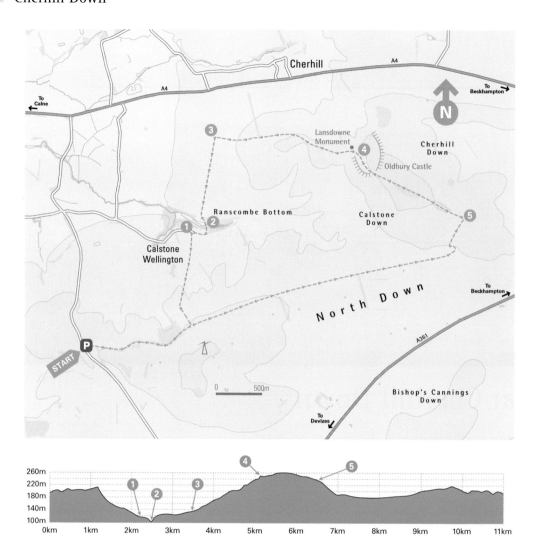

Route Description

🏃 START Take the steps out of the car park onto the byway leading E. After 1.1km, take the footpath leading steeply downhill on the left and follow it 1km to South Farm. ❶ Turn right (E) onto the lane. After 150m, take the footpath signposted off to the left and follow it down to and across a stream. ❷ Directly after the stream, take the bridleway leading steeply uphill to the right. The bridleway soon reaches open fields, follow it N alongside two large fields until you reach a footpath signposted to the right. ❸ Follow the footpath uphill (past a bridleway that crosses) to the Lansdowne Monument at the summit. ❹ From the Lansdowne Monument, take the righthand of the two paths leading away; this follows the ramparts of Oldbury hillfort. When you reach the end of the hillfort, continue E for 1km across access land, following the fence. The fence ends at a junction with a byway track; cross the gate to join this. ❺ Follow the byway downhill (S) for 400m to where it joins a larger byway track. Turn right (W) and follow the byway for 4km back to the start. Be careful not to miss the signposted turn-off for the car park, on your left.

Trip Planning

Smallgrain Picnic Area is located just past a golf course entrance, reached by heading along the A361 from Devizes towards Avebury, and then turning left when you see signs for Calne.

There is nothing here but you, the downs and the views; for civilisation, backtrack to Calne or Devizes, or perhaps head to Avebury to enjoy a National Trust cream tea.

Other Routes

A shorter run out and back run to Cherhill Down's summit could be enjoyed from either Cherhill or Calstone Wellington.

Crossing the road from Smallgrain Picnic Area, it's 3km along the White Horse Trail to Oliver's Castle and Beacon Hill, the skyline behind Devizes. Or you could head 6km ESE along the Wansdyke to join up with Route 62.

The White Horse and Lansdowne Monument

Events

The Marlborough Downs Challenge has 20 and 33-mile options; the longer route takes in Cherhill Down.

Iron Age hillforts in the South West

Why do so many routes in this book pass through hillforts? Partly because the author unashamedly loves running along their raised banks and sunken ditches, but mainly because it's really hard to get away from them. There are about 4,100 across Britain, with most prominent high points in the South West hosting one; except for central Dartmoor, Exmoor and Bodmin Moor, clearly deemed too cold and grim by our ancestors. Britain's largest and most sophisticated hillforts are to be found in Dorset and Wiltshire, heart of the Iron Age 'Wessex Culture'. Additionally, the coast is dotted with 'cliff castles' (at least 33 in Cornwall), hillforts which make use of headlands and promontories to minimise bank construction; the most impressive is at Rumps Point (Route 7).

Hillfort construction and design is surprisingly elaborate, as anyone who has run around the multiple vast walls of Maiden Castle near Dorchester can attest. Archaeologists classify hillforts as univallate, bivallate or multivallate, depending upon the number of enclosing banks. What were they for? Clearly they had a defensive function, but the illogical defences or impractical locations of some (e.g. those on waterless rocky headlands) suggest this may not be the whole story. Hillforts may have been as much about status, culture and religion as about keeping enemies out. Go run around one and ponder for yourself.

Maiden Castle

Cherhill Down from Morgan's Hill

The White Horse

62 The Pewsey Downs

Distance	13km (8 miles)	**Ascent**	300m (985ft)
Map	OS Landranger 173 OS Explorer 157		
Navigation ●●●	Well-trodden and signposted routes		
Terrain ●●●	Mostly grassy underfoot, but some long uphills		
Wet Feet ●●●	The tow path gets pretty puddly after rain		
Start/Finish	Alton Barnes SN8 4LE/SU 106 620		

From a secluded canal onto the roof of Wiltshire

The Pewsey Downs are the summits of Wiltshire's rolling chalk topography ... and they're rather pleasant! A steep scarp rises 180m above the plain, adorned with a White Horse carved into the turf. Actually there are *thirteen* white horses in Wiltshire, but regardless: this feels like a special place.

This route starts with a gentle potter along the Kennet and Avon Canal, before heading 'inland' from the water to gradually ascend Tan Hill, Wiltshire's answer to Mount Everest. En route you pass a massive chambered tomb which is not quite as ancient as it appears (it's a modern replica) and a small (genuine) hillfort. The run along the summit ridge is a joy; you can take in the views whilst running atop the pagan-named Wansdyke (*Woden's Dyke*), a large Dark Age earthwork which actually stretches over 30km in length. All around, orchids sprout. Pewsey Downs National Nature Reserve is described as, *'one of the finest remaining areas of Wiltshire's iconic chalk downland habitat'* and we see no reason to quibble with

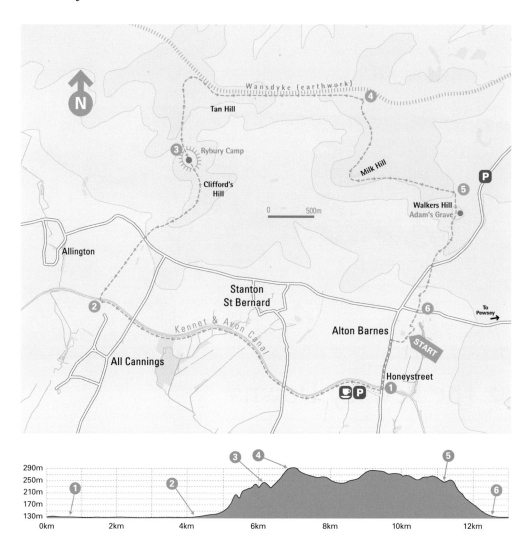

that. After passing above the white horse, you ascend Adam's Grave – possibly the best situated burial mound anywhere – and then commence the long and fast grassy descent back to the start.

Route Description

START Head W along Church Farm Lane to the junction with the main road. Turn left and follow this for 325m to the canal bridge (Careful! No pavement). **1** Cross the bridge and descend to the canal towpath. Follow this W for 3.5km. **2** Cross the canal at the fourth bridge (no. 128) and take the footpath immediately to the right (not the byway ahead). Follow this past Cannings Cross Farm and cross the road. Follow the bridleway opposite uphill for 200m to gates; take the footpath leading off to the right. Climb steeply on the footpath following the fence. After 1km, pass Rybury hillfort and descend to join the bridleway. **3** Climb on this bridleway to the top of Tan Hill. Cross the summit of the hill past the trig point to the huge earthen dyke. Turn right (E) and follow the bridleway along this for 2km. **4** Turn right at a sign for 'Pewsey Downs National Nature Reserve' onto a footpath heading S. The footpath contours around the

Ascending Tan Hill

rim of Milk Hill, turning E and passing above a chalk White Horse. ⑤ 500m after the horse, you reach a junction: follow the path up the prominent hill ahead topped by a mound (Adam's Grave). Take in the view and then descend S following the obvious footpath. When you reach the road, cross carefully and climb up the bank on the other side. Head 25m back uphill and turn right onto the footpath (footpath is un-marked, you need to climb over the fence to access it), follow this downhill to a lane. ⑥ Turn left onto the lane and follow it a short distance to the junction with Brown's Lane. Turn right onto this, follow it until you see a footpath leading off to the left. Follow this for a short distance along a wall foundation back to Church Farm Lane.

Trip Planning

Parking space in Alton Barnes is limited, but it is free. Pewsey Downs car park at SN8 4JX/SU 115 637 is an alternative high altitude start point, 400m across the road from ⑤. Another alternative start point is the canal side Barge Inn at ① SN9 5PU/SU 100 616; this is for customers only, so would commit you to eating and drinking some of their fine wares after running, no hardship! The Barge Inn is well known to generations of D of E groups for its campsite; however at time of writing (2018) this is closed.

Other Routes

There is plenty of leeway to extend your run along the ridge of the Pewsey Downs; it stretches 10km east from ⑤ to Savernake Forest (Route 64), whilst following the Wansdyke along the ridge 6km ENE from ③ will bring you to Cherhill Down (Route 61).

The Kennet and Avon Canal is lovely enough to warrant a run in its own right; see next page.

The descent to Alton Barnes

Events

The Marlborough Downs Challenge has 20 and 33-mile options, both ascending Tan Hill. The LDWA run the Pewsey Downsaround hereabouts, with distances of 10 to 35 miles.

The Kennet and Avon Canal

Completed in 1810, the Kennet and Avon Canal was built to connect Bath and Reading. Its 92km route is a small miracle for trail runners; at least, those who seek the mildest gradients! The K and A's tow path offers a continuous trail bridging Southern England from the River Thames to the River Avon, alternately boasting open views of the countryside or sinking into overgrown cuttings. The western parts delve through valleys peppered with disused mills of Cotswold stone. After the amazing

The Kennet and Avon Canal

flight of 29 locks at Caen Hill, the canal weaves through the Marlborough Downs between Devizes and Hungerford, summiting near Savernake Forest at 140m above sea level; this is a glorious stretch that could make for a great overnight camp adventure. Further east to Reading (and outside this book's remit), the canal loses a bit of its lustre but continues to be a green corridor worthy of your precious running time.

The Ridgeway's ruts

63 Avebury

Distance	20km (12.5 miles)	**Ascent**	230m (750ft)
Map	OS Landranger 173 OS Explorer 157		
Navigation ●●●	Well signposted throughout		
Terrain ●●●	Ridgeway heavily rutted, rough pathless section descending off it		
Wet Feet ●●●	The Ridgeway's ruts hold water long after rain!		
Start/Finish	Avebury National Trust car park SN8 1QT/SU 099 696		

Gentle hills touring a Prehistoric landscape and World Heritage Site

Avebury is famous as the village set within the world's largest prehistoric stone circle. For many, this complex of ditches and stone circles is a more engaging place than its not-too-distant cousin, Stonehenge. This run takes you on a tour of the surrounding prehistoric landscape, which is simply incredible: no hyperbole. First port of call is Silbury Hill, an enormous artificial mound. You then venture into the dark mouth of West Kennet Long Barrow, a chambered tomb overlooking the mound. The Sanctuary is the site of a timber (and later stone) circle complex, which marks the start of the Ridgeway, an ancient route across England and now a National Trail. The Ridgeway passes numerous burial mounds and also loosely scattered sarsen stones, the peculiar sandstone blocks used to create the stone circles at Stonehenge and Avebury. The penultimate Prehistoric treat is windswept Windmill Hill; the earthworks here are Britain's largest causewayed enclosure; these were circular ditches seemingly used for feasting and ritual ... there are no fewer than three here. All this, and you still need to run around the Avebury stones to finish off.

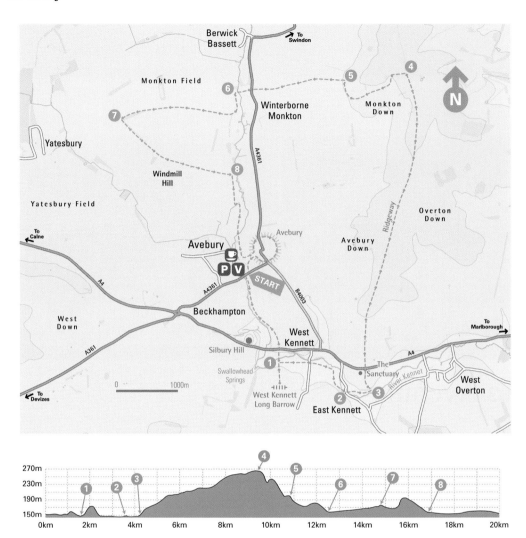

Route Description

🏃 **START** Leave the car park at the road entrance, cross the road to the bridleway just to the right. After 700m the bridleway turns sharp right; continue straight ahead on a footpath to the A4. Cross and follow the footpath opposite. ❶ After 200m on the footpath, an out-and-back diversion 400m uphill to visit West Kennet Long Barrow is recommended. After this side-trip, follow the footpath E along the valley, crossing a lane after 500m. After another 600m, turn left onto a bridleway. Follow this 200m to a lane. ❷ At the lane, cross the bridge and then immediately turn right onto the bridleway again. After 350m turn left onto a byway. ❸ Follow this byway uphill and cross the A4, then continue ahead (N) for 5km on the Ridgeway. 250m after bridleways join the Ridgeway from the left and then right, a single bridleway leaves the Ridgeway on the left: take this. ❹ After 250m the bridleway passes through a stile to a sloping field (you'll see sarsen stones down the slope), and becomes indistinct: follow the wall to your right, past trees, to a gate leading W out of the field. Continue 400m to another wall, pass through the gate and head downhill to a line of trees at the base. Turn right (N) and follow these trees to a much more obvious bridleway path which turns off left (W). **⑤** Follow this bridleway downhill until it joins a lane, the A4361 is joined after 1.5km. Cross and follow the lane ahead to its end. Continue through the front garden of a house onto a footpath. **⑥** Turn left (S) on the footpath and after 250m (before reaching the church) look for a sign pointing W marked 'Byway to Yatesbury'; follow this direction. After 1.4km this byway track reaches a crossroads beside woodland; continue ahead for 300m to a second crossroads at the end of the woods, and take the left (SE) turn onto a bridleway. **⑦** Follow the bridleway for 800m to the foot of

Avebury

Windmill Hill: climb ahead to the summit! From the summit, head ESE following paths through earthworks and then descend following a fence. 500m from the summit, the bridleway path reaches a crossroads; turn right onto a footpath. **⑧** Follow the footpath for 1.3km through four fields to Avebury. When you reach the lane, head E towards the church. The car park is 300m S of the church, but first why not run clockwise around the ditches and stones encircling the village?

West Kennet Long Barrow

Trip Planning

The car park is just off the A4361 and is well-signposted for miles around. It's pay and display, or free to members of the National Trust. For a cheapskate free alternative, try the viewpoint parking or the layby beside Silbury Hill on the A4, starting your run at **①**.

The National Trust run a decent café beside the stones; their hotpot revived the author nicely after one particularly wet and windy run. Visiting the visitor centres is worthwhile whilst there, but those wishing to get a better understanding of this remarkable landscape could do worse than start by reading through the bumf on English Heritage's website.

Descending from the Ridgeway

Other routes

This can be shortened by descending from the Ridgeway back into Avebury, 3km after **③**.

A scenic alternative or extended run can be enjoyed by following the Ridgeway further north from **④** to Barbury Castle hillfort (parking available here) and then looping south on the byway towards Ogbourne Maizey, and then back W to the Ridgeway.

Windmill Hill

Avebury

Events

The Avebury8 is (confusingly) a 9-mile trail race starting and finishing at Avebury. The Neolithic Marathon starts at Avebury and crosses Salisbury Plain to end at Stonehenge (Route 59). This is organised by Wiltshire Wildlife Trust. Avebury is the finish point for various ultra-distance events along the Ridgeway; see page 306.

Silbury Hill

Silbury Hill is the largest prehistoric mound in Europe. But what on earth was it for? Rather wonderfully, no one really has a clue. The known facts are that it is 30 metres high and flat-topped with flattened sides; the effect is not unlike an earthen pyramid, although it may originally have been rounded all over. It was built in stages between 2470 and 2350BC, from half a million tonnes of chalk and turf. Investigatory tunnels were bored into the hill during the eighteenth, nineteenth and twentieth centuries and discovered ... nothing.

Silbury Hill

Grey Road

64 Savernake Forest

Distance	12km (7.5 miles)	Ascent	125m (400ft)
Map	OS Landranger 173, 174 OS Explorer 157		
Navigation ●●○	One tree looks much like another, definitely take a compass		
Terrain ●○○	Little gradient; tracks and paths of gravel, earth and grass		
Wet Feet ●●○	A few muddy sections lurk in the forest		
Start/Finish	Savernake Forest car park SN8 4ND/SU 199 680		

A lifetime's worth of trail exploring in a beautiful forest

A total contrast from Wiltshire's open downland. Savernake Forest sprawls across 1,100 hectares of chalk plateau above the River Kennet valley, close to the market town of Marlborough. Savernake is the largest privately-owned hunting forest in England, having been in the hands of the same family since the Norman Conquest. However, some of the oaks are older than that!

This route offers a taster of the varying trails, woodland and landscapes to be explored within Savernake. The trails vary from hard wide tracks to winding rooty paths, with a fair bit of bogginess to negotiate at times. Despite my 'one tree looks much like another' oneliner above, various ancient or significant trees are flagged up by signage, and there is huge diversity to be enjoyed by arboreally informed folk. Some hint of Savernake's past as a landscaped park can also be gleaned from the planned out 'rides'; these are die-straight trails converging on the Ailesbury Column and Eight Walks junction.

Top tip: run here in autumn.

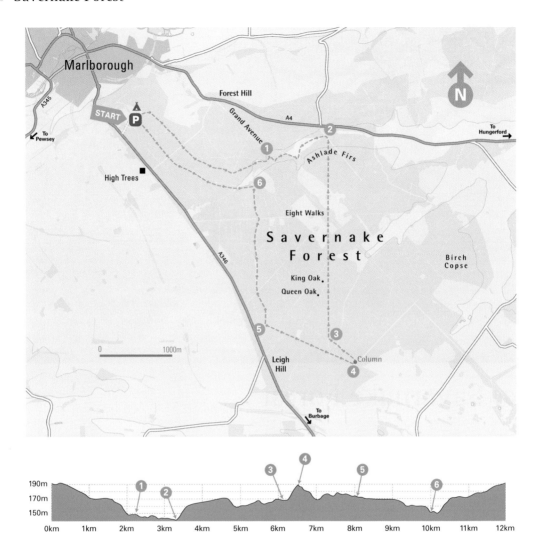

Route Description

START From the parking area beside the toilets, continue ahead (NE) along the track (Long Harry) past barriers to where it becomes unsurfaced. Continue on Long Harry, ignoring all turn-offs and going ahead at all junctions. After 2.2km it ends at a T-junction with a major track (Grand Avenue). **1** Turn right and follow Grand Avenue for 100m to a crossroads. Turn left off Grand Avenue and follow this track (Red Vein Bottom, it narrows to a path at times) for 400m to a T-junction where you turn left (N). After 500m Red Vein Bottom ends at a T-junction with a track (Ashlade Firs Road). **2** Turn right (SE) onto Ashlade Firs Road and after just 80m turn right onto a track heading directly S (Twelve O'Clock Drive). After 1km an eight-way junction is reached (Eight Walks), cross and continue ahead for 1.6km to the first crossroads encountered. **3** Turn left (SE) onto this track (Charcoal Burners Road) and follow it for 400m to where it ends at a T-junction with another track (Three Oak Hill Drive). **4** The Ailesbury Column is across Three Oak Hill Drive; head 20m right to find the entrance to the column, then take the track directly opposite this entrance, a right turn (heading WNW) off Three Oak Hill Drive. **5** Follow the track for 1.3km to a junction; at the junction follow the track around a bend to the N (on the left of the bend is a tree signposted 'Cluster Oak'). Follow this track (New Road Bottom) ahead for 2km, ignoring all turn-offs and going ahead at all junctions, until you reach a barrier across the track in front of the drive for Braydon Hook House. ⑥ Turn left (W) before the barrier and follow a path along a clearing. After 200m it forks, take the right fork (Grey Road) and follow this ahead for 1.8km back to the start.

Trip Planning

The car park is reached by following the A346 Salisbury Road south from Marlborough. One kilometre from town (and shortly after a steep climb), 'Forestry Commission Postern Hill' is signposted on the left. Turn off onto this track and then turn off again onto the track immediately on the right (carrying on ahead leads to Postern Hill Campsite). Follow this track (known as 'Long Harry') until you see a toilet block on your left and an information board on your right. This is the start point, park nearby.

The Forest can be accessed from various alternative spots, for example cars are allowed along the (unsurfaced) Grand Ave, where there are numerous spots to park. Access this from the A4 east of Marlborough. Note that this is closed for one day annually, usually the first working day of the year. This is to preserve the private status of the road. Access to the forest on foot is unaffected.

As noted above, there is a campsite near the start at Postern Hill. There is also a toilet block at the route start point. For all other facilities and needs, Marlborough is just a kilometre away, downhill.

Other routes

Seriously, where to start? The tricky thing here is keeping to the outlined route and *not* creating your own route (inadvertently). The potential for exploration is vast, run free and just remember to take a compass so that you can always find your way (north-west-ish) back to the start.

Long Harry

Red Vein Bottom

Twelve O'Clock Drive

Charcoal Burners Road

The Column

New Road Bottom

Outside the Forest, a pleasant 8km loop can be run from Great Bedwyn around the Kennet and Avon Canal. Follow the canal south-west to the lake of Wilton Water, follow this lake to Wilton and then loop back to Great Bedwyn via woodland bridleways.

Events

The Savernake Fun Run starts at a local school and offers 3km and 10K routes into the Forest, including some areas not usually accessible.

Savernake Forest

Savernake ('Seven Oaks') has belonged to the same family since the Norman Conquest, when it became a Royal Forest; a private hunting ground for the monarch. However, the Big Belly Oak which is prominent beside Burbage Road probably dates from Saxon times! Henry VIII met Jane Seymour whilst hunting in the forest. In the eighteenth century the forest was remodelled as a landscaped park, with the 6km Grand Avenue of beeches planted (the longest in Britain), the Ailesbury Column built and the riding trails converging on Eight Walks planned out. During the Second World War, Savernake was used as an ammunition store, with some wartime buildings still remaining. The Forestry Commission have managed Savernake since 1939.

Sugar Hill

65 The Aldbourne Circular Route

Distance	13km (8 miles)	Ascent	225m (740ft)
Map	OS Landranger 173 OS Explorer 157		
Navigation ●●●	Signposted for most of the way		
Terrain ●●●	Rutted byways, tracks, field boundaries		
Wet Feet ●●●	Add an extra star in winter, when the ruts fill		
Start/Finish	The Square, Aldbourne SN8 2DU/SU 264 756		

Quiet undulating downs on the Ridgeway's fringes

The waymarked Aldbourne Circular Route is designed to be a taster of The Ridgeway National Trail and its landscape; outlined here, is an even shorter taster of this circuit. This, the most easterly route in this guidebook, is selected as an easy to access and easy to navigate 'quick' hill run. The M4 and Swindon are just minutes away from the ACR, but once you set out you are quickly immersed in green downland which appears to ripple endlessly in all directions, with only the occasional barrow mound to break up the skyline. Only a short part of this route follows The Ridgeway National Trail, but the byways that you follow up onto the ridge still offer an authentic flavour of the National Trail, because of their ruts. Anyone who has run on the Ridgeway west of the River Thames will be familiar with these ruts. Are these ruts preferable in summer when they are firm but overgrown making it hard to place your feet, or in winter when the ruts flood with cold water? You really need to sample both states to decide.

The Aldbourne Circular Route

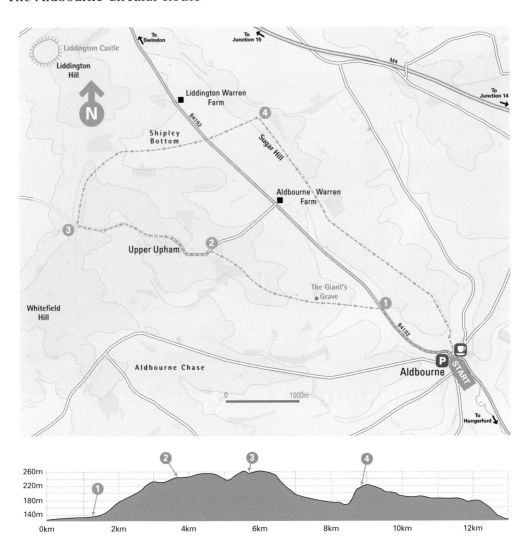

Route Description

🏃 **START** From the Crown at Aldbourne pub, head 80m SE along The Square (towards the Post Office) and turn right at the B4192 main road. Follow this for 500m (no curb at times, be careful) and turn left onto a byway track. **1** Follow the byway for 200m until it splits, take the right fork. Follow this uphill for 2.3km to a lane in front of Upham House. Turn left onto the lane. **2** Follow the lane for 800m until it becomes an unsurfaced byway track, then continue 1.2km ahead across a valley and uphill to a crossroads with the Ridgeway. **3** Turn right onto the Ridgeway and follow it 600m to a fork. Take the right fork, signposted 'short cut'. Descend on this byway track to the B4162, cross, and then continue following the byway to steeply ascend Sugar Hill. **4** At the summit of Sugar Hill, look for a bridleway leading off to the right and follow this along the ridgetop. After 2km you pass between four burial mounds, and then the track descends into Aldbourne to reach the Crown at Aldbourne after 1.3km.

The first climb

Trip Planning

There is plenty of free parking space in central Aldbourne, most of it opposite the Crown Inn. If you arrive to find this occupied (e.g. around Sunday lunchtimes), simply head up the road a bit to find a space. Aldbourne's nicest bet for food is The Crown whose menu includes 'rustic' chips, crayfish sandwiches and pulled pork, all of which a sure sign that you are nearly in the South East. There is also a café across the Square from the Inn. For supplies, the Village Stores (and Deli) are also on the Square, whilst the Co-op is just a short walk away.

Other routes

The full Aldbourne Circular Route is about 20km: just after ❷, a byway heading S adds an extension via Snap Farm before following the Ridgeway N to re-join this route at ❸; 600m after ❸, ignore the right turn at the fork (signposted as a short-cut) and continue N on the Ridgeway past Luddington Castle hillfort to the B4192. After crossing this, turn right off the Ridgeway, follow ACR signs S to re-join this route at ❹.

Upham House

Barbury Castle Country Park is about 10km west of Aldbourne, with parking beside the Ridgeway. Short runs around this hillfort offer great views (also there are views of Swindon). A loop taking in this spot from the village of Ogbourne St Andrew offers an outing of similar character to the ACR.

Internal ruts, near The Giant's Grave

The Aldbourne Circular Route

Leaving the Ridgeway

Events

The Aldbourne 5K Fun Run is held on lanes and trails to the east of this route.

The Ridgeway National Trail

Routes 63 and 65 both utilise parts of The Ridgeway National Trail. This Prehistoric road follows the high ground for 140km/87 miles west between Ivinghoe Beacon in Hertfordshire and The Sanctuary at Avebury in Wiltshire. The 71km of the Ridgeway east of the River Thames (outside this book's region) are quite varied in terrain and surface. The western half featured in this book is characterised by rolling ridgetops with mild ascents and descents. The trail surface of the western Ridgeway is notable for its parallel lines of narrow, deep and uneven ruts. These are testing to runners in dry conditions and nothing short of purgatory in the wet. It doesn't help that byway sections of the trail are used by city-dwelling 4WD owners to test out their expensive white elephants. But don't be dissuaded! The masochism of tackling these challenges offers a certain satisfaction. The Trail Running Association hold the Ridgeway Challenge, covering the entire Ridgeway; this solo event is

The Ridgeway

also the UK Ultra Distance Trail Running Championship. The author entered and somehow completed this, but don't be too impressed; it took 22 hours. A less extreme variant is the Race to the Stones, clocking in at a mere 100km. This event can be completed in stages, has more of a 'festival' feel and was voted the UK's 'best endurance event' in 2016. Marlborough Running Club organise the Ridgeway Relay, a team relay race along the entire Ridgeway. There is also the LDWA's Ridgeway 40 (miles).

Bristol and Gloucestershire

At the north-east extremity of the South West (don't think too hard about that statement) are the limestone Cotswold Hills, which present a dramatic frontage towards the Severn Estuary, in the form of a long high scarp. The great trail running routes featured here serve as merely an introduction to the Cotswolds, which are in truth worthy of far more extensive trail running explorations. Also featured is a run around Bristol's impressive Avon Gorge, which is actually just across the border in Somerset, but don't tell anyone. Sadly, the trails of Gloucestershire's lovely Forest of Dean and Wye Valley will have to await a future guidebook, as (being located north of the River Severn estuary) they arguably stretch the definition of 'South West' just a little too far.

Coaley Peak (Route 68)

View from Stokeleigh Camp

Purple trail

66 Leigh Woods

Distance	8.5km (5.5 miles)	**Ascent**	275m (900ft)
Map	OS Landranger 172 OS Explorer 154		
Navigation ●●●	Well-signed paths, route easy to follow		
Terrain ●●●	Mostly wide firm tracks, some steep rocky or rooty paths		
Wet Feet ●●●	No problem dodging the occasional puddles		
Start/Finish	Leigh Woods car park BS8 3QB/ST 552 739		

Wooded trails along a plunging gorge, close to central Bristol

Trail runners in Britain's eighth most populous city are blessed with a spectacular natural landscape to explore, right beside the city centre. Leigh Woods cling to the precipitous limestone cliffs of the Avon Gorge, overlooking Brunel's Clifton Suspension Bridge. A hundred metres below, the River Avon constantly surges between muddy tidal shores. This oak and lime woodland was donated to the National Trust in 1909, basically to stop it becoming a housing estate; it is now a National Nature Reserve.

This route takes in as many different elements of the landscape (and running surfaces) as possible; the start and finish make use of marked woodland trails. A run through the arboretum (look out for the Giant Redwood) leads into a rough descent to the gorge floor, emerging beside the River Avon. You follow the River Avon Trail upstream and re-enter Leigh Woods just before passing under the Clifton Suspension Bridge; then commences a rocky and admittedly murderous climb up Nightingale Valley. Finally emerging

Leigh Woods

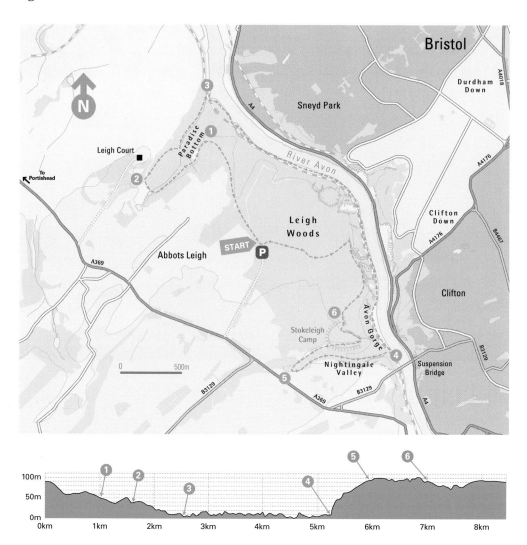

on top again, a grassy run out to Stokeleigh Camp (an Iron Age hillfort) gives a great view of the bridge before heading back to the start.

Route Description

START From the car park, follow the signposted blue trail which continues downhill from the end of the road. **1** After 1km, the track bends left whereas the blue trail turns off right; keep on the track and follow it for 750m past two ponds to a small car park. **2** Follow the path behind the car park information board, downhill through the Arboretum. After 400m the path reaches a pond (Paradise Bottom), pass this and take the small path following the left bank of the stream downhill. Pass beneath the railway to reach the River Avon. **3** Turn right and follow the footpath along the river for 2.7km. **4** About 200m before passing under the Clifton Suspension Bridge, turn right uphill into Nightingale Valley (entrance marked by an NT 'Leigh Woods' sign). Ascend the footpath and steps until a fence blocks the route ahead. **5** Turn sharp right to follow the path along the rim of the hilltop, bearing right at junctions until you reach Stokeleigh Camp hillfort. Pass through the earthworks to a view point overlooking the Clifton Suspension Bridge. ⑥ From the viewpoint, follow the path along the edge of the hill until you reach a junction with the signposted purple trail. Turn right and follow this 1.5km back to the start.

Paradise Bottom

Trip Planning

The main parking area is free, accessed by following signs off the A369. It is very popular; at weekends you may have to park some way back along the track. The car park closes at dusk. There is a tea van on duty more or less permanently, but no toilet facilities. For all other needs, there is a major city not very far away.

The trails close to the car park can get clogged with child buggies, yappy dogs and hipster parents; be considerate and remind yourself that you won't have to run far to find personal space. Note also the mountain-biking trails around the car park; these are not for trail runners! If you are feeling touristy, cross the Clifton Suspension Bridge after running (it's a toll bridge) for an impressive perspective of Leigh Woods and the Avon Gorge. The 360 Café at the nearby Clifton Observatory offers the best view in the city, alongside your lunch.

Nightingale Valley

Other Routes

The National Trust website suggests various routes and a map can be downloaded. The purple and red marked trails offer pleasant non-hilly routes of 2.5 and 1.2km, respectively. There is also a permanent orienteering course.

The plethora of paths within Leigh Woods of course offer plenty more exploring, whilst the River Avon Trail can be followed for as far as suits in either direction.

Ashton Court Estate (a country park owned by Bristol Council) is a short distance away and worth visiting to extend your run. At ⑤ follow North Road west to Abbots Leigh Road (A369). Turn left onto this and follow it for 550m to the park entrance.

Events

Wild Night Run organise Back to Black, a series of 1km to 10K night races around Leigh Woods. Don't forget your headtorch! Another local night trail race (must be a Bristol thing) is the Towpath 10K, organised by Great Western Runners. At the far end of the distance spectrum is the Green Man Ultra, with 30 or 45-mile distances following Bristol's Community Forest Path (see next page).

Leigh Woods

River Avon

Bristol trail running

Whilst Leigh Woods offers the best of 'Brizzle's' trail running, there are plenty of other decent spots to explore around the city. Just across the A369 from Leigh Woods, Ashton Court Estate has various trails to explore, and hosts a parkrun (albeit on some of its surfaced trails). Ashton Court is managed by Bristol Council, who maintain numerous other parks giving access to Bristol's hilly terrain; Blaise Castle Estate is 260 hectares of engaging landscape (including a gorge and a hillfort), while Stoke Park occupies a ridge (around the grotesquely ugly BT tower) overlooking the M32, near the University. Maps and routes are downloadable from the Bristol Council website.

Across the gorge from Leigh Woods, the parkland of Clifton Down and Durdham Down have enough space for short runs. Further west along the gorge rim, Shirehampton Park is owned by the National Trust and has great views but is marred by a golf course.

The River Avon Trail follows the river 37km upstream along various surfaces from Pill (near Gordano Services on the M5) through Bristol to Pulteney Bridge in Bath. It is intersected by the 29km Frome Valley Walkway which heads up that river to meet the Cotswold Way at Old Sodbury. Guides for both routes can be downloaded from their websites.

Bristol's paths and green spaces are tied together by the Community Forest Path, a 72km circuit; completing this behemoth in a day is known as the Green Man Challenge.

The National Trust's Tyntesfield estate is just 5km from the city centre. There are 180 hectares of hilly woodland and parkland to explore, with a fortnightly 4-mile run laid on known as Feel Good Friday, as well as a monthly Trust10 (10K run).

Lock on the canal

67 Cotswold Water Park

Distance	15km (9.5 miles)	Ascent	25m (80ft)
Map	OS Landranger 163 OS Explorer 169		
Navigation ●●●	Well-signposted, however numerous junctions to keep track of		
Terrain ●●●	Largely flat grassy or stony paths and tracks, some tarmac		
Wet Feet ●●●	Numerous mud patches and puddles to hop, skip or jump		
Start/Finish	Cotswold Water Park Gateway Centre GL7 5TL/SU 072 970		

Flat trails winding through a complex waterworld

Cotswold Water Park is a huge complex of over 150 lakes spanning 5,000 hectares, the UK's largest marl lake system. The lakes are artificial, a consequence of limestone gravel quarrying from the 1930s to the present. The River Thames flows through the midst of all this, a small innocuous stream which is hard to reconcile with your image of the London River. Numerous paths and tracks weave amongst the lakes and streams, offering a great opportunity for runners to get a decent waterside trail fix (with minimal gradient!). This is a landscape created by industry, some of which still continues. Surprisingly though, the result is a beautiful environment, a quiet green haven for all manner of aquatic wildlife. Whilst running, you'll certainly encounter wildfowl and other water birds; the more keen-eyed (or lucky) will spot kingfishers, otters or water voles. This route is effectively a grand tour of all facets of the Water Park; lakes, an active quarry, back lanes, disused tram and railways, winding paths following streams (including the Thames itself) and a final engaging stretch along a dried-up canal bed.

Cotswold Water Park

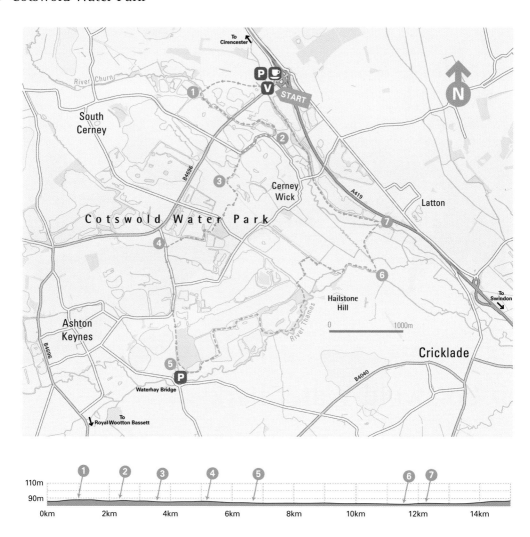

Route Description

START   Leave the car park by passing under the B4696 on the footpath beside the canal. After 100m, take the footpath leading off on the left, signposted 'South Cerney'. After 800m the footpath crosses a bridge, take the footpath on the left following the River Churn downstream. **①** Follow the footpath along the river. After 600m the B4696 is reached, cross this and rejoin the footpath on the opposite bank of the river. After 300m the footpath crosses the river via a bridge, after another 300m a T-junction is reached. **②** Turn right and follow this footpath a short distance to a lane. Turn right and follow the lane 500m to a right bend. Take the footpath on the left and follow this past a gravel works to a bridleway on a disused railway. **③** Turn left (SE) and follow the bridleway for 230m to where a footpath leads off right. Take this footpath and follow it through numerous bends. After 500m Wickwater Lane is reached; follow this right for 50m to rejoin the footpath for another 1km to Fridays Ham Lane. **④** Turn left and follow Fridays Ham Lane S for 1km to a right bend. Take the bridleway on the left of the bend. After 700m a bridleway track on the left is signposted as the Thames Path. **⑤** Take the bridleway track and follow the Thames Path signage for 5km through lakes and along the River Thames, until you climb an embankment to reach a crossroads of trails at a disused bridge. ⑥ Turn left onto the bridleway atop the embankment (a dried-up canal), leaving the Thames Path. Follow the bridleway (becomes a footpath) along the canal to a large building, pass this to the right and cross the River Churn just before reaching the A419. ⑦ Turn left and follow the footpath alongside the canal 2.5km back to the start, crossing a lane halfway.

Trip Planning

Parking at the Gateway Centre is free. It is found just off Spine Road on the left, shortly after you turn off the A419 for South Cerney. The Centre has displays on the wildlife, geography and history of the park, and can supply information on activities and suchlike. There is also the Relish Café which can supply necessary calorific energy for your run in the form of cakes (you can't argue with science). Incidentally, next door to the Centre are the national headquarters/flagship shop of the Cotswold Outdoor chain, ideal if you have forgotten any kit.

A quieter start to this route is possible at the Waterhay car park near Waterhay Bridge, just after ⑤. It charges, though, and is subject to flooding in winter.

Other Routes

Cotswold Water Park have produced a leaflet outlining possible routes, all shorter than this one. All of the routes start and finish at the Gateway Centre, where you should be able to pick up a copy of the leaflet. This can also be found on their website.

This route can easily be shortened by nearly half, by continuing SE on the bridleway (an old railway line) after ③, until you join the Thames Path.

The Thames Path National Trail of course offers all sorts of possibilities; see next page.

Events

Triathlon events of various distance are held in the park, organised by TriFerris.

Lake in former gravel pit

The railway

Cotswold Water Park footpath

The River Churn

The River Thames

The Thames Path National Trail

The Thames Path National Trail follows the river for 296km/184 miles from the source to the Thames Barrier. The first 40km of the TP (to Lechlade, on the Gloucestershire-Oxfordshire border) are within this guidebook's area, offering some lovely (downhill!) rural trails. The source of the Thames is basically a non-descript stone marker in the corner of a field, with little sign of water for much of the year. This is only a

few kilometres from the village of Kemble, where there is a useful railway station. From here to Cricklade (including part of Route 67), the odd feature of the TP is how often the River Thames is nowhere nearby! However, the section alongside the Thames through the western part of Cotswold Water Park, with lakes also either side, is a highlight. Down to Lechlade, the TP follows the river more faithfully, but also includes some unexciting road sections.

The source spring

Shuttling between Kemble, Cricklade or Lechlade using public transport is possible but rather awkward, involving changes at either Cirencester or Swindon.

Inevitably, there are numerous race events which utilise this National Trail for excessive ultra-distance masochism. Most are located along sections of the TP within the South East, but the T184 (T Series Racing) and the Thames Challenge (Ultrarunning Ltd) both tackle the entire National Trail; the former ending and the latter starting at the source. The T184 offers a relay option and the Thames Challenge divides up the 184 miles over four days. So, they are easy, really ...

View from Coaley Peak

68 Coaley Peak

Distance	12km (7.5 miles)	Ascent	375m (1200ft)
Map	OS Landranger 162 OS Explorer 168		
Navigation ●●●	Fairly simple, only a couple of junctions where attention is needed		
Terrain ●●●	Easy stony tracks, a steep grassy climb, rooty narrow paths		
Wet Feet ●●●	Cotswold Way notably slippy and squelchy in damp times		
Start/Finish	Coaley Peak Picnic Site and Viewpoint GL11 5AU/SO 794 012		

Cotswold gold

This cracking run manages both to steer clear of civilisation throughout (crossing only a handful of roads) and to immerse you in a decent mix of Cotswold-flavoured landscapes. The key to its crackingness lies in the combined use of the hidden Woodchester Park valley, and the always rewarding Cotswold Way.

You start by legging it down the estate tracks of Woodchester Park, descending past the Gothic gables and chimneys of Woodchester Mansion and a series of ornamental lakes. What goes down has to come up however (is that right?) and you next face a long climb up and over Bown Hill, before dropping into beech woodland for a rooty and winding blast along the hillside back to the start. Note the Nympsfield Long Barrow (prehistoric grave) alongside the parking area; people have been enjoying the views from Coaley Peak for at least 6,000 years.

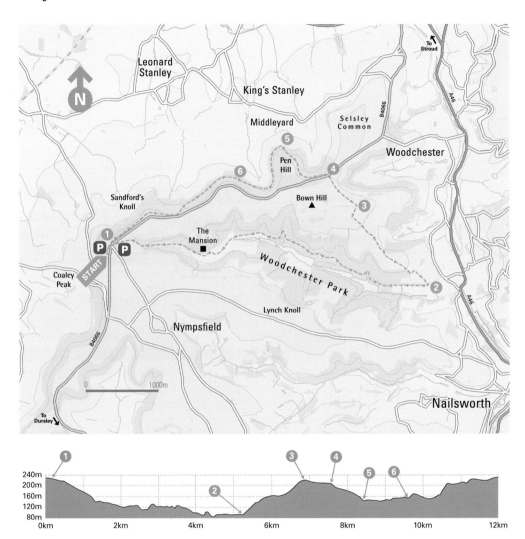

Route Description

START Leave the car park and turn left (N) onto the B4066, follow this along the verge for 100m to a junction with a lane on the right. Cross the B4066 to the lane. You will see a gate signposted for Woodchester Mansion, go through this. **1** Follow the track downhill into the woods, stay on it for 5km (Woodchester Mansion is passed on the right after 1.2km) until you reach a gate which is the park entrance, with a footpath signposted uphill on the left. **2** Follow the footpath steeply uphill through a series of fields. The second and third fields are vineyards; bypass them by keeping to the left edge. **3** When the footpath ends at a junction of lanes, cross the first lane and follow the lane heading NW. After 600m the lane reaches the B4066, cross and go through the gate 50m to the left marked 'Pen Wood' to a permissive bridleway. **4** Follow the permissive bridleway downhill through the woods. After 300m take the footpath signposted on the left and follow this downhill (joining another bridleway en route) to reach a junction with the Cotswold Way footpath. **5** Turn left onto the Cotswold Way. **6** After 1.2km you'll see steps on the left, signposted 'Stile-free alternative permissive footpath for Coaley Peak'. Ascend the steps and follow this path; after 1km it comes close to the B4066. Keep following paths ahead until you emerge on the open land beside Coaley Peak viewpoint.

Buckholt Wood

Trip Planning

Coaley Peak Picnic Site and Viewpoint offers free parking and is signposted off the B4066 midway between Dursley and Stroud. An alternative is to use the National Trust car park GL10 3UP/SO 798 013 in Woodchester Park, free to members.

There are no facilities or opportunities for refreshment along the route (the National Trust offer only picnic benches). However the nearby towns of Dursley, Stroud and Nailsworth will cater for any normal needs.

Bown Hill

Other Routes

A pleasant short extension is to head NE at ④ for a loop around Selsley Common.

There isn't really a way to shorten the loop, but just confining your run to Woodchester Park means that you can explore the numerous trails around the valley; do take note of ongoing forestry work. The National Trust have also marked out several trails, from 3 to 11km in length.

If you are staying in the area, the hills south and west of Dursley have some lovely trails offering great views; check out Nibley Knoll and Stinchcombe Hill.

Woodchester valley

Events

Stroud and District Athletics Club organise the 8-mile Woodchester Park Race, around the valley. See their website for details of their other trail events. The Stroud Trail Events organised by Iamoutdoors Running is a running festival including quarter, half, full and ultra marathon distances, with routes around Stroud and the Frome Valley.

Entrance to Woodchester valley

Bown Hill

Woodchester valley

Woodchester Park

This wonderfully secluded valley has for centuries been a private playground for its privileged owners. The park and lakes around Woodchester Mansion were inspired by landscape gardener Capability Brown in the eighteenth century, and when the Ducie family sold the mansion and estate in 1843, it was advertised as *'everything the most fastidious Gentleman can desire'.* The new owner, a ship-builder, demolished the previous mansion and started work on the current Gothic effort; however, he ran out of money and it is unfinished! In the following century, the estate changed hands several times and commercial conifers were planted. Since the National Trust acquired the val-

Woodchester Mansion

ley in 1994, they have been working to reduce the coni-fers and restore the parkland views. There are numerous trails to explore (some are suggested on the National Trust's website); just take heed of ongoing forestry work. Woodchester Mansion is not owned by the National Trust, but can be visited on Fridays, Saturdays and Sun-days through the warmer months.

Painswick Beacon

69 Painswick Beacon and Crickley Hill

Distance	17km (10.5 miles)	Ascent	500m (1650ft)
Map	OS Landranger 162, 163 OS Explorer 179		
Navigation ●●●	Almost entirely on the heavily signposted Cotswold Way		
Terrain ●●●	Wide tracks, narrow rooty and stony paths, grass.		
Wet Feet ●●●	Huge mud potential, but there is usually an option to dodge the worst		
Start	Painswick Beacon car park GL6 6SU/SO 867 117		
Finish	Cheese Rollers bus stop GL51 4TN/SO 918 182		

Superb trails traversing the Cotswold Way's limestone escarpment

The Cotswold Way National Trail (see page 328) is widely recognised as an outstanding trail-running experience; why else would folk sign up for the non-stop 164km Cotswold Way Century every year? The route suggested here has slightly more modest aims, sampling a short(ish) section of the National Trail which has been selected both for its accessibility by public transport and for its showcasing of what makes the CW so great.

The first port of call is Painswick Beacon, a hillfort and viewpoint giving you the lie of the surrounding land! You soon descend via rooty muddy trails into the beech woodland which clings to the sides of the Cotswold Edge, not emerging from this sylvan seclusion until the latter third of the run. The final part emerges out into the sunshine up on the Edge, with grand views from The Peak and then Crickley Hill

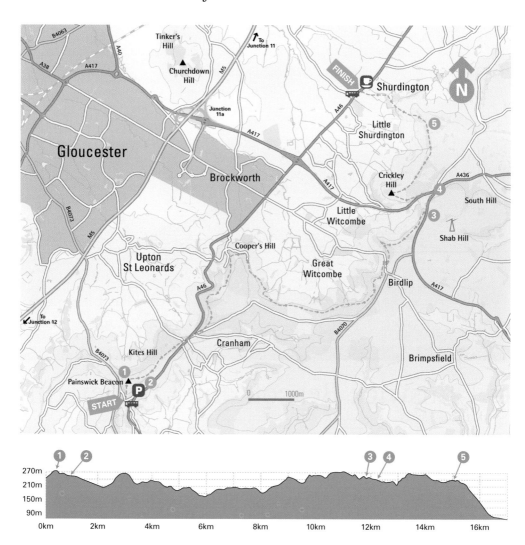

Country Park before a rapid descent down to the main road. This route is a tremendous taster for the Cotswold Way; the author will admit that when he ran this section, he struggled to tear himself away from National Trail and descend to the finish.

Route Description

START From the parking area, follow the lane uphill to where the Cotswold Way (CW) is clearly signposted. Turn left (N) onto the CW. Immediately take the path on the left to detour off the CW to the summit of Painswick Beacon. Follow the hillfort walls to the summit trig point. **1** Continue around the fort walls until you see a path descending to rejoin the CW. **2** Turn left (NE) onto the CW and follow it for 11km. After 1km you cross a road, followed by another road crossing a short road section. After 4km there is a short road section through a village. The following 5km is continually in woodland (with a road after 4.5km), you then leave the woods and pass Barrow Wake car park before reaching the A417. **3** When you reach the A417, turn left and follow the CW along the A417 for 350m to a roundabout. Turn left and carefully cross the first road turning off the roundabout (again the A417) to the Cotswold Way sign. ❹ Follow the CW for 2.8km, along the scarp edge and through Crickley Hill Country Park to Greenway Lane. ❺ Turn left (downhill) and follow Greenway Lane for a short distance to a footpath on the right. Take the footpath and follow it downhill (ignoring a footpath on the left after 150m) through successive fields to Shurdington. When you reach Farm Lane, turn left to reach the Cheese Rollers Inn.

Trip Planning

Painswick Beacon car park is simply an extended road-side space, free to use, on a small lane which links the A46 and B4073; the junctions for both are signposted 'Painswick Beacon'. It gets busy with golfers, so perhaps arrive early.

This trip is based around using local buses to shuttle back after (or before) running. The route finishes at the Cheese Rollers Inn, where there is a bus stop. You need the number 66 bus which arrives hourly (but check before running!) and will take you to the bus stop named 'Paradise, opposite Adam and Eve House' GL6 6TW/SO 870 117. This stop is 2km after the bus climbs and then passes over the Cotswold edge. Across the road from the bus stop, a footpath leads 250m uphill to Painswick Beacon car park.

Whilst waiting for the bus in Shurdington, an obvious option is to eat at the Cheese Rollers Inn. A cheaper option is to wander a few hundred metres into Shurdington; there is a supermarket on Yarnolds with a small friendly café (which is confusingly also a beauty spa) next door.

Other Routes

Of course, there are various spots at which you can descend to the A46 and cut this run short. Continuing a few kilometres further on the Cotswold Way at ❺ to Leckhampton Hill lets you see the Devil's Chimney, a

Crickley Hill Country Park

Barrow Wake

The Peak and Cooper's Hill from Crickley Hill

Cotswold Way near Birdlip

Shurdington Hill

tall limestone spire, but this means lots of tarmac as you descend into Cheltenham to catch the bus. It's about 17km around and above Cheltenham to Cleeve Hill (Route 70), highest point in the Cotswolds. To the south of Painswick Beacon, the CW offers more lovely woodland and scarp running of similar character as it loops around Stroud but is more awkward to shuttle using public transport.

Those wanting a short run with excellent trails and views could do far worse than just turn up at Crickley Hill Country Park and run around the Edge.

Events

The LDWA run the 26 or 18 miles Cotswold Challenge around this stretch of the CW. If you feel like a bit of silliness, Iamoutdoors Running's Rudolphs Rampage is a 7km fancy dress trail race around Painswick, near Christmas time.

Cleeve Hill ascent

70 Cleeve Hill

Distance	7km (4.5 miles)	Ascent	150m (500ft)
Map	OS Landranger 163 OS Explorer 179, OL45		
Navigation ●●●	Simple line-of-sight navigation, in clear conditions		
Terrain ●●●	Grassy and stony paths and tracks, few obstacles		
Wet Feet ●●●	Paths drain well, puddles easily avoided		
Start/Finish	Cleeve Hill car park GL52 3PW/SO 989 271		

Epic vistas from the highest point in the Cotswolds

The author has arbitrarily decided that the South West terminates at 330m Cleeve Hill (sometimes called Cleeve Cloud), the highest point in the Cotswold Hills and Gloucestershire. 7km further north is Worcestershire, effectively the Midlands. Here in the far north, winter lasts year-round and snow drifts make running a challenge. Don't be scared off by the photos though, as long as you wrap up warm the huge undulating plateau of Cleeve Common is a wonderful place to run, with open access and immense views.

Cleeve Common is a precious environment, 400 hectares of 'unimproved' limestone grassland. Such environments formed over a third of the Cotswolds less than a century ago; today the figure is just 1.5%. This route is relatively easy in terms of gradient and ascent, cherry-picking the best of the Common with a traverse atop a line of limestone cliffs (newcomers are always surprised to learn that the Cotswolds have cliffs!) through a hillfort, with the Malvern Hills and distant Welsh mountains beyond.

Cleeve Hill

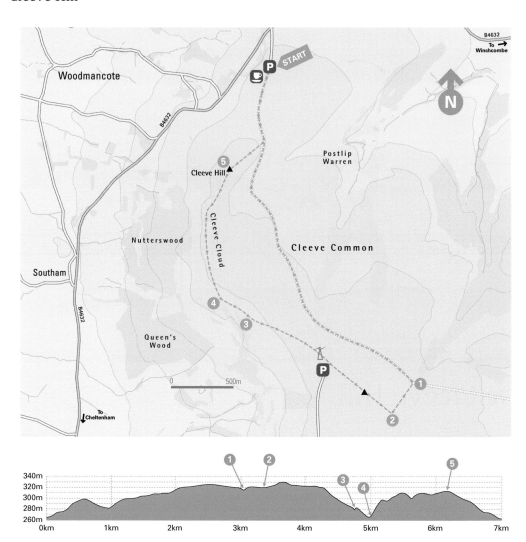

Route Description

🏃 **START** From the car park, follow the main track uphill (S) through the golf course. Follow this (the Winchcombe Way) for 3.1km until you reach a wall and gate at the boundary of Cleeve Common. **1** Don't go through the gate. Turn right and follow the wall for 200m. When the wall bends away left, continue ahead for another 100m to the southern boundary of the Common. **2** Turn right and follow the fence 1.4km (past the summit trig point and three communication masts) to a gate and sign. **3** Don't go through the gate but continue following the fence uphill. In a short distance the fence ends and is replaced by a steep scarp (cliffed in places) dropping away to your left. Choose and carefully follow paths N along the edge of this scarp. **4** After following the scarp edge for 800m, choose a path (there are several) to climb the prominent high point ahead. **5** From the summit trig point, the car park is visible; descend through the golf course.

Trip Planning

The car park is reached by heading north out of Cheltenham on the B4632 Stratford-upon-Avon road, and turning right following the brown sign for Cleeve Hill Golf Course. The car park is at the end of this lane, just past the Golf Club building. Note that it is locked at 8pm in summer, and 5pm outside British Summer Time. There is no charge.

Cleeve Hill Golf Club has a restaurant which is open most days; using this might be a convenient excuse to use their car park and avoid getting locked in the public car park. Otherwise, the town of Cheltenham is of course directly downhill and offers all facilities.

Interesting information about Cleeve Common's management and precious ecosystems can be found on their website. There are no restrictions to runners other than (obviously) to leave the place as you found it.

View from Cleeve Hill

Cleeve Common

Other Routes

Cleeve Common is Access Land, so if this route does not suit, then feel free to deviate freely!

A hillier 10K can be enjoyed by heading E along the bridleway towards Postlip from the start, and rejoining this route at . This is also a popular walking route, known as the Cleeve Hill Common Ring.

The Cotswold Way (which this route is adjacent to, but largely avoids) can of course be used to significantly extend your Cleeve Hill run. For example, you could start your ascent from Winchcombe along the CW and return via Birdlip.

Cleeve Hill viewpoint

Mountain biker on Cleeve Hill

Events

Cheltenham Harriers' Cleevewold is a long-established and tough 14-mile race centred on Cleeve Common. The same folk also organise the 5.5-mile Cleeve Cloud Cuckoo, later in the year. The Naunton Nearly Nineteen, organised by Cotswold Running, is held nearby (the name refers to the mileage). Winchcombe is the base for Maverick Race's Inov8 Original Gloucestershire Race, with 7km, 17km and 23km distances. The LDWA's Winchcombe Way Challenge covers 21 miles of the eponymous trail.

Cotswold Edge

The Cotswold Way National Trail

The Cotswold Way winds 164km/102 miles south-west from Chipping Campden to the city of Bath. Early on, it briefly leaves Gloucestershire (and the area of this guidebook) to ascend Broadway Hill in Worcestershire, but otherwise it can truly be labelled a South West gem. The route largely traces the north-west edge of the Cotswolds. This is the Cotswold Escarpment (AKA the Cotswold Edge); here the underlying limestone has been lifted up and has literally broken off at the edge, exposing steep slopes and cliffs leading down towards the River Severn Estuary.

Cotswold Way signage

The CW is easy to access with numerous car parks and reasonably good public transport links for much of the route. Intermittently the route follows the summit (with fantastic views); more often it traverses the slopes of the scarp to explore beech woodlands and sleepy villages of yellow-brown stone.

Numerous long-distance events take on sections of, or the entire, CW. The Cotswold Way Challenge (based on the well-established Ridgeway Challenge) offers 100km, 50km and 25km courses, with team and multi-day options. This is not to be confused with the 100 Mile Run Cotswold Way Challenge, which covers the whole CW over four days. The Cotswold Way Relay breaks the trail into ten sections. The Cotswold Way Ultra is 44.5 miles and the Broadway Challenge and Heineken Race to the Tower are mere double marathons, whilst only The Cotswold Way Century from Cotswold Running dares to cover the entire National Trail, non-stop. The record for completing the CW is a ridiculously fast 20 hours, 36 minutes and 48 seconds, set in 2015.

Resources

Public Transport

Traveline South West – timetables and journey planner for all bus, rail, coach, air and ferry services in the region *www.travelinesw.com*

National Rail – train services *www.nationalrail.co.uk*

Car Journey Planning

Google Maps *www.google.com/maps*

Bing Maps *www.bing.com/maps*

Traffic England – up-to-date information on closures, roadworks and traffic jams *www.trafficengland.com*

Weather

UK Met Office – general and upland area forecasts *www.metoffice.gov.uk*

Metcheck – general forecasts *www.metcheck.com*

Magic Seaweed – surf forecasts and tidal information, useful for checking sea conditions before coastal runs *www.magicseaweed.com*

Accommodation

Visit England – national tourist information organisation with information on travel, accommodation and places to visit *www.visitengland.com*

Visit South West – regional tourist information *www.visitsouthwest.co.uk*

Tourist Information Centres – contact information *www.visitengland.com/plan-your-visit/tourist-information-centres*

Many regions and communities have their own websites with information on local accommodation and businesses.

Mapping

Paper Maps

Ordnance Survey – 1:50,000 Landranger and 1:25000 Explorer maps *www.ordnancesurvey.co.uk*

Harvey Maps – 1:40,000 British Mountain Maps, 1:25,000 Superwalker maps for popular areas and National Trail Maps *www.harveymaps.co.uk*

Mapping Software

Software such as Memory Map or Anquet Maps allows users to look at Ordnance Survey Maps and plot routes on their home computers. Runners with GPS devices can download plotted routes to their devices or upload recorded routes *www.memory-map.co.uk www.anquet.co.uk*

There are also many similar online-only applications; *www.bikehike.co.uk* or *www.gmap-pedometer.com* provide simple interfaces which enable users to plot and download their own routes. Online communities store large databases of public routes uploaded by their members. These include Ordnance Survey OS Maps (their previous Getamap service has discontinued) *https://osmaps.ordnancesurvey.co.uk/osmaps/* Garmin Connect *https://connect.garmin.com/en-US/* and MapMyRun *www.mapmyrun.com/gb/*

Online grid conversion tools can usefully convert grid references into post codes for use with sat navs *www.gridreferencefinder.com www.streetmap.co.uk/gridconvert.html*

Access

The Countryside Code gives guidance on responsibilities for those who visit and those who manage the countryside *www.gov.uk/government/publications/the-countryside-code*

Detailed guidance on Rights of Way and access to the land is available from *www.gov.uk/topic/outdoor-access-recreation/rights-of-way-open-access*

Natural England's website gives details of CRoW Access Land where you can run freely *www.openaccess.naturalengland.org.uk*

Running Clubs

There are running clubs all across the region packed with enthusiasts of all abilities. Joining a club is a great way to become a better runner, whilst also making friends and discovering new routes. Find a local club through the searchable map on the England Athletics website *www.englandathletics.org* or from other online sources such as *www.goodrunguide.co.uk/ClubFinder.asp*

Specialist running shops often organise group runs or can provide contact details for local clubs and groups. Every club is different so it is worth enquiring about the running speed of club runs, coaching sessions and the club's emphasis on road, off-road and social activities.

Run Together is a recreational arm of English Athletics and has groups all over the country. Run Together aims to make walking and jogging accessible to everyone including absolute beginners *www.runtogether.co.uk*

Orienteering combines running with navigation and is a good way to develop the skills needed for more remote off-road runs. Find a club or local events by contacting British Orienteering *www.britishorienteering.org.uk*

Racing

Trail races are increasing in number. Most events are listed in the Southern Running Guide which is free from many sports centres and running shops. Their listings are also available online at *www.southernrunning guide.com* Other useful sources of event listings include *www.tra-uk.org*, *www.runnersworld.co.uk* and *www.therunningbug.co.uk*

The Fell Runners Association *www.fellrunner.org.uk* run a handful of events in the region.

Numerous trail marathons and ultra-marathons take place in the region, some extending over multiple days. The 100 Marathon Club *www.100marathonclub.org.uk* list most events.

The Long Distance Walkers Association (LDWA) run numerous 'Challenge' events which are entered by runners (don't be fooled by the 'walkers' title, these events can get quite competitive!). The Challenge events function as very cheap but well organised trail runs. The LDWA's events are listed on their website *www.ldwa.org.uk* and also in their member's handbook. Membership is not usually necessary to join their events.

Adventure Races and other endurance events which combine running with other outdoor activities are growing in popularity. A good source for event ideas is the Sleep Monsters website *www.sleepmonsters.com*

Parkruns *www.parkrun.org.uk* are a fast-growing phenomenon! These free, weekly 5K runs are held in numerous locations and are a great way to develop confidence in running and to track personal progress. However, although they are held in parks, many are held on tarmac or other hard surfaces.

Training, Coaching and Guiding

Most clubs organise training sessions as well as social runs. These usually include activities such as hill reps or fartleks. Many coaches work with clubs and it is also possible to hire personal coaches for individuals or small groups.

Confident and accurate navigation only comes through practice, but the basic techniques can be taught on courses intended for orienteers or hill walkers. Suitable courses are run by a number of outdoor centres within the region. A useful instructional tool is *Mountain and Moorland Navigation*, Kevin Walker, Pesda Press 2016 ISBN 978-1-906095-56-7.

A handful of companies within the region offer coaching and guided running, for example Wild Running *www.wildrunning.co.uk*

New Route Ideas

Books and magazines

Trail Running is the only UK magazine dedicated to off-road running.

Although there are few trail running guidebooks for the UK at present (and none previously focusing on this region), books and other information aimed at walkers and mountain bikers can be a useful source of ideas for new routes. Outdoor shops, bookshops and tourist information centres usually sell a range of such guidebooks.

Online communities and databases

Online communities (see Mapping) can provide ideas of where other people go running in particular areas. Many online communities or route databases intended for walkers and mountain bikers are also useful for trail and hill runners. New websites for runners, walkers and bikers appear all the time so an internet search is the best way of finding suitable sites.

Regional and local information

Tourist Information Centres and other visitor centres often have free leaflets describing local walking routes. Many of these are also available online through local or national websites.

The Forestry Commission *www.forestry.gov.uk* promote trail running and offer suggestions for routes on their land (see page 182).

National Trails *www.nationaltrail.co.uk* invariably offer fantastic route opportunities (with special mention for the South West Coast Path!). The websites for each trail include ideas for shorter routes which utilise the trail.

The Long Distance Walkers Association (LDWA) *www.ldwa.org.uk* are an excellent source of information for waymarked or named long-distance routes which do not have National Trail designation.

Acknowledgements

Many thanks to Susie Allison, whose outstanding guidebook *Scottish Trail Running* (Pesda Press 2017 ISBN 978-1-906095-62-8) provided both the inspiration and the model for this volume. Thanks to also Franco Ferrero at Pesda Press, Vicky Barlow for her great design work, Ros Morley for her meticulous proofreading and Don Williams of Bute Cartographics for the stunning maps.

All manner of friends came along and ran with me during the research of the book. Cheers for your help all, you are all great company and make the miles so much easier; for the Second Edition though, I will definitely hire better-looking models for the photos.

Index

Index